THE DEAF EXPERIENCE

THE DEAF EXPERIENCE

Classics in Language and Education

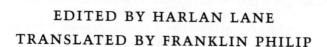

EDITED BY HARLAN LANE

TRANSLATED BY FRANKLIN PHILIP

HARVARD UNIVERSITY PRESS

CAMBRIDGE, MASSACHUSETTS
AND LONDON, ENGLAND

Library of Congress Cataloging in Publication Data
Main entry under title:

The deaf experience.

Includes bibliographical references and index.
1. Deaf—France—History—Addresses, essays, lectures.
2. Deaf—Education—France—History—Addresses, essays, lectures.
3. Sign language—History—Addresses, essays, lectures.
I. Lane, Harlan L.
HV2736.L36 1984   362.4'2'0944   84-26420
ISBN 0-674-19460-8 (alk. paper)

ACKNOWLEDGMENTS

WE GRATEFULLY ACKNOWLEDGE the assistance of the Bibliothèque Nationale in providing photocopies of the original works translated here and all the photographs in this volume, except the bas relief of Jacob Pereire, which is reproduced from the Zeitschrift für Bildende Kunst, 1881. The preparation of this translation was made possible by grant 0989-80 to Northeastern University from the Translations Program of the National Endowment for the Humanities. We are also indebted to the Northeastern University Psychology Department and Academic Computer Services for assistance in word processing.

CONTENTS

ILLUSTRATIONS

CHRONOLOGY

1760s
Epée's school opens in Paris

1765
Saboureux de Fontenay's *Autobiography* is published

1779
Pierre Desloges's *Observations* is published

1784
The abbé de l'Epée's *True Way to Educate the Deaf* is published

1789
R. A. Sicard succeeds Epée

1800
Jean Massieu's *Autobiography* is published

1800
The abbé Sicard's *Course of Study* is published

1817
First American school for the deaf opens

1817
R. A. Bébian's *Essay on the Deaf* is published

1840
F. Berthier's *The Deaf and Epée* is published

INTRODUCTION

THE RELATIONS between a minority using one language and the enveloping society using another are often the subject of heated dispute. The daily papers report protests by speakers of Spanish in the United States, by speakers of Basque in Spain, by speakers of French in Canada. Foremost among the rights demanded by language minorities is typically the conduct of their children's education in their own language, at least in part. In the United States the community using the manual sign language of the deaf and the surrounding community speaking English are no exception to the pattern. The relations between them have been the subject of impassioned debate for over a century, ever since the deaf Frenchman Laurent Clerc and his American colleague Thomas Gallaudet created a network of residential schools for the deaf throughout the land where a single language, evolving from the manual, or sign, language of the deaf in France, served all the purposes of daily life, including worship and instruction. And once again the debate centers on education: shall the children of the signing community be educated, at least in part, in their minority (manual) language or shall spoken English exclusively prevail? Thus the history of the deaf in the United States is the history of a struggle in which, by a bitter irony, the community of signers is pitched against their would-be benefactors, those English-speakers charged by the nation with improving the plight of the deaf.

Speakers of a majority language commonly view those who use another language in their midst as deficient; to be thus demeaned is the unhappy lot of the French community in Canada, as Wallace Lambert has shown so incisively, the Basque community in Spain, and the signing community in America—to cite a few examples. Speakers of the American Sign Language of the Deaf, however, have been particularly oppressed, because their language was so alien to English speakers, and also because their varying degrees of hearing impairment seemed to justify viewing them as deficient.

The United States has a long history of grappling with the ills of the body politic by construing them as illnesses of the individuals concerned. In the same manner, for over a century our nation has sought to address the social problems of deafness with a model that pathologizes all consequences of deafness, tidily placing the blame for the ills of the deaf on a cruel nature and invoking the health establishment to deal with them while disturbing the rest of society as little as possible. For this model to be coherent, the manual language of the deaf had to be branded a pathetic pantomime—just what it seemed to the uninitiated—a fallback, even an atavism, in the absence of real language. Thus the deaf could not be an indigenous language minority and their failure to make appropriate use of the national language had to be attributed to pathology, as it is with retarded persons. An "enlightened" society would provide the deaf, therefore, not with bilingual teachers giving them at least some instruction using their primary language but rather with "special" educators, speech pathologists and the like, who directed their efforts almost exclusively to rehabilitation. The same government agencies that support research and training for the education of retarded people who have no primary language do likewise for the deaf who have, while those agencies that address the needs of minority language groups in the United States have nothing to do with the half-million or so Americans whose primary language is the American Sign Language of the Deaf.

The deaf community itself, however, has historically spurned this pathological model of its situation, favoring instead a social model: deaf signers have seen themselves not as deficient but as different, and what makes the difference is not their hearing loss but their ostracized language, a language that has been actively banished for over a century by the hearing establishment concerned with the deaf. The deaf themselves were too familiar with all the functions perfectly served by their manual language, for them ever to abandon it, and they were too injured by the sacrifice of education in the name of rehabilitation for them to embrace this substitute goal.

It is no accident, then, that the seminal works concerning the deaf deal mostly with the conflict between the pathological and social models of deaf people's condition, hence with the status of the sign language that forces a choice between them. The conflict has imposed on deaf history wide swings between these polar conceptions of the deaf condition; hearing action and deaf reaction have seesawed back and forth ever since the eighteenth century, when European societies first came to grips with the signing communities in their midst. The trend, however, has moved unmistakably against signing communities and their languages. Consider France: in the mid-nineteenth century there were 160 schools for the deaf, and the manual language of the signing community was the language of instruction in all of them; by the turn of the century, it was not allowed in a single one. Similarly, at the end of the American Civil War there were twenty-six schools for the deaf with American Sign Language (ASL) the language of instruction in all; by 1907 there were 139 schools and in every one ASL was forbidden. Indeed, a few years later the National Association of the Deaf, fearing the total extinction of American Sign Language in the hostile environment that had prevailed for some decades, commissioned a series of films of great American deaf orators, to preserve a record of their language for future generations.

The ostracism of sign language continues largely unabated to this day, although two developments have provoked a reexamination, which this collection reflects, and augur a shift toward the social model espoused by the deaf community. First, the manual communication of the American deaf came under the scrutiny of language scientists, beginning in the 1960s with William Stokoe's analysis of word (sign) formation and continuing in the 1970s with Ursula Bellugi and Edward Klima's description of sentence construction. The linguistic structures discovered at the two levels were, to be sure, quite unlike those in English. Parallels came from other languages, but structural principles did exist, and it quickly came to be known that ASL shared the duality of patterning characteristic of natural human languages, hence invited the same kind of scientific examination. There were studies of children learning ASL as a native language, of the dialects of ASL and its social registers, of its historical evolution, of its similarities and differences with other sign languages, of its mechanisms for borrowing from oral language, of its stylistics and poetics, of its neurological organization and functioning in the production, perception, and recall of messages—and more. This work soon led to journals such as *Sign Language Studies*,[1] collections such as *The Signs of Language*,[2] and syntheses such as *Recent Perspectives on American Sign Language*,[3] to name but one of each. National and international conferences, courses in the structure of sign language, and textbooks and videotapes based on the linguistic findings were not long in following, with increasing involvement by deaf organizations and native signers. Scholars had discovered, in a word, that language is a capacity of the mind that, if blocked in one avenue of expression, will take another. And if the signing community is indeed using a natural language, then it is, of course, a linguistic minority, as the deaf have contended at least since 1779, when Pierre Desloges published the first book by a deaf person. Linguistic minorities do indeed have handicaps, foremost among them the conduct of their education in a language they have not mastered, hence poor educational achievement. To this must be added unequal opportunity for jobs, unequal access to health care and government services, and many more such handicaps, but the handicapping condition lies in the society that has created these barriers and not in the individual hurtling himself against them.

The second reason for a shift toward the social model of deafness is the dramatic failure of the pathological model. Even the most arduous and timely efforts at oral rehabilitation typically fail to confer speech on those who have never spoken, or to restore speech once lost. Tireless efforts to teach the deaf child to glean from the lips the messages of a language he never knew or no longer uses are equally frustrated. Meanwhile, classroom instruction proceeds in spoken English, which the teacher may or may not accompany with isolated signs. No wonder that in a recent study deaf high-school students performed at the fourth-grade level in reading and writing and sixth-grade level in arithmetic (their best subject).[4] No wonder that the 1974 census of adult deaf Americans found 30 percent could not read and write and 80 percent engaged in manual or unskilled labor.[5] Under these conditions few indeed of the thousands of students with boundless ability to learn in their primary manual language can get through high school, not to mention college. In Europe, where educational standards are less flexible, the situation is even worse: rare indeed is the deaf Frenchman with even a high school diploma.

The pathological model has a long history dating from at least the sixteenth century when Pedro Ponce de Leon, a Spanish monk, taught the deaf scions of a noble family to speak, read, and write—to the astonishment of scholars in Spain, and as word spread, throughout Europe.[6] Just what his means and accomplishments were have proved difficult to reconstruct, for his manuscript describing them was lost. There is reason, however, to believe it served indirectly to guide the three men generally considered to have founded oral rehabilitation: Jacob Pereire in the Romance-speaking countries, John Wallis in the British Isles, and Jan Conrad Amman in the German-speaking nations. All three labored under conditions similar to those of Ponce, as did their many disciples well into the nineteenth century. A wealthy family has a deaf son (deaf daughters were commonly sequestered at home or in convents). The family hires a tutor, often a man of letters, who works to maintain, perhaps restore, the boy's speech and to expand his knowledge of arts and sciences. The boy makes progress; a philosopher notes it; the tutor publishes letters announcing his achievement but withholding his method. The tutor goes on to other things; the boy, generally, does not.

Jacob Pereire, the most famous "demutiser" in history, was twenty-six when he taught speech to his first deaf pupil—his own sister. His second pupil was a thirteen-year-old apprentice tailor born profoundly deaf; in one hundred lessons extending over a year, Pereire taught him to articulate all the basic speech sounds plus several words and phrases, such as "hat," "madame," and "what do you want?" This achievement brought him Azy d'Etavigny, the eighteen-year-old son of a wealthy family, who had been born deaf and treated by the leading physicians of Europe to no effect. In 1746 the boy's father drew up a year's contract: Pereire would closet himself with the son at the abbey where the boy was attending school and would receive a handsome sum in three payments, each contingent on the boy's progress. The prior of the abbey also contracted to discover Pereire's method, which the teacher called "a secret I think I ought to keep entirely in my family." At the abbey Pereire found his pupil to be an intelligent youth who could read and write, having received instruction in French through sign language from a deaf monk.

In eight days Pereire had the boy saying "mama" and "papa," and in a month, fifty words. In a year he spoke over a thousand words and a few sentences—which reflected, however, the grammar of his sign language. The contract ended, the father withdrew his son, but the boy's speech deteriorated rapidly and Pereire was called in again. This time he took the boy to live with him in Paris; after a month he displayed him before the most prestigious scholarly body in the land, the Academy of Sciences, which called Pereire's efforts worthy of the strongest encouragement, cited the boy's good intonation, but lamented his slow, guttural, and choppy pronunciation. The duke of Chaulnes, head of the Academy, presented pupil and teacher to the king, who later appointed the polyglot Pereire as one of his official interpreters. More important, the duke gave Pereire charge of his deaf godson, Saboureux de Fontenay.

Saboureux, born hard of hearing, was thirteen when he joined Azy d'Etavigny in Pereire's home. In but two and a half months Pereire went before the Academy again to display his latest pupil, and the Academy again acclaimed his achievement; Saboureux pronounced distinctly all the sounds of French, understood many common expressions in writing, and could read aloud with the intermediary of his teacher's fingerspelling, which represented the words phonetically. Saboureux spent five years with his teacher, then continued his education on his own, becoming the most famous of Pereire's half-dozen pupils and securing for him renown throughout Europe and an income for life. Pereire died in 1780, taking the secret of his method with him to the grave. Diligent efforts by scholars since then have uncovered little more than is to be found in Saboureux's account of his instruction, translated in this volume for the first time.

In his later years Pereire became bitter and disappointed; he abandoned the cause to which he had devoted his life, for he witnessed the birth, development, and success of an entirely different conception of the deaf, viewing them as a social class, therefore, addressing them through the medium of their manual language, seeking to educate the many poor and not the few rich, and paying lip-service to oral rehabilitation while devoting all effort to intellectual growth. His rival's school soon won the protection and support of King Louis XVI and attracted heads of state, scholars, and disciples from all Europe. The first public school for the deaf in history, founded in the 1760s, it was the inspiration and model for hundreds soon to follow. It created educated leaders among the deaf, instilling pride in themselves and their language, as well as giving them an elevated vision of what the deaf could become. It earned for its founder, the abbé Charles-Michel de l'Epée, the gratitude of deaf people down to the present, whose spokesmen have called him "the father of the deaf."

"Every deaf-mute sent to us already has a language," Epée wrote. "He is thoroughly in the habit of using it, and understands others who do. With it he expresses his needs, desires, doubts, pains, and so on, and makes no mistakes when others express themselves likewise. We want to instruct him and therefore to teach him French. What is the shortest and easiest method? Isn't it to express ourselves in his language? By adopting his language and making it conform to clear rules, will we not be able to conduct his instruction as we wish?"

As this last sentence intimates, Epée was misled, as many scholars have since been, by the great differences between the structure of his own language and the manual language of the deaf community. Because French grammar relies heavily on word endings and word order while sign language does not, conveying many of the same ideas instead by systematically modifying the movements of the signs themselves, Epée thought French Sign Language (FSL) lacked rules. What better structure to impose on it than that of French? Thus, with the aid of his pupils, he undertook to choose or invent a sign for all the word endings in French, for all the articles, prepositions, and auxiliary verbs, and so on, until virtually every French sentence had its counterpart in this manual French, could be transcribed into it, and could be recovered from it. Where the oralists sought to replace sign language with spoken French, Epée sought to convert it into a kind of manual dialect of the national language. Replacement or dialectizing—these are the alternative avenues traveled whenever a society seeks to supplant rather than embrace the language of a minority.

In Epée's lifetime he had seen a dozen schools for the deaf founded by his disciples throughout Europe—from Rome to Amsterdam, from Madrid to Vienna. During his successor's career that number would grow fivefold. In the end Epée is recognized as the founder of deaf education not so much because of his method, which would rapidly evolve in the hands of others, but because of his humility: he started by learning the language of the deaf, and was thus able to learn some of what they have to teach hearing people about themselves, their observations, their language, the nature of oppression, the condition of man.

The failing of Epée's strength coincided with the end of the French monarchy. In December 1789 he lay dying, rich in universal acclaim, poor in worldly goods. The man who gave the deaf his genius, his heart, and his labor had not withheld his funds, spending his modest inheritance on the salaries of his assistants and on food and lodging for his pupils. A delegation from the National Assembly joined the pupils at his bedside to tell him that his most fervent wish, the certain continuation of his school, was assured; the new republic had proclaimed it a national institution. Then Epée blessed his pupils in sign for the last time.

"There are congenitally deaf people, Parisian laborers, who are illiterate and who have never attended the abbé de l'Epée's lessons, who are so well instructed about their religion, simply by means of signs, that they have been judged worthy of admission to the holy sacraments . . . No event in Paris, in France, or in the four corners of the word, lies outside the scope of (their) discussions." Thus did Pierre Desloges affirm what is supported by other evidence, that the Parisian deaf community had a common manual language before Epée began his labors. Indeed, it appears that Epée's first pupils were taught some elements of religion in that language by a certain Father Vanin.

Many other precious insights into the deaf community of Paris are afforded by Desloges's book written, he tells us, in order to defend his beloved sign language from the false criticisms of it published by a disciple of Pereire, the abbé Deschamps. Thus Desloges's work, translated here for the first time, is the first in a long series of ringing defenses of sign language by deaf people.

The leading disciple of the abbé de l'Epée, and the man who would carry forward the education of the deaf on the master's death, was yet another abbé, Roch-Ambroise Sicard. Sent by the bishop of Bordeaux to study under Epée for a year, Sicard, forty-three, then returned to that city to open the second school for the deaf in France. About three years later Epée died, and, to announce his candidacy as Epée's successor, Sicard published a memoir on the instruction of the deaf. In it he severely criticized his teacher's methods for producing rote copyists able only to transcribe written sentences into manual French and back again without any understanding and without any ability to formulate a sentence of their own. Indeed, the abbé de l'Epée had at one time sent a note urging him to give up the hope that the deaf can ever express their ideas in writing. "Our language is not theirs; theirs is sign language. Let it suffice that they know how to translate ours with theirs." Sicard reasoned that for the deaf to comprehend and formulate sentences in manual French, in which familiar signs are scattered among invented ones in an unexpected order, the deaf would have to learn the grammar of French, and to study the rules of order that determine the composite meaning of the separate words. This he had undertaken with the aid of a gifted assistant, and he now had one pupil, a congenitally

deaf shepherd boy named Jean Massieu, whom he believed superior
to any of Epée's students. Therefore he proposed that Epée's successor be chosen in a public contest before the French Academy, a
competition in which each candidate would display his best student
and explain his methods of instruction. Sicard was staking everything on Massieu and on his own phenomenal abilities as an orator.

It came to pass as Sicard had hoped, but on taking over his mentor's
school he found it in desperate straits, housed by the government
in decrepit quarters and short of staff, fuel, and even food. Sicard
again used Massieu, appearing with his pupil before various com-
mittees of the Legislative Assembly. They were mightily impressed:
"Massieu understands all our ideas and can express all his own,"
records the minutes. "He knows all the intricacies of grammar and
even of metaphysics perfectly. He is thoroughly familiar with the
rules of mathematics, celestial mechanics, and geography. He has a
knowledge of religion, knows the principles of the Constitution . . ."
Funds were soon provided, Massieu was appointed head teaching
assistant, and the school was relocated in a refurbished seminary.
It was to serve as a beacon that would illuminate the lives of countless deaf people in Europe and America for over half a century.
Massieu's moving account of his childhood and of the changes in
him under Sicard's tutelage is translated here from two addresses
he gave to the Society of Observers of Man, the first anthropological
society. For his part, the abbé Sicard, wishing to provide his disciples
with an account of his methods and to call attention to his achievements and the cause of the deaf, published a detailed description of
how he taught Massieu. It was the first and, for decades, only textbook on educating the deaf; despite its metaphysical bombast and
self-serving calumny of the uneducated deaf, it became a guide for
the scores of schools for the deaf that opened in Europe and America
in Sicard's lifetime. The first four chapters are translated here.

Seven years before Sicard's death in 1822 a Protestant minister,
Thomas Gallaudet, was sent by philanthropists from Hartford to
London to acquire the art of instructing the deaf from the heirs of
Thomas Braidwood, an oralist and follower of John Wallis. The Braidwood family, which had a monopoly on the education of the British
deaf, was unwilling to disseminate their method, however, so Gallaudet had recourse to the abbé Sicard who, as it happened, was then
in London presenting his star pupils, Massieu and a certain Laurent
Clerc, to members of Parliament and large crowds of interested spectators. At Sicard's invitation Gallaudet joined them in Paris and

spent several months studying Sicard's method, receiving lessons in
manual French from Massieu and Clerc, and attending their classes.
In the end he asked Clerc to return to Hartford with him; there, in
April 1817, they founded the first school for the deaf in America.
Naturally, they started with Sicard's methods and his manual French,
which during the long transatlantic voyage they had partially adapted
to English.

The man whom Laurent Clerc called "the greatest hearing friend
the deaf ever had," who was the first to urge educating the deaf in
their own language, and who eventually changed the character of
their education in Europe and America, R. A. Bébian, was born in
Guadeloupe the year Epée died (1789). When he was only eleven he
was sent to Paris to be educated by his godfather, the abbé Sicard.
He became close friends with the deaf pupils, learned French Sign
Language from them (which Sicard never did), and after finishing
high school, attended Laurent Clerc's classes. Soon he was appointed
monitor, then teaching assistant, finally head of studies. In 1817
Bébian published an essay on the deaf and their language, translated
here, and a few years later a prize-winning eulogy of the abbé de
l'Epée in which he roundly and incisively criticized Epée's and Sicard's system of manual French, urging instead that the instruction
of the deaf be conducted in their sign language. "There is no more
sure, direct, and effective way to initiate the deaf into our written
language than with their sign language," Bébian wrote in the first
manual for the education of the deaf predicated on their language.
Until Bébian's reform, instructors in Hartford or New York as in
Paris or Bordeaux would first express some thought in the language
of the deaf community—for example, "Try to understand me." Then,
using that language, they would teach the vocabulary and explain
the grammar, coming up with ten signs required by manual English
(or French) to express the same thought: *try* + second person +
plural + imperative + *to* + *under* + *stand* + infinitive + *I* +
accusative. Finally they would write the corresponding sentence in
English (or French) on the blackboard: "Try to understand me." The
labor involved in teaching the ten signs was the very labor again
required to teach the corresponding written sentence; there was no
need for the intermediate step, and under Bébian's impetus the attempt to dialectize the languages of the deaf communities faded on
both sides of the Atlantic.

Thereby was ushered in a golden era in the education of the deaf
toward the middle of the last century. Instructed in the national

language and all the traditional branches of knowledge through the vehicle of their primary sign language, deaf children throughout Europe and America completed elementary education in growing numbers. "High classes" were then launched by the Hartford, New York, and Paris schools among others; students gifted in the liberal arts pursued their schooling for another four years, many going on to become themselves teachers of the deaf. At midcentury nearly half of the teachers in American schools for the deaf were deaf themselves; today they are a rarity. To allow graduates of the high classes to continue their education, Thomas Gallaudet's son Edward Miner Gallaudet founded at Washington, D.C., in 1864, the first college for the deaf in the world.

The deaf intellectual who symbolized and left his mark on this era perhaps more than any other was a Frenchman, the brilliant pupil of Bébian and Clerc, Ferdinand Berthier, who was born deaf. After completing the Paris curriculum he became a monitor, then teaching assistant, then professor at twenty-six, finally dean of professors. Witty, elegant, and modest, Berthier was polyglot—he knew French, Latin, and Greek, but he preferred his own sign language above all these. "How few men," he wrote, "have deeply studied its immense resources . . . so clear, so positive, so reliable." Like Clerc and Massieu before him, Berthier was a living argument for his cause. His wide knowledge, refined use of language, and sincere and lively style won him many readers and the cause of the deaf many friends. He was a prolific writer: he wrote voluminous biographies—still the definitive works—of Epée, Sicard, and Bébian, a concise history of the deaf, translated in this collection, a refutation of the slander of deaf character by a leading physician of the time, a book explaining the Napoleonic Code to the deaf, numerous encyclopedia entries on deafness, and countless newspaper articles assailing the unequal treatment of the deaf in French society. Berthier founded the first social organization of the deaf, which took initiatives in legal reform, adult education, and charitable gifts. He was vice-president of the first welfare organization of the deaf and a member of various literary and historical societies. Toward the end of his career he received the Legion of Honor, never before conferred on a deaf person.

By the time Berthier died in 1886 the tide had turned against education of the deaf minority in their language and in favor once again of their oral rehabilitation. In America the New England aristocracy resisted the education of their deaf children, most of whom had once spoken, in the ranks of the poor congenitally deaf and by the exclusive means of sign language. Moreover, with the rise in immigration in the late nineteenth century and the shift in its sources to poorer southern Europe, the "old" immigrants, particularly those from Britain and Germany, clamored for restrictive immigration laws, for eugenic reduction of the "unfit," including the deaf, for language uniformity, and for English-speaking day schools for the deaf. The nation's leading champion of all these causes was Alexander Graham Bell, and he put his vast wealth, prestige, and energy behind them. In Europe a series of international congresses on the welfare of the deaf—from which the deaf were excluded—were launched by Jacob Pereire's millionaire son and grandson. Their espousal of oral rehabilitation fomented a veritable revolution in European practices, culminating in the closing words of the 1880 Congress of Milan: "Long live speech!" By the turn of the century, the sign languages of Europe and the Americas were driven out of the classrooms and into the washrooms, out of sight, but of course not out of the lives of deaf people.

The seminal works in deaf history translated in this collection were consigned to oblivion. In their place there began the tradition of presenting deaf history as the untiring efforts of hearing people across the ages to teach the deaf to speak. Compendious surveys of oralism such as Thomas Arnold's in 1888[7] and more concise treatments based on his, such as Kenneth Hodgson's[8] and Ruth Bender's,[9] misled the teachers of the deaf and then the deaf themselves. The lessons of the golden era of deaf education that ended with Berthier, the cries of the "silent press" (newspapers published by and for deaf people), and the proceedings of a score of deaf congresses were totally ignored. The pathological model of deafness seemed to tell the whole story.

Yet the renewed appreciation of cultural pluralism in our society today invites us to reexamine the conviction that others should speak as we do. Many Americans can recall their initial shock when they realized fully for the first time that other people were conducting their lives in an entirely different language. Perhaps that shock reflects a kind of egocentrism that it is in our common interest to overcome, for the growth of social consciousness, like that of the child, is largely a series of triumphs over egocentrism.

As I am not less but more when I recognize the heliocentric movement of the planets and the biological continuity of the species, so I am not less but more when I recognize that there are other languages, manual and oral, on a par with mine. That recognition opens the way to collaboration with people who speak another language and who can teach it to you. Sicard called this collaboration a happy exchange: "Thus by a happy exchange Massieu taught me the signs of his language and I taught him the signs of mine." Laurent Clerc called this collaboration a useful employment. "We spent the voyage to America in useful employment. I taught Mr. Gallaudet the methods of signs, and he taught me the English language." May this collection aid the reader to begin that happy exchange and useful employment. Only then will we be equal to the challenge confronting us which is, clearly, to find a synthesis of the pathological and social models better suited to the reality of the deaf experience than any single model has proven.

I

SABOUREUX DE FONTENAY

In January of 1751, midway between his twelfth and thirteenth birthdays, Saboureux de Fontenay was presented to members of the Royal Academy of Sciences in Paris. The academicians had been convoked to examine the deaf boy's astonishing command of spoken French. Their report states that he pronounced "clearly and distinctly" all the French vowels and consonants, including the "complicated" nasal sounds. He also recited the Lord's Prayer in Latin, and demonstrated that he understood a few French expressions conveyed to him by fingerspelling. This impressive achievement by the second talking deaf person to be observed at the academy was taken to confirm the pedagogical talents of their teacher, Jacob Rodriguez Pereire. As a consequence of this examination, and as a reward for bringing greater glory to the most enlightened nation on earth and to its language, King Louis XV granted Pereire an income for life, securing his reputation as the greatest "demutiser" of the deaf in Europe.

At the time of this first public appearance, Saboureux had only recently begun his instruction in speech. For Pereire the boy represented "the most splendid gift of my life." The gift had been given by the duke of Chaulnes, the boy's godfather, who had introduced the teacher to his future student in the city of Versailles where the boy lived, his father being an officer in the king's guard, and where Pereire was employed as an interpreter at court. Saboureux studied with Pereire for some five years.

The writings of both pupil and teacher indicate that they at first used what signing the boy already knew, but they minimize its importance. Instead, they lay emphasis on the manual alphabet published in 1620 in Pereire's native Spain (from which he had emigrated, via Portugal, to escape persecution as a Jew). Pereire augmented the alphabet so it included handshapes corresponding to French sounds as well as French letters. Saboureux already had a little knowledge of reading and writing before his instruction by Pereire. As he relates in this memoir, he had been sent at the age of six or seven to school in the south of France, where a certain M. Lucas befriended him, taught him fingerspelling, and gave him some reading knowledge of French.

By the time Saboureux left off his education with Pereire, he tells us, he was pursuing studies on his own, learning several other languages. In his mid-twenties he wrote the autobiographical letter translated and slightly abridged in this volume, "Lettre de M. Saboureux de Fontenay, sourd et muet de naissance, à Mademoiselle * * *, Versailles, le 26 décembre 1764." It was published in the Suite de la Clef ou Journal historique sur les matières du tems [Journal de Verdun] [98] (1765): 284–298, 361-372, making him the first deaf person whose writings appear in print. Later on he published a treatise on meteorology. In addition, he himself undertook the education of another deaf person.

Although Saboureux first gained fame as a deaf person who could speak, reports of his later life have it that, once his lessons with Pereire were over, Saboureux ceased speaking and communicated with pen and paper. A linguist who met him at age thirty found "not a trace of his speech lessons." When Pierre Desloges later claimed to be the first deaf person to publish a book, Saboureux sent him an angry letter stating that he was the first to publish, and also the first to declare war on the practice of conversing with gestural signs.

Jacob Rodriguez Pereire, teacher of Saboureux de Fontenay

EXTRACT OF A LETTER FROM
SABOUREUX DE FONTENAY,
A CONGENITALLY DEAF PERSON,
TO MADEMOISELLE * * *

Versailles, 26 December 1764

Mademoiselle,

You ask how I could learn to read, write, speak, and make myself understood. It will be a genuine pleasure to give a clear explanation of this and, even though this topic involves some metaphysics, I shall avoid technical terms and use only the language of everyday conversation.

There is a special relation between the ears and the tongue such that people born deaf are also mute. In what follows I explain this fact as succinctly as I can. People have a natural tendency to imitate what they see; we rightfully pride ourselves on being the monkeys of nature. The sounds falling on our ears are easily expressed by language. To comprehend my ability to read and so forth, you must necessarily reflect on the way a toddler learns to speak, a fact everyone soon forgets.

The hearing son from a farming or laboring family learns to speak his father's language because he is constantly hearing it, because his memory is continually picturing it, and he is forever repeating it. Without any parental instruction the boy uses the same words and phrases, uttering them in the same tone of voice. Thus without any initial plan or lesson in the subject the child learns, merely through hearing speech, to speak. This fact gives rise to the apt maxim that nature is an excellent schoolmistress who teaches to good effect. Our sense organs are all more or less interconnected: a certain movement stimulates the ear, and the tongue experiences the urge, so to speak, to move in a way that is the complement of the movement just made in the ear. We hear some words sung or spoken, and our vocal organs seem to make an effort at singing the same tune or uttering the same words. Nature has made us avid to say what we are thinking, and the desire for intercourse with our peers about our needs means that we have an ardent desire to know what others are thinking. We love company precisely because it provides material for learning, and that is why we take pleasure in speaking, and in hearing speech. The desires of children are even more pressing than ours, so they learn languages more easily. It is not difficult to imagine how a child learns his father's language and speaks in the same manner and with the same tone of voice. His father, giving him some bread or other commonplace object, has repeatedly stimulated his ear with the sound "bread"; the sound of the word has become connected in memory with the idea of something called bread, and the child acquires the tendency to utter the word, learning that when he does so, he will receive the thing it designates.

According to this principle the deaf child's total lack of hearing seems to prohibit him, necessarily, from ever learning to speak like the normal child. The sounds—the language itself, even—are completely arbitrary (this is proved by the multiplicity of languages in the world), and the letters of the alphabet function merely to represent the sounds uttered (informing the eyes about what is meant). The formation, order, and reading of these letters are different in different countries, because letters, like sounds, are also arbitrary. We can readily assume that deafness is just an impediment to hearing the sounds as they should be heard, entailing no difference in intelligence or inclination, and that all we need do is, for the ears, substitute the eyes, and for sounds, written or fingerspelled letters, and then to apply to the deaf the universal system by which normal children learn through hearing, and they will learn language through usage, the way hearing children and foreigners settling in Paris learn French, that is, through ordinary conversation. By this means, the deaf experience the same effects, emotions, mental processes, and so on, that we note in children who learn through hearing. To this end, the only method possible is practice and the kind of education given to young people of both sexes. Hence the truth of the Latin epigram that means *practice is the ruler of languages*. This education must, I would add, take into account the nature and development of reason and the mind.

That is why, consistent with the way a child learns French, M. Pereire, seeing I was nearly thirteen, went about teaching me common words and phrases, for example, "open the window," "shut the window," "open the door," "close the door," "light the fire," "put out the fire," "get a log," "set the table," "give me some bread," and so on. Deciding that I was sufficiently well versed in everyday dialogues, which we fingerspelled with his enlarged and improved Spanish manual alphabet, he shunned the use of gestures. This was to get me accustomed to language, to rid me of the habitual use of my own signs, to train me in understanding sentences, to enable me to carry out all sorts of things consistent with my understanding of the language, and to answer both easy and difficult questions. So that I might formulate thoughts by myself, he had me describe every-day occurrences, to report what was said, to talk, to converse, to reason, to argue with people about various things that came to mind, to write letters to friends, to write back to people, and so on. In this way I reached a clear and automatic understanding of the meaning of pronouns, conjugations, adverbs, prepositions, conjunctions, and other parts of speech, of which M. Pereire then presented a goodly number of striking examples to get me to produce still others.

At the end of six months M. Pereire, pleased with my progress in mastering everyday expressions, began teaching me to conjugate verbs, then to decline nouns, and finally to construct grammatically proper sentences expressing everything I needed to say, describe, and the like. It was during the seventh month that my uncle Lesparat, later a lawyer at the high judicial court, assumed benevolent re-sponsibility for my religious instruction, applying himself on Sun-days and holidays to the explanation (without gestures or drawings) of the catechisms of Paris, of Montpellier, and of the abbé Fleury. Because he was only seven years my senior, my uncle had discus-sions with M. Pereire and with the late Father R. P. Vanin, priest of the Christian Doctrine of Saint-Julien-des-Ménétriers-de-Paris, about the best way to catechize me and to explain the language of religion. After giving precise definitions and explanations of all the standard French words and phrases, my uncle had me recite from memory the catechismal replies to the questions he asked with the manual alphabet. He taught me how to express the same basic idea in a thousand different ways. The following phrase, for example, "to live in a Christian way," is variously expressed as "to live by prac-ticing the good that the Christian church commands and by abjuring the evil that it forbids," "the Christian lives in a way that brings God's grace on himself," "to live according to the rules of the Chris-tian doctrine," "to live consistent with the spirit of the Christian religion," "to live following the principles of the Gospel," and so forth. My uncle's aim was to further my understanding of the fig-urative and sublime language that is customarily devoted to religion, and to get me to appreciate its logic and proper use. To explain the intellectual ideas expressed in words and phrases, he gave fairly concrete examples of what is happening at every moment in the mind. To explain the word "justice," for example, seeing that I had witnessed the execution of criminals, he pointed out that if a mur-derer were not put to death he would kill other men; that is why he was put to death, to make everyone good and to take from him the power to do evil to anyone. Justice was further explained as the faculty of punishing the wicked and rewarding the good, of preventing people from doing evil and of leading them to do good. Personal circumstances added to explanations clinched my understanding of the idea behind the word. With comparisons and examples my uncle explained many difficult matters at length. To test my command of language, he had me explain the lessons in other words; he urged me, in turn, boldly to ask him questions and, with him and other acquaintances, to take part in mutual reflection and discussions about religion; he took pleasure in arguing with me.

Both M. Pereire and my uncle enjoyed taking me to observe experiments in physics, to look at collections of scientific curiosities, to visit different houses, and to go for walks in the country. Their main purpose was for me to learn to answer people's questions appropriately, to understand conversational French, and to acquaint me with social customs. I took frequent advantage of my leisure to go by myself into the houses where, I knew, friends would be glad to converse and instruct me in everyday matters; in this way I learned the meaning of many terms and phrases not used by M. Pereire or my uncle. This was the chief aim, I have since realized, of my tutors' attempts to make language intelligible through practice, which they thought an excellent teacher, and to get me to appreciate terms for sensory impressions, circumstances, and persons. In company I began to get the idea of figurative speech, verbal elegance, delicacy of expression, embellishments of discourse, and so on. After taking my leave of my uncle and M. Pereire, I would develop this idea through diligent reading of books written in a sublime and lofty style.

Finally, around the fourth year of my instruction, when I had sufficient background in grammar, Christian doctrine, and the Bible, my godfather and protector the duke of Chaulnes, who during the first three years of my instruction had tested me and given me guidance, did me the honor of suggesting that I write composition books. Then M. Pereire and my uncle had me fill notebooks on selected subjects; they had me identify errors of French and other mistakes in the notebooks, which I then corrected. This was the way that, thanks to the Creator of men's minds, I succeeded in mastering French and in expressing myself easily on paper. At the end of the fifth year I took my leave of M. Pereire and my uncle. Since then I have enjoyed reading all sorts of books, both printed and handwritten, to familiarize myself with the difficult French that was barely comprehensible to me when I was with M. Pereire. I also enjoy talking with people for the purpose of learning and understanding different kinds of French, and of deciphering the different ways in which French is written despite the rules of spelling.

I believe I can, without fear of grave error, say that throughout my experience in studying French, it was by practice, aided by first principles, that I actually learned the language, and that my education did not seem mechanical. We used—and still use—three methods to encourage my constant use of French: writing, spelling in the Spanish manual alphabet, and signs in the usual manual alphabet. I say "aided by first principles" because of a certain M. Lucas, royal building-contractor for water-works, who in 1746 was sent from Paris to Ganges, a small town of the Bas-Languedoc some seven leagues from Montpellier, to oversee the building of a barracks. There he met me (I had arrived there from Paris some two years before). Shortly thereafter, knowing I was eight and a half, he decided to devote his leisure time to my education; he began by teaching me to write and to use the signs of the manual alphabet so that I could read books to him. Then he explained a number of commonly used words and the names of friends and places. (I say "friends" because in Ganges I was always on my own and without relatives.) He taught me to count, to do arithmetic, and to write place names, days of the week, months, and years. But upon completion of the barracks in the spring of 1749, M. Lucas departed for Paris, leaving my education unfinished. During these earliest lessons I watched various people, strangers and people I knew, to determine whether their understanding of my written words was the same as mine. I asked these people to write down the names of things I showed them. Because of my naturally retentive memory I was able to report these names to my dinner companions. I was greatly surprised when they showed me the very same things originally designated by the names; everyone was perfectly in accord, I found, about the words, but not about my habitual signs. So I set about noting the effects of spoken conversation, reading, writing, and so on. From these activities I glimpsed the apparent impossibility of my becoming as educated as any other child my age, despite my observations in the diocesan schools of Montpellier and Assais where my entire day was spent copying out passages from the New Testament and other books without learning a thing (during M. Lucas's stay in Ganges and after his return to Paris). My observations made clear the teacher's labors and the student's problems, and led me to conclude that nothing in this study was easy for beginners, that the main thing necessary for retaining the difficult material was a good memory improved through diligent practice, time, and contemplation of nature's spectacle, and that patience and perseverance were required to endure the study's pains and difficulties. I had already memorized many sections of the New Testament, and I took pleasure in making natural, physical, economic, and other kinds of observations.

About five months after M. Lucas returned to Paris, I went for my usual stay in the Cévennes Mountains, which at the behest of the duke of Chaulnes I left toward the end of September 1750, to return to Paris. Some three weeks after my arrival at my birthplace in Versailles, the duke placed me under the direction of M. Pereire. At M. Pereire's home in Paris I saw him use the signs of his manual alphabet to converse with M. d'Azy d'Etavigny, his first pupil, and both extolled the value of the linguistic knowledge M. Pereire was to impart to me, and to encourage me to study hard, they showed me the drawbacks of my usual signs. I was quite willing to be instructed, as I had learned that my friend M. d'Azy d'Etavigny was, like me, congenitally deaf. Eventually overcoming with patience and persistence the tedium and difficulty of the study which at first set me trembling, I began to understand and repeat French, and by grasping the intellectual, abstract, and general ideas designated by words, sentences, and turns of phrase, I gave up the idea that it was impossible for the congenitally deaf to become as knowledgeable, educated, capable of reasoning and thinking as others—an idea that had been confirmed by the example and confession of a friend who had trouble remembering words, expressing himself, and understanding either people or books. The manner by which I achieved an understanding of language and of various topics is nothing other than a continual repetition of the same words, phrases, and ways of speaking, applied in every conceivable manner, at every opportunity, and in every encounter. It is a wise teacher who can make a prudent choice of what is valuable and who can adroitly and continually give the most needed words without bothering us with the less common ones which, nevertheless, he gradually and painlessly teaches through experience with things or through their connection with words that are already familiar.

For the congenitally deaf who have been taught language, everyday communication is still an excellent portrayer of thought. Indeed, at the sight of a picture, the eyes, rightly called the mirror of the soul, communicate to the deaf person the whole thought of the person who painted it (by writing or fingerspelling or signs or whatever means), much as his mind imagined it, by combining all the parts into a single indivisible whole, despite its extension, and so quickly that the need for the senses is scarcely detected; and seemingly without sensory or artistic help, the thought goes from the person imagining it to the person receiving it.

But you should realize that print, signs, words, phrases, conversation, and the reading of books give deaf persons as much pleasure as hearing people get from the sounds of speech and conversation. Indeed, deaf people find instruction a kind of diversion, not unlike the experience of normal children who constantly hear speech, whereas this instruction may be a torment for others, being highly metaphysical and very difficult and laborious for the teacher. As this sort of activity naturally causes the deaf person to confront in the prescribed manner the difficulties that he feels can be overcome with time, the method of instruction requires much patience, intelligence, caution, and shrewdness on the part of both teacher and pupil to guess what is happening in each other's mind. The quality of instruction varies depending on the teacher's skill in explaining and instilling in the pupil's mind the language of sensations, circumstances, and persons, commensurate with the pupil's memory, intelligence, and determination to meet the challenges posed by the genius of the language and the spirit of the subject matter and his motivation to hear, read, speak, write, and repeat the language.

It is accurate to say about the education of deaf people, or of hearing people, that when it comes to conceptualizing—particularly about intellectual, abstract, and general matters—older people have several advantages over younger ones. Children of six or even younger, however, begin to understand many small matters that allow the teacher to give his young deaf pupils appropriate training for their tongues, memory, and comprehension, and gradually to lead them to a knowledge of weightier matters. This task is all the easier as the teacher has led the children to use speech, writing, and the manual alphabet naturally, and they will express themselves with an ease that adults can acquire only with much more practice. There is a very great difference (even greater among the deaf) between knowing how to speak, knowing how to read, and knowing how to write. This difference usually escapes people who are inattentive to it or who have not learned a foreign language. When we reflect about this as we should, we see that, except for distinctions between concrete things, almost all the words in a dictionary are very hard to explain to the deaf, who usually get only confused and inadequate ideas about purely intellectual, abstract, and general things. These claims of mine about the education of the deaf suggest that, generally speaking, for a full appreciation of both language and other subjects, nothing could be harder or more trying than the usual instruction given to the young. But if our explanations of many common words and phrases take the form of recreation, and if the deaf pupil frequently repeats these expressions, he will get such pleasure from this activity that the tedium associated with education will scarcely be felt at all . . .

Habit becomes so incredibly strong that we lose sight of the way we first learned to speak, to read, to write, to think, to reason, and to reflect. Following this argument we see clearly that normal children learn an infinity of things, practicing them for life without being able to explain how they learned them. Speech itself is a clear example of this. Everyone learns to speak, everyone speaks. Practically no one, however, understands the nature of speech sounds and the mechanisms of the speech organs, or even the art of putting the different parts of speech in the proper order. How hard put any learned man would be to explain how he had gone about learning the elements of the very subject in which he excels, or to teach them to others! Wouldn't teachers attribute the success of their methods to their pupils' aptitudes, and pupils attribute their great good fortune to their teachers' methods, talents, and example? Even so, despite their good will, neither teachers nor pupils can give exact answers to questions about the faculties needed to obtain a good education, for they lack a knowledge of this subject. They say not a word about memory, understanding, the wit to guess what is continually happening in the mind, practice, time, the contemplation of the spectacle of nature. Reflecting carefully on this, we realize that to give a deaf person a superficial education requires: (1) getting him to understand the words for everyday concrete things such as goods, clothes, the parts (both furniture and structures) of a house, and the like; (2) teaching him short phrases; (3) leading him to describe actions happening in the immediate environment; (4) explaining to him everyday dialogues; (5) providing the remaining instruction. This is hard to practice and very costly in mental exertion—by "remaining instruction" I mean a proper elucidation of the words contained in all parts of speech, of their appropriate use, of writing according to grammatical rules and the special genius of the language, of grasping subject matter and expressing the same stock of ideas, thoughts, and arguments in a thousand different ways. I tell you, mademoiselle, that the clear, precise explanation of intellectual, abstract, and general terms is one of the thorniest areas of education and potentially disheartening for both teacher and student. It forces the teacher to look at everyday events for a way to get the pupil to appreciate these ideas . . .

You will have realized that a knowledge of concrete objects and of history provides the ladder, as it were, for scaling intellectual, abstract, and general ideas. Despite these comments of mine about the education of the deaf, almost no one can imagine the extent of the difficulties encountered in the study of language. There is a considerable difference between the way a deaf person without a knowledge of language learns the speech of his society, and the way in which another person trained in spoken language studies a foreign language. My sense of this difference is all the keener as I have some knowledge of Latin, Italian, Hebrew, and other languages—languages that I learned by myself during my leisure and without anyone's help. As for the method of teaching language and religion by gesticulations and other signs, I must tell you, mademoiselle, that Father Vanin used signs and drawings to teach me sacred history and Christian doctrine and in this way explained the words and phrases found in the captions. I thought that God the Father was a venerable old man residing in the sky, that the Holy Ghost was a dove surrounded by light, that the Devil was a hideous monster who lived beneath the earth, and so on. So my ideas about religion were concrete, physical, and mechanistic. But after I left Father Vanin, M. Pereire found me fairly advanced in the understanding of everyday language, and so he refrained from using these sorts of signs, making it a fortunate necessity to pay precise attention to the meaning of nouns, verbs, participles, prepositions, sentences, and the import of the order of phrases. He had me express myself in French without my usual signs, and informed me that he had no trouble understanding what I was trying to say, even without these signs. Thereafter, finding me well versed in everyday French, the brothers Pereire and my uncle spoke to me either aloud or, to explain themselves better, with gestures assisted by fingerspelling, in a way much like that of talking with speech sounds. Moreover, they and other persons concerned for my educational progress were pleased to talk with me informally in their homes or the homes of acquaintances, in the street, in public buildings, on walks, at fetes, and so forth, and to have me converse with others. In this way I came to realize how inadequate is the method of religious instruction through signs, above all when it comes to intellectual, abstract, and general ideas, and how cumbersome is the system of assigning a given sign to a given word, which would consequently give us as many signs as there are words and word endings. If we continue to use this method without planning the gradual suppression of these sorts of signs, if we do not get the pupil to explain a lesson, a question, or a passage from a book, in other words, to reply to easy or difficult questions without his teacher's help, and finally to ask questions in words of his own choosing, then memory alone, refreshed by imagination, allows him to respond accurately while his mind has almost no understanding of the intellectual, abstract, and general ideas designated by gesticulations. As the sign determines too narrowly the idea of the word whose use makes the meaning more extended, we may regard this instruction as mechanistic and nearly identical to the training of animals. I base this claim on the experiment carried out with myself, and I note that the manual alphabet is not employed in signed conversation with the deaf, who naturally find it hard to retain language, to use it appropriately in different circumstances, to express themselves properly, and to understand people or books during their instruction.

I ought to explain the manual alphabet used by M. Pereire to spare himself the inconvenience of holding a pen and to avoid the slowness of handwriting, and used by my uncle to teach me about religion.

This kind of Spanish manual alphabet involves the fingers of one hand; it consists of twenty-five signs for the letters of the alphabet, excluding *k* and *w* which are not used in French, and of the signs invented by M. Pereire to make it conform to the rules of French pronunciation and spelling. Hence there are as many speech sounds (thirty-three or thirty-four) and as many clusters in normal writing (thirty-two or more, each cluster making a single speech sound) as there are signs in the manual alphabet, which for this reason I call *dactylology*, the term adopted by M. Pereire. It is true that some letters and clusters vary in sound depending on the words in which they occur. In dactylology, all these different sounds are expressed with a single letter or with a cluster of letters; altogether, the system includes more than eighty signs. The hand is used like a pen for making drawings in the air of the periods and accent marks and to indicate the capitals and small letters and abbreviations. The finger movements mark the long, medium, short, and very short pauses observed in speech. Dactylology includes the signs for numbers and arithmetical operations. It is as rapid and convenient as speech itself, and as expressive as good writing. Other signs can be added freely to accommodate the rules of prosody, music, poetry, and the like.

We can, if we like, retain a manual alphabet with just the signs for all the sounds of speech, which would be valuable for uneducated people. If anyone takes exception to the signs of a manual alphabet, I reply that with regard to the signs from an unfamiliar dactylology, this person is in the same position as deaf persons with regard to the inaudible sounds of speech. With dactylology we can speak to the deaf-and-blind as well as the deaf. Once M. Pereire and I found ourselves in a room at an hour when the night was so dark that we could not make each other out. He wanted to speak to me, and took my hand and separately moved my fingers according to the rules of dactylology. Because my sense of touch was stimulated by the movements of my fingers controlled by his hand, I understood clearly everything he was trying to tell me. He sometimes used this way of speaking throughout the dark days of winter, and when the light was insufficient I understood him just as well. So the use of dactylology deserves to be as widespread as normal writing.

So, mademoiselle, this essay should make it clear that anything we have to say can be evoked in the other person's mind with the help of hearing or sight or touch. Your own further reflections on this matter will inform you better than I could. Developing this line of reasoning, you will soon realize that we could just as easily, though less conveniently, communicate ideas with smell or taste— as we do with hearing or sight or touch. To this end it is enough to make an agreement with some people that a particular smell have the meaning of a particular speech sound or printed letter, and to bring these meaningful smells successively close to the nose so as to present anything we wish to say. We can do likewise with a choice of easily discriminable tastes to represent the sounds or letters, putting them in the mouth in order to get ideas into the mind. With the proper understanding of this whole essay, we will clearly perceive that everything in the world is pure convention and that diligent habit provides the marvelous strength to retain the signs of ideas and of operations of the mind, and naturally helps to recall them.

Every day we read and hear poems, eulogies, panegyrics, and the like, to the memory of great men, heroes, saints, benevolent sovereigns, able ministers, and upright judges; with how much greater reason ought we to pay the one Author of nature the tributes of love, gratitude, praise, of good acts, and even of fidelity and devotion to do everything He requires of us and to avoid anything that displeases Him!

With deep feelings of consideration I am . . .

II

PIERRE DESLOGES

THE FIRST PERSON to publish a defense of the sign language of the deaf, championing it as the proper vehicle for their instruction, was a deaf man, Pierre Desloges, who in 1779 *wrote the short book translated in this volume: Observations d'un sourd et muet sur 'Un Cours élémentaire d'éducation des sourds et muets,' publié en 1779 par M. l'abbé Deschamps* (Amsterdam and Paris: Morin, 1779). The editor (the abbé Copineau, canon of the Church of Saint-Louis-du-Louvre) claims in a preface that this is the first book ever published by a deaf man.

Born thirty-two years earlier in the town of Le Grand-Pressigny in the Loire Valley, Desloges had an attack of childhood smallpox and attributed to it both his deafness and his mutism. Before the illness, when he was seven, he had some knowledge of reading and writing; afterward he received no further formal education, although he continued to study written French on his own. He came to Paris when he was twenty-one, and living in considerable adversity he took up the trade of bookbinding and paperhanging. It was not until he was twenty-seven that he learned the sign language used in the Paris deaf community.

Desloges "took up his pen," he tells us, to defend deaf people's sign language against the scathing attack just published by the abbé Deschamps, canon of the cathedral at Orléans and something of a disciple of the great speech teacher of the deaf, Jacob Pereire. Pereire's most famous pupil, Saboureux de Fontenay, in turn criticized Desloges's book and thus the manualist-oralist battle was joined.

Desloges's book is important to students of deaf history not only for its closely reasoned arguments on behalf of sign language by one of its users and for its early but fragmentary description of that language, but also for the evidence it provides that a sign language of wider communication was in use by the Paris deaf before the abbé de l'Epée adapted it when he inaugurated a formal course for the instruction of the deaf.

A DEAF PERSON'S OBSERVATIONS ABOUT
AN ELEMENTARY COURSE OF EDUCATION FOR THE DEAF

EDITOR'S NOTICE

Authors often give their books titles appropriate to fiction, either in order to mislead their readers, or to publicize their work more strikingly, or for other reasons. This essay is not of that kind; it was actually written by a young deaf man with whom I became acquainted through my dear friend the abbé de l'Epée.

This young man has never been a student of Epée's, but as he has written his essay in defense of Epée's method, he thought it fitting to honor him. He even wanted Epée to read the essay, checking it for publication. The virtuous ecclesiastic's obligations—perhaps his great modesty—prevented him from doing so. So M. Desloges came to me for this service and I performed it with great pleasure.

Here is exactly what I contributed. I corrected the young man's quite faulty spelling. I pruned some repetitions and softened a few words that could have given offense. Aside from these minor emendations, the essay is entirely the work of the deaf Desloges.

These are his thoughts, his style, and his arguments.

I felt that the chief interest of this essay would come from its author, that perhaps for the first time a deaf-mute had the honor of being published; such a phenomenon had to be presented to the public in a form as close to its original as possible. Therefore the only liberty I took was to add a few notes to the text at points where they seemed pertinent.

To satisfy the public's curiosity, I advised M. Desloges to give some personal information, the causes of his infirmity, his ideas of sound and speech, and the like. He discusses these matters in the following preface.

AUTHOR'S PREFACE

Most writers of books add a prefatory note begging the public's indulgence and giving the good or bad reasons for taking up their pen; here are the reasons that prompted me to write this short volume.

My line of work obliges me to go into many homes[1]; once inside I am invariably questioned about the deaf. But most often the questions are as laughable as they are absurd; they merely prove that almost everyone has gotten the falsest possible ideas about us; few people have an adequate notion of our state, our resources, or our way of communicating with each other in sign language.

To add the last straw to the public's errors, a new teacher of the deaf, the abbé Deschamps, publishes a book in which, not content to condemn and reject sign language as an instructional medium, he advances the oddest paradoxes and most erroneous criticisms of it.

As would a Frenchman seeing his language disparaged by a German who knew at most a few words of French, I too feel obliged to defend my own language from the false charges leveled against it by Deschamps and at the same time to justify the abbé de l'Epée's method, which is entirely based on the use of signs. I attempt, moreover, to give a more than usually accurate idea of the language of my comrades the congenitally deaf who are illiterate and whose only sources of instruction have been common sense and the company of their own kind. Here, in brief, is the whole aim of this short book.

As the whole of my subsistence comes from my daily work, while my writing must be done during the time I have for sleeping, I have trained myself to be very terse. So I shall leave unmentioned many things I disapprove of in Deschamps's book although my opinion of them is no higher than of those I have faulted. For the same reason my presentation of sign language is limited to a simple outline of it, with no claim to a full explanation of its mechanism. That would be an immense enterprise requiring several volumes. Indeed, sometimes a particular sign made in the twinkling of an eye would require entire pages for a description of it to be complete. Moreover, I fear that these details would soon become boring to the delicate ears accustomed to the winsome sounds of speech. I fear that this language, which has so much strength and energy in its performance, would weaken under my beginner's pen.

In the hope of gaining a wider public for this short essay, I say just enough to put thoughtful readers on the right path; I may, however, return to this topic and give a more detailed account of the way we can render ideas we wish to express visually, if this meager essay should have the good fortune to be well received by the readers.

It has been judged that a writer as unusual as I may be permitted to say a few words about himself. I have taken this advice and shall conclude this preface with some personal details.

I became deaf and mute following a dreadful attack of smallpox at the age of seven. The two accidents of deafness and mutism occurred at the same time and, so to speak, without my realizing it. During my illness, which lasted nearly two years, my lips became so slack that I can close them only with great effort or the assistance of my hand. In addition I lost all my teeth; it is chiefly to these two causes that I attribute my mutism. Beyond that, it happens that when I try to speak, air escapes and the sound I make is just inchoate. I can utter long words only with great hardship, by constantly breathing in new air which, again escaping, makes my pronunciation unintelligible to strangers. One can reproduce my speech fairly accurately by trying to speak with the mouth open, without closing lips or teeth.[2]

I have been asked a million times whether I still have some idea of sounds, particularly the sounds of speech. Here is everything I can say about that.

First, at more than fifteen or twenty paces I detect all fairly loud sounds, not from using my totally blocked ears, but from the simple disturbance. In my room I can distinguish a passing coach from the beating of a drum.

When I put my hand to a violin or flute being played, I can hear some indistinct sound, even with my eyes closed.[3] I can easily distinguish the sound of a violin from that of a flute, but without my hand on the instrument I can make out absolutely nothing.

It is the same with speech. I cannot hear a speaker unless I have my hand on his throat or the back of his neck. With my eyes closed

I can still hear him talking into an empty cardboard box in my hands but it is impossible for me to hear any other way. I can also easily distinguish the sound of the human voice from any other sound. I have even tried to see whether I could not manage to form a fairly distinct idea of the various articulations of my acquaintances which would enable me, by putting my hand on their throats and the back of their necks, to recognize them in the dark. I was unsuccessful in doing this but it still seems to me possible.

Furthermore, the different ideas I have of sounds are the same as those of my deaf comrades, some of whom hear much better than I. I do not know whether they use their ears or detect the simple disturbance, for several do not have stopped-up ears like mine.[4]

At the beginning of my infirmity, and for as long as I was living apart from other deaf people, my only resource for self-expression was writing or my poor pronunciation. I was for a long time unaware of sign language. I used only scattered, isolated, and unconnected signs. I did not know the art of combining them to form distinct pictures with which one can represent various ideas, transmit them to one's peers, and converse in logical discourse. The first person to teach me this useful art was a man congenitally deaf, Italian by nationality, and illiterate; he was employed as a servant in the household of an actor in the Italian Comedy. He later worked in several great houses, notably that of the prince of Nassau. I became acquainted with this man when I was twenty-seven, eight years after I had settled in Paris.

I think that this is enough talk about me and that a longer treatment of such a minor subject would try my readers' patience.

Parisian society, and indeed all of Europe, rang with praises rightfully due the abbé de l'Epée and his simple, ingenious method of teaching the deaf in sign language. The worthy teacher gives public lessons; this way a crowd of onlookers could appreciate the excellence of his method which leads his pupils with incredible speed and ease to reading, writing, and a knowledge of several languages, then to the pronunciation and understanding of spoken language through the inspection of the movements of the vocal apparatus. Several monarchs have deigned personally to verify the wonders of this far-famed method. One of the chief and most august potentates of Europe [Emperor Joseph II] wanted to go into the most minute details of the work. He came away from the abbé de l'Epée filled with admiration, saying that of everything he had seen in his many travels, nothing had so touched and delighted him as the spectacle he had just witnessed. On returning to his homeland, he concerned himself with the establishment of a similar institution there and sent a worthy ecclesiastic to Epée to take lessons from him and to become familiar with his method.

Nor has our own august monarch [Louis XVI], who gloriously follows in the steps of the good and great Henri IV, neglected this art so precious to humanity. By his own account he has taken this institution under his royal protection, has already assigned it certain funds, and has taken measures to found, for the benefit of the deaf, an educational institution using the abbé de l'Epée's method.

It is at this moment that *An Elementary Course of Education for the Deaf* appears in which the author Deschamps explicitly rejects this method and claims that it should be supplanted by another method, one requiring the deaf to attend to the various movements of the vocal apparatus and to imitate these movements. Before all else, this method begins with teaching the deaf person to make various speech sounds by giving him practice in performing the different mechanics of these sounds so that he is actually speaking for hearing people, and it teaches him to read speech sounds in the movements of the speaker's vocal apparatus as if he were reading them from a book. Deschamps suggests that the deaf person can then proceed to reading and writing proper and eventually to the understanding of whatever language has been chosen as the basis for instruction. This is, at least, the clearest idea I could get of his system and procedure.

First let us see what the author himself thinks of his method:

"Our lessons are not accompanied by pleasure; far from it, they seem to feature a great deal of boredom and distaste; they are unhealthy . . . To these annoyances, add the inherent distastefulness that this instruction necessarily entails . . . the mutual impatience of teacher and pupils seeing the lack of progress produced by repeated effort, the most exact attention, the best will" [introduction, p. 4].

Elsewhere Deschamps says: "The repugnance of deaf people to having us put our fingers in their mouths and to consenting to put their fingers in our mouths can only be overcome with considerable vexation, determination, and patience . . . We must work at it all the more energetically as otherwise it is impossible to give them the use of speech" [p. 155]. He then naively depicts the extreme resistance encountered in persuading the deaf to employ these movements which must initially seem bizarre and utterly incomprehensible to them.

Finally he has the good faith always to represent his method as infinitely tedious, for the teacher as much as the pupils. His prefatory letter ends with these words:

"So I gradually accustom my pupils to writing and speaking . . . To reach this degree of perfection, we must find in the pupils a great desire to learn, intellect, memory, and judgment; and in the teacher, extreme sweetness and accommodation . . . It is impossible to give an idea of the patience required at the start of instruction" [p. 31].

I doubt that such an admittedly boring method, one that conspicuously reverses the natural order of instruction (beginning with the most difficult things and having the pupils work for a long time with no understanding of what is required of them), a method whose successful use demands qualities that are extremely rare in either teacher or pupil, can have many advocates. So I am unsurprised to find Deschamps expressing the desire "that the publication of this book can bring about another, shorter, and easier method" [p. 4].

How could he be so blind as not to recognize that this method was already at hand, long practiced with singular success by the abbé de l'Epée?

Indeed, once Epée had conceived the noble project of devoting himself to the education of the deaf, he wisely observed that they possessed a natural language for communicating to each other. As this language was none other than sign language, he realized that if he managed to understand it, the triumph of his undertaking would be assured. This insight has been justified by success. So the abbé de l'Epée was not the inventor or creator of this language; quite the contrary, he learned it from the deaf; he merely repaired what he found defective in it; he extended it and gave it methodical rules. The learned teacher considered himself like a man suddenly transported to a foreign people to whom he wanted to teach his own native language; he judged that the best way to manage this would be to learn the country's language so as to give easily understandable instructions.

I ask of the abbé Deschamps himself: supposing he were planning to learn English or some other foreign language, how would he go about it? Would be begin by reading a grammar in English of which he understood not a word? Certainly not; he would choose an English grammar written in French, and would learn the new, unknown language easily with the help of his native language.

That is precisely the route taken by the abbé de l'Epée. Could he do anything more sensible or rational? He did not require, as the abbé Deschamps believes [p. 37], a great deal of time, pain, and labor to create his instructional system using natural signs. Order in his ideas, rightness in his observations, a concern to follow nature as a guide in everything—these are the means he made use of, this is the whole magic of his art.

I, no less than the abbé Deschamps, hold speech in great veneration and am mindful of its benefits for the deaf. For that very reason, I take exception to his condemnation and proscription of sign language, for I am persuaded that it is the surest and most natural means for leading the deaf to an understanding of languages, nature having given them this language to substitute for the other languages of which they are deprived.

But is it certain that sign language is natural for the deaf?

Deschamps piles up the most shocking contradictions about this question. He affirms both the positive and the negative.

"Not only does a common inclination lead the deaf to make signs; but all men make use of them naturally: this penchant determines that we who enjoy the use of speech and hearing make use of signs among ourselves without our notice" [p. 1].

Two pages further on we read: "No one can deny it, signs are natural to man."

After such a formal declaration he seriously asks, on the very next page, whether signs are a product of nature or of education. He repeats the same question [p. 8], and finally [p. 12] he solemnly resolves it with these words: "So this inclination is the effect merely of education and not of nature."

The reader then has to choose between these two contradictory opinions: "sign language is natural to the deaf" and "sign language is not natural to the deaf." Whichever opinion the reader embraces, he is sure of having the same opinion as either the abbé Deschamps on page 3 or the abbé Deschamps on page 12.

The author greatly exaggerates the difficulty of sign language [p. 32ff]. If he had given its nature more thought, he would have seen that all men possess its essential basis; for everyone can, when he wishes, use gesture to depict and hence explain the ideas and affections that concern him and that he wants to communicate to others. The belief that sign language is difficult is prompted only by a lack of practice in it.

So what happens to the abbé de l'Epée when he explains the principles of sign language? Spectators at his demonstrations all agree that nothing could be simpler and easier, that anyone could do it.

An adequate acquaintance with sign language requires no more than six weeks of training. Now what language could even the greatest genius profess to learn in six weeks? Wishing to devote himself to the education of the deaf, Deschamps should perhaps have begun by getting instruction for a like period of time in the abbé de l'Epée's school. This unusually honest and open teacher would have delighted in sharing his knowledge with him. With more knowledge of sign language, the abbé Deschamps would have spoken more accurately about it than he does in his book.

He commits a major error in suggesting [pp. 12, 18, 34] that, for the deaf, sign language is limited to physical things and bodily needs.

That is true for those who are deprived of the company of other deaf people or who are abandoned in asylums or isolated somewhere in the provinces. This also unquestionably proves that we usually do not learn sign language from hearing people. But matters are completely different for the deaf living in society in a great city like Paris, for example, which we can rightfully call the epitome of the marvels of the universe. On such a stage as this our ideas are elaborated and extended by our opportunities for constantly observing new and interesting objects.

Therefore, when a deaf person encounters other deaf people more highly educated than he, as I myself have experienced [preface, p. 11], he learns to combine and improve his signs, which had hitherto been unordered and unconnected. In intercourse with his fellows he promptly acquires the supposedly difficult art of depicting and expressing all his thoughts, even those most independent of the senses, using natural signs with as much order and precision as if he understood the rules of grammar. Once again I must be believed, for I have been in this situation myself and speak only from my own experience.

There are congenitally deaf people, Parisian laborers, who are illiterate and who have never attended the abbé de l'Epée's lessons, who have been found so well instructed about their religion, simply by means of signs, that they have been judged worthy of admittance to the holy sacraments, even those of the eucharist and marriage. No event—in Paris, in France, or in the four corners of the world—lies outside the scope of our discussion. We express ourselves on all subjects with as much order, precision, and rapidity as if we enjoyed the faculty of speech and hearing.

So it would be a gross mistake to regard us as some species of automata fated merely to vegetate in the world. Nature has not been as cruel to us as is commonly assumed; it always compensates in one of the senses for what is absent in the others. The privation of hearing makes us more attentive in general. Our ideas concentrated in ourselves, so to speak, necessarily incline us toward reflectiveness and meditation. The language we use among ourselves, being a faithful image of the object expressed, is singularly appropriate for making our ideas accurate and for extending our comprehension by getting us to form the habit of constant observation and analysis.[5] This language is lively; it portrays sentiment, and develops the imagination. No other language is more appropriate for conveying great and strong emotions.

To promote the development of the language the abbé Deschamps seems to advocate a dictionary of signs [p. 33]. A book like this would indeed be a suitable aid to the imagination; it could be the seed of a universal language for all the peoples of the world, since all objects have the same features in all countries. Surprisingly, scholars concerned with many different subjects, often with trifles, are still unaware of this undertaking. In the meantime, however, while we await the enjoyment of this dictionary, let us agree that it exists potentially, for everything, absolutely everything in nature carries with it its own sign. In sign language we find verbs, nouns, pronouns of every kind, articles, genders, cases, tenses, modals, adverbs, prepositions, conjunctions, interjections, and so on. Finally, there is nothing in any part of speech that cannot be expressed in sign language.[6]

The abbé Deschamps, always restricting sign language to physical and material things (to suit his ideas, apparently), claims that if we allow sign language to express morality, the past, and the future, the expression of a single word entails paraphrases and perpetual circumlocutions of signs [p. 18].

He could not have chosen a worse example to support this claim. If we want, he says [p. 19], to use sign language to express the idea of *God*, we will indicate the sky where the Almighty resides. We will say that everything we see is the work of His hands. Then who can assure us that the deaf person will not take the firmament for God Himself, and so forth?

It is I who can assure him, for when I want to designate the Supreme Being by indicating the sky, which is His dwelling place or rather His stepping-stone, I accompany my gesture with an air of adoration and respect that makes my intention quite evident. The abbé Deschamps himself could make no mistake about it. On the other hand, if I want to speak of the sky or the firmament, I will make the same gesture unaccompanied by any of these auxiliaries. So it is easily seen that the two expressions "God" and "firmament" contain no ambiguity or circumlocution.

Nor is there any greater ambiguity or circumlocution in the expression of the past or the future; often our expression in sign will even be shorter than in speech. We need, for example, only two signs to express what you say in three words: *la semaine prochaine* [next week], *le mois qui vient* [next month], *l'année dernière* [last year]. The phrase *le mois qui vient* contains four words; nevertheless I use only two signs for it, one for the month and one for the future, the signs for the article *le* and for the relative pronoun *qui* being superfluous (although these latter signs are on occasion necessary). In addition, all these signs are at least as brief as speech.

It can be truly asserted that Deschamps's claims about sign language are inconsistent and contradictory. After all his harangues against it in twenty places in his book, after first declaring and continually repeating that its employment is highly restricted and that, outside the narrow confines of natural needs and physical ideas, sign language was just a tissue of ambiguity, arbitrariness, difficulty, complications, and so on, here is his justified praise of it [p. 38]. Referring to the abbé de l'Epée, he writes, "In this language of signs he discovered the art of portraying all ideas, all thoughts, all sensations. He has made signs as combinable and variable as the languages we normally use to portray all things in the moral or physical world. Abstract ideas, as well as those we form with the help of the senses—anything lies within the province of sign language . . . Sign language can supplant speech. It is quickly performed, clear in its principles, without too many difficulties in its execution."

After this splendid encomium, wouldn't anyone think that the abbé Deschamps was retracting his erroneous claims about sign language? Be not deceived, reader. Here, directly following the praise you have just read, in his conclusion.

"However wonderful this method, we still do not follow it." One is not expecting such a come-down; it is worthy of a person who could suggest that "deaf people's inclination to express themselves in signs does not prove that this is the best medium for their education" [p. 11]; "the meaning of things is no more difficult for the deaf to acquire through speech than through signs" [p. 21], and so on, and so on.

It would be a waste of time to refute assertions like this. The mere mention of them is enough to bring out their falsity. Moreover, the abbé Deschamps readily lends himself to refutation, for as we have already seen many times, all we have to do to set him in opposition to himself.

One of his strongest objections to sign language is that it is useless in the dark [p. 163]. At first blush this claim seems plausible; nevertheless, it is as ill-founded as the others. Put me in a dark room with a deaf friend, and I will tell him with signs to run some errand, in Paris or in the outskirts; I will inform him about any event you like and I will need no more signs than I use in daylight. The signing would simply take somewhat longer; but it will be a hundred times quicker and easier than the two procedures that our author has invented [p. 163], which consist in touching the speaker's lips or in fingerspelling in the deaf person's palm.

To demonstrate the tedium of these procedures, let us take some of the commonest conversational words such as *applaudissement* [applause], *aplatissement* [humiliation], *assoupissement* [drowsiness], or the like.

These three words together contain at least forty-one letters that must be lipread one by one with the touch method or felt to be written on the palm with the second method. What intelligence, what memory, what a fine tactile sense, how much time it will take to express and remember them all!

Even in total darkness sign language requires only four or five signs to convey these same words, and these signs will be as expressive as speech and as rapid as the wind. This is the whole secret of signing. When I am in darkness and wish to speak to a deaf person, I take his hands and with them form the signs that I would be making with my own hands if I were in daylight. When he wishes to answer me, he in turn takes my hands and forms them into the signs he would be making with his own if we could see clearly.

Despite Deschamps's seemingly unreflective aversion to signs, he still makes frequent use of them in his method of education through speech.

Explaining in his preface or preliminary lesson how he teaches his deaf pupils the names of things, he says [p. xxx]: "I always get them to combine the sign for the thing with the verbal expression so as to make them understand the thing when it alone is not by nature sufficiently palpable." He continues: "The conjugation of verbs presents a host of problems; person, numbers, tenses, and so forth . . . It is true that for this I had recourse to signs to make myself understood."

He discusses [p. 67] how he explains and elaborates the idea of God to his pupils, adding: "We fully realize that signs are of great help in this exercise." He also says [p. 69]: "after getting them to read these details several times and having explained them to them by natural signs," and so on; see also [p. 125] a long passage where he tells how he always explains pronouns by means of natural signs, and so on and so on.

Here again Deschamps's own practice belies his principles, and indeed what means other than signs could he use for explaining words and ensuring that his pupils understand them? I tell him emphatically: if in the education of the deaf we suppress the use of signs, it is impossible to make the pupils anything but machines that speak.

Deschamps uses bits of thread to explain how syllables must be connected. These bits of thread are signs, but they are signs of his own invention. It would have been easy to find some simpler, less cumbersome signs. He seems to have a great dearth of signs. Perhaps he also uses bits of thread to explain in class the mystery of the Holy Trinity.

From the abbé Deschamps's own practice, we must conclude that the chief instrument in the education of the deaf must be sign language and that, like it or not, we will always come back to this method for the compelling reason that sign is their natural language, the only one they can understand until with its help we have taught them another one. So it was a great deal of trouble for nothing to make so much hullabaloo against this poor language of signs!

The abbé Deschamps too often forgets that the abbé de l'Epée's goal is not exactly the learning of sign language. This language is the means, not the end of his instruction. The wise Epée overlooks no branch of education for which the deaf are suited. Thus in addition to religion—the first of the subjects for his thorough instruction—and in addition to reading, writing, basic mathematics, plus the three or four languages of which he gives a smattering to his most apt pupils, he also concentrates on getting them to speak; like the abbé Deschamps, he familiarizes them with guessing or reading speech through lip movements.[7] But he prepares his pupils for these two exercises by reading, writing, and an understanding of words. Now who does not suppose that once the deaf understand perfectly the meaning of words, they will find it easy to make the transition from reading to speech, or rather, to put it more accurately, they will learn without difficulty both reading and speech at the same time?

Deschamps makes a great mystery of the supposedly wondrous art of hearing with the eyes, that is, understanding speech from the movements of the lips, tongue, and cheeks. All my acquaintances know that the persons I live with scarcely speak to me in any other way, without needing to make a sound, provided that the articulation is clear and distinct. Nonetheless, I have received no instruction in this matter. Nature alone has been my guide.

Lipreading is so simple that any deaf person can learn it by himself once he knows the meaning of the spoken words. The only thing needed is for persons wishing to address him this way to speak deliberately and distinctly, to open their mouths enough for the deaf person to observe the mechanism of their speech, and finally, to put fairly strong stress on each constituent syllable, and to pause briefly at the end of each word. I believe I have now said enough to effect a reconciliation between the abbé Deschamps and sign language. Nevertheless, to throw still more light on this language, I shall, as I have promised, [preface, p. 3], briefly explain how my friends use sign language without taking lessons from any teacher except nature.

Furthermore I would like to declare, before I go any further, that it is not my intention to belittle the author whom I have taken the liberty of criticizing. I laud and respect his zeal for a kind of work that cannot be overencouraged. He is too good a thinker to take offense at my remarks, and if he considers them unprejudicially, he will soon recognize that I had no intention of slighting him. In addition, he confesses [p. iv] that he has taken only a few steps forward in this difficult field, so he still has a chance to regain the proper course and to acquire a better idea of this inadequately investigated language; this is the main purpose of the new observations that we are going to read about here and that will conclude this book.[8]

The abbé Deschamps is not alone in supposing that [p. 37] the abbé de l'Epée was the creator of sign language. But this opinion is untenable, for I have already shown that my illiterate comrades who do not attend the gifted teacher's school make extensive use of sign language, that they possess the art of giving a visual representation of their thoughts and ideas, and even the ones most independent of the senses.

Here are some examples that explain in greater detail the wonderful but simple and natural mechanism of this language as we use it.

(1) To designate some close acquaintance, we need only two or three signs. First, we make a general sign indicating the person's sex by putting the hand to the hat or breast; we then make a special sign for individuating this person. But more signs are needed to name more distant acquaintances of whom we have only a rough idea or whom we know only by reputation. First, we indicate the person's sex (this sign must always come first); then we make the sign for the person's social class as determined by his birth and fortune. Then we individuate this person with signs taken from his profession, residence, and the like. This operation requires no more time than is required to mention, say, "M. de Lorme, draper, rue Saint-Denis."

In further conversation we have no need to repeat the same number of signs to designate the same person. In fact, that would be as pointless as always repeating someone's first and last names plus all his attributes.

(2) We have two different signs for designating nobility. We divide it into two classes, upper and lower. To mention the upper nobility, we move the flat of the left hand to the right shoulder and draw it down to the left hip. Then we spread the fingers and place the hand over the heart. We designate the lower nobility by tracing a small band with the fingertip and a cross on the buttonhole of the suit. Then, to indicate someone from either class of nobility, we use signs taken from his occupation, coat of arms, livery, and such, or the most natural signs for individuating him.

(3) If I wanted to designate an acquaintance who had the same name as some familiar object, such as *L'Enfant du Bois, La Rivière* [Woodchild, River], I would avoid using the sign for a child, wood, a river, or the like; I would certainly meet with incomprehension by my deaf friends who would see no connection between a man and a river, and so on, and would laugh at me. But knowing that our language depicts the proper idea of something and not the arbitrary names given them in spoken language, I would designate these persons by their individual characteristics, as I explained a short while back.

Similarly, if I wanted to mention a prince of the blood, then once I had made the signs for a lord, I would be ill-advised to make the sign for the blood running through our veins—that is merely the sign for a word. I would take my signs from the degree of relationship between the prince and the sovereign.

(4) The sign for the class of tradesmen is different from the sign for manufacturers who sell their own products, for the deaf have the good sense not to confuse these two occupations. They regard as true tradesmen only people who buy something in order to resell it as is. The generally sign we use to designate these tradesmen gives the idea of *as is*. With the thumb and index finger, we take the hem of a garment or some other object and present it the way a tradesman offers his merchandise; we then make the movement for counting money with our hands, and cross our arms like someone resting. The combination of these three signs denotes the class of tradesmen in the strict sense.

The action of working is the sign common to the class of manufacturers, artisans, and laborers. An additional sign is required to show that the object of discussion is a supervisor. Then we raise the index finger and lower it in a commanding way—that is the sign common to all supervisors. We also use it to talk about a shopkeeper as distinct from a street vendor. If we want to indicate directly someone from these classes, we need merely designate the tradesman's type of business or the manufacturer's product along with his residence, or the most appropriate sign for individuating him.

Thus, when necessity or expressive clarity demands, we always mention the social class of the person we are speaking about or wish to introduce.

You will realize that this simple, natural means of communication spares the imagination a great deal of trouble and work. We guide the imagination this way—as if by degrees—toward the object we wish to represent. This procedure puts order in our ideas and enables us to understand who is being referred to with fewer signs than spoken words giving his first name, last name, and individual characteristics.

With procedures similar to this, we will need merely two or three signs to designate any one of a family with some ten children.

(5) But I am committed to proving an even stronger claim. Paris is so large that one is obliged to have a written address for people whose residence one is trying to find for the first time, and despite this precaution it is often difficult to locate the dwelling in question. Nevertheless, I can successfully direct any illiterate deaf friend of mine to any building in Paris, whether shop or townhouse or first

or sixth-floor room, provided that I have once seen it myself. I would use fewer signs to give him the person's address than I would write in words.

(6) What I have said about signs for each social class can also be extended to any object that we want to indicate individually when the idea of it is remote or the natural sign for it does not immediately present itself or, finally, when the natural sign by itself is insufficiently expressive. In this case we make the general sign for this object. If, for example, I am talking about a piece of pastry the sign for which also applies to some object, I would precede the sign with the sign for the general category of pastry. Then a deaf person could not be mistaken about the sign expressing the kind of pastry I am talking about, for his imagination will be focused on the particular class I have in mind.

I recall once being with a hearing person holding a small black cane and asking her in sign language what the cane was made of. She answered aloud, "of whale." Uncomprehending, I entreated her to explain it to me in sign. She made several ridiculous gestures that could apply to a number of animals. As she perceived that I did not understand at all, she asked for a pencil to write the word down. A deaf friend of mine who was present and who had recognized the substance, immediately made the gestures for a fish swimming and then for a gigantic animal. These two signs were sufficient to make clear to me that the cane was made of whalebone, for the first gesture had indicated the general category of fish. Such are the general and particular signs we use in our language.

We can reduce all signs to three general classes, and by combining and uniting them, we can express every possible idea.

(1) *Ordinary* or *basic* signs. These are signs in frequent conversational use all over the world for a multiplicity of ideas for which a gesture is handier and more expressive than speech. We generally find them in all parts of speech, especially pronouns and interjections. As I have stated, these signs are natural to all people, but hearing people make them unreflectively and without thinking about them, whereas the deaf always use them deliberately to present their ideas and make them palpable.

I am not thereby claiming that my deaf friends have an exact understanding of the function of a pronoun or article or verb or any other part of speech. They are as utterly ignorant of all this as are three-quarters of all hearing people. Even so, if we asked them the reasons for the three signs they make to express the phrase *je le veux* [I want it], they would have no trouble answering that: they place their index finger on their breast to indicate that the matter is *in them* and *of them alone*; they raise and lower the same index finger with a commanding air to express their *will*; they point the same index finger at the thing they have in mind so as to indicate the *object* or *term* of their will.

(2) *Reflected* signs. They represent objects that have—in absolute terms—their natural signs, but still require a bit of reflection before being combined and understood. I have given several examples of these signs in my discussion of general and particular signs.

(3) *Analytic* signs. These are the signs rendered natural through analysis. They aim to represent ideas that do not, strictly speaking, have any natural signs and so in sign language are based on analysis. It was analytic signs especially and also reflected ones that the abbé de l'Epée subjected to methodical rules so as to facilitate instruction.

Here is my explanation of how this analysis works. I have no knowledge of metaphysics or grammar or the sciences requiring advanced study. But good sense and reason tell me that it will seem impossible at first to produce a visual representation of the idea, alone and isolated, of an object absolutely independent of the senses.

If, on the other hand, I can imagine secondary ideas to accompany this first idea, I find a host of natural signs that I combine in a twinkling and that express this idea very clearly. I have previously given an example (p. 21) when I dealt with the word "God."

It is the same with ideas that are more concrete but that can still be expressed only with the help of analysis. For example, in talking about an ambassador I may not immediately hit upon a natural sign for the idea, but in going back to the secondary ideas I make the signs for a king who sends a lord to another king to discuss weighty issues; then a deaf person from Peking will get the idea as fast as a deaf person from Paris.[9]

The abbé de l'Epée gives a good explanation (*Instruction of the Deaf*, p. 144) of the signs needed to express the idea *dégénérer* [degenerate], the same signs as those used by my deaf comrades. So we always find signs for a main idea by the analysis of its auxiliary ideas.

I cannot understand how a language like sign language—the richest in expressions, the most energetic, the most incalculably advantageous in its unversal intelligibility—is still so neglected and that only the deaf speak it (as it were). This is, I confess, one of those irrationalities of the human mind that I cannot explain.

Several famous scholars have worn themselves out in the vain search for the elements of a universal language as a point of unification for all the people of the world. How did they fail to perceive that it had already been discovered, that it existed naturally as sign language, that all that had to be done was to improve the language and subject it to a methodical procedure, as the abbé de l'Epée has done so well?[10]

Moreover, let not what I say here, in favor of a language made necessary for me by my infirmity and in favor of the abbé de l'Epée's method based entirely on sign, be regarded as the effect more of enthusiasm than reflection. I am going to show that the most searching linguistic investigators have judged this language and this method as favorably as I have.

One such scholar is M. Court de Gébelin, author of a *Universal Grammar* (Ruault, 1774); the second is the author of *Synthetic Essay on the Origin and Formation of Languages* (Ruault, 1774); the third is the abbé de Condillac, author of *A Course of Education for the Prince of Parma* (Monory, 1776). The most fitting conclusion to this essay will thus consist of quotations from these three writers.

Court de Gébelin expresses himself as follows in Chapter 9, "On various ways of picturing ideas":

"The deaf, who are currently taught with a splendid, simple method to understand and to write compositions in any language whatever, and whose exercises we cannot witness without emotion, had had no other instruction. Not only were they taught to express their ideas with gestures and in writing in various languages, but they were raised to an understanding of the principles that make up the universal grammar and that, taken from nature and the order of things, are invariable and determine all the forms in which ideas are depicted in all peoples and all methods" (p. 16).

In another passage from this book, he says: "With gesture we can form a language subject to the same principles, the same operations, and the same rules as spoken language, for gesture can depict the same objects, the same ideas, the same sentiments, and the same passions" (p. xxii).

In the *Synthetic Essay* the author proposes his answer to the important question of how men manage by themselves to create a language. He observes (p. 21) that one of the first languages would be that of signs, for sign language (which is largely independent of convention) represents or recalls the idea of things by signs that are not arbitrary, but natural.

The learned author says:

> This language is a kind of painting that puts objects before our very eyes, so to speak, by means of gestures, attitudes, different postures, bodily movements, and actions. This language is so natural to mankind that despite the help we get from spoken languages to express our thoughts and all their nuances, we still make frequent use of it, especially when we are moved by some passion, and we leave off using the cold and measured tone prescribed by our institutional training, to bring us closer to the tone of nature.
>
> This is also the common language of children. It is the only language that mutes can use among themselves, and it is an established fact that with it they can go far in the communication of their thoughts.

The author adds the following note to the passage just cited:

> As for the perfectibility of sign language, we know the surprising things reported about the mutes of the sultan [harem eunuchs]. If anyone has the slightest doubt about the possibility of the fact, let him attend the daily lessons given by the abbé de l'Epée, and with admiration mingled with poignancy he will see him surrounded by a crowd of mutes whom he instructs with disinterested zeal. His primary means of instruction is a mimic or sign language so perfected that every idea has its own distinct sign, always taken from nature or something as close to it as possible. Analogous ideas are represented by analogous signs suitable for making their interconnections and interrelations concretely felt. With these signs, his pupils understand and give precise expression to the subtlest metaphysical analysis of language and the most abstract ideas. It is a kind of simplified, improved hieroglyphic language that includes everything and employs gestures to depict what the Chinese language depicts with characters. (p. 22)

The abbé de Condillac distinguishes two kinds of action language, one a natural language whose signs are given by biological constitution, the other an artificial language whose signs are given by analogy. He remarks:

> The abbé de l'Epée, who displays a singular wisdom in instructing the deaf, has made the action language into a simple and easy and systematic art for giving his pupils ideas of all kinds—ideas, I venture to say, more exact and precise than those usually acquired with the help of hearing. Because in childhood we are reduced to judging the meaning of words from the circumstances in which we hear them uttered, it frequently happens

that we grasp this meaning only approximately—we have only a loose grasp of it and we make do with this approximation all our lives. It is different with the deaf instructed by the abbé de l'Epée. He has only one way to give them ideas that lie beyond the senses; namely, to analyze and to get his pupils to analyze the ideas with him. So he leads them from concrete ideas to abstract ideas by simple and methodical analyses; and we can see how advantageous his action language is over the spoken sounds of our governesses and tutors.

The abbé de l'Epée teaches his pupils French, Latin, Italian, and Spanish. And he dictates to them in these four languages with the same action language. Why so many languages? To enable foreigners to judge his method, and he flatters himself that he may find someone in authority to found an establishment for the education of the deaf. He himself has created one, sacrificing some of his own funds. I thought it my duty to seize the opportunity to give due credit to the talents of this generous citizen who, I believe, does not know me, although I have been at his school and have seen his pupils, and he has given me full information about this method (Vol. I, footnote, p. 11).

III

CHARLES-MICHEL DE L'EPEE

The guileless, gentle, devout person who first gathered numerous deaf children under one roof for instruction using sign language—and thus was responsible for founding the education of the deaf as a social class—was born Charles-Michel de l'Epée in 1712. His father was an architect in the service of Louis XIV at Versailles. The young man's career in the church was arrested at the deaconhood, for he refused to sign a profession of anti-Jansenist faith. Then he began and later abandoned a legal career. When Epée was in his late forties, living a quiet life of leisure in Paris, the mother of two deaf daughters appealed to him to undertake their religious instruction and so gave Epée the inspiration for his ultimate vocation as teacher of the deaf. It occurred to him that the deaf could be taught written French by using their sign language, just as he himself had been taught Latin using his own native French. In the next two decades the number of deaf pupils coming to Epée's home for instruction grew from two to over sixty.

To gain public recognition of his pupils' achievements, and thus to promote the education of the deaf throughout Europe, Epée began, in 1771, to hold public demonstrations in a chapel installed in his home. The pupils would write out texts dictated in a version of their sign language that Epée had altered to make it more similar to French. Epée describes this "methodical sign" language and how it was taught in *La Véritable Manière d'instruire les sourds et muets, confirmée par une longue expérience* (Paris: Nyon, 1784). The American Francis Green published an English translation of this book in 1802; the language of the translation is now archaic, and Green had to take considerable liberties with the original to make it a textbook for the teaching of English; the first five chapters in a new translation are presented here. This book was the touchstone for the worldwide dissemination of Epée's method of using sign to educate the deaf; in his lifetime his disciples founded a dozen schools for the deaf throughout Europe, which in turn gave rise to hundreds more.

Despite his burgeoning celebrity Epée never accepted any personal remuneration, and he in fact exhausted his modest inheritance in the upkeep of his pupils and assistants, who spread the tale of his doing without comforts like heat so as to spare more wood for keeping them warm.

On his deathbed in 1789 Epée learned that the revolutionary National Assembly was to take his school under its protection and thus to ensure the continuation of his work.

Abbé de l'Epée

THE TRUE METHOD OF EDUCATING THE DEAF, CONFIRMED BY MUCH EXPERIENCE

AUTHOR'S PREFACE

The work published here is, properly speaking, a second edition of a book that appeared in 1776 with the title *Institution des sourds et muets par la voie des signes méthodiques* [*Educating Deaf-Mutes Using Methodical Signs*], which is now out of print.

Religion and humanity inspire me with such a great interest in a truly destitute class of persons who, though similar to ourselves, are reduced, as it were, to the condition of animals so long as no attempts are made to rescue them from the darkness surrounding them, that I consider it an absolute obligation to make every effort to bring about their release from these shadows.

It is to perform this essential duty that I am here setting forth my procedures for enabling many deaf persons to take part in public exercises in which children hitherto regarded as semiautomatons have demonstrated beyond question an intelligence higher than that shown by most young people of the same age.

The book will show, as clearly as possible, how to go about bringing in through the window what cannot come in through the door; namely, to insinuate into the minds of the deaf through the visual channel what cannot reach them through the auditory channel.

May the discussions of these procedures fall into the hands of all people whose compassion is sufficiently aroused at the sight of the sad, deplorable state of the deaf to resolve with generosity and Christianity to undertake their education, a task less difficult and laborious than is commonly thought.

Much of the content of the first edition of this book has been expunged in this second edition; hence the change in title. The deletion is not, however, due to any material defect that I have perceived, or that others have pointed out, in the first edition. I would be glad to publish the book precisely as it appeared in 1776 if I were now in the same position as at its first appearance; but as my circumstances have since completely changed, what was then necessary has become totally superfluous.

When I first undertook the education of two deaf twin sisters for whom no tutor could be found after the death of Father Vanin (the occasion of my attempting this kind of instruction), I did not know that a teacher in Paris [Pereire] had been working with the deaf for several years and had gained disciples. Yet he had acquired some reputation owing to the commendation bestowed on him by the Academy of Sciences, and his method for enabling the deaf to speak was considered a justly praiseworthy resource.

This person was not the originator of this method, however. It had been practiced about a hundred years before by Wallis in England, Bonet in Spain, and Conrad Amman, a Swiss physician in Holland, who had all published excellent treatises on the subject. He [Pereire] had, however, profited from their work, and his skill in this endeavor merits the approbation he obtained.

Because neither my studies nor my profession had heretofore brought these illustrious authors to my attention, I hadn't the slightest desire to get my two pupils to speak, and did not even suspect that it was feasible. My only goal was to get them to think systematically and to combine their ideas. I supposed this might be brought about with representative signs reduced to a method from which I constructed a kind of grammar.

M. Pereire, the teacher of the deaf I am alluding to, and his ablest disciple, neither of whom I had any knowledge of, were soon informed of my method. They deemed the project that I had conceived impossible, and the idea I was attempting to realize more likely to obstruct than to facilitate my pupils' progress.

Because this skepticism gained some public support from M. Pereire's reputation, I felt it was necessary to combat the prejudice against my method of teaching when it was published, as I believed myself commanded by Providence to render the unfortunate deaf every service within my power for the benefit of current and future generations.

I therefore argued that these gentlemen's reasoning was invalid, and even ventured to show that although M. Pereire's system for teaching—called dactylology or fingerspelling—could lead the deaf to speak, it was nevertheless utterly worthless for teaching them to think.

M. Pereire responded in the newspaper that he would answer my allegations as soon as his leisure permitted. Although he lived for several years after offering to take up the challenge, he never replied. Indeed, he never, in my opinion, had any real intention of doing so. His ablest disciple remained equally silent. Everything on this subject in the first edition, being now no doubt superfluous, would therefore swell the present edition to no purpose.

But I had other, more formidable adversaries to combat, namely, those theologians, rationalistic philosophers, and academicians of various nationalities who held that metaphysical ideas were inexpressible by signs and hence necessarily beyond the understanding of the deaf.

It required considerable time, argument, public exercises on abstract matters (in more than one language), daily lessons attended by scholars from all over Europe, and above all clear and precise and unrehearsed explanations by the deaf of the metaphysics of every regular verb, to convince every reasonable person that: (1) because every word means something, then anything, no matter how abstract, can be clearly explained by an analysis in simple words that ultimately need no explanation; (2) this analysis can be presented in speech or writing to a person with normal hearing, for hearing or reading the simple words in it reminds him of the signs made to him since childhood, without which he would have no more understanding of the words originally heard or read than if they had been in German or Greek or Hebrew; (3) the deaf can be offered the same analysis only in writing, but it will be just as valid because reading the simple constituent words readily calls to mind the meanings of the words that have become as familiar to them as they are to us, being in constant use in intercourse between them and us.

If some scholar is still inclined to dispute or to doubt these principles, not having witnessed our demonstrations, I urge him to honor us with his attendance. I do think it unsuitable, however, to weigh down the second edition of this book with every claim from the first one just to invalidate a claim since generally disproved.

Therefore, I thought it appropriate to omit more than half of the first edition, and to introduce new procedures that have in eight years' experience proven effective.

This new method has three parts. In the first I explain procedures enabling the deaf to continue their education by themselves, through reading good books. In the second part, drawing on the work of Bonet and Amman as well as my own thoughts, I describe steps for teaching the deaf to *speak*; I repeat almost verbatim the claims made about this in my *Methodical Instruction*, for the repetition is definitely necessary.

The third part concerns a serious dispute that arose between the teacher of the deaf in Leipzig [Nicolai] and the teacher in Vienna [Storck] and me. Scholars from all countries, I trust, will be grateful for the documents from this literary contest, carried on in Latin, as well as for the judgment made after a full discussion by the Academic

Society of Zurich, to which I applied for a decision about the controversy so that M. Nicolai could not complain that his judges were
French. The academies or literary societies of Leipzig, Vienna, Upp-
sala, and Saint Petersburg were similarly consulted, but they did not
grant us a reply.

The third part is of particular interest for the deaf because it may
determine which method, that of Leipzig or that of Paris, is better
for teachers of the deaf.

PART I

Teaching the deaf is less difficult than is commonly supposed. We
merely have to introduce into their minds by way of the eye what
has been introduced into our own by the ear. These two avenues
are always open, each leading to the same point provided we do not
deviate to the right or left, whichever one we choose.

CHAPTER 1. HOW THE INSTRUCTION OF THE DEAF IS TO BEGIN

In any language, we do not learn the meaning of words merely
from hearing them uttered. Words like "door" or "window" could
be repeated hundreds of times without our ever attaching any idea
to them if the objects designated had not simultaneously been shown
to us. A sign from the hand or eye was the only means for learning
to combine the idea of these objects with the sounds stimulating
our ears. Whenever we heard these sounds, the same ideas came to
mind because we remembered the signs made when those sounds
were uttered.

We must use the same procedures with the deaf. The instruction
begins with a manual alphabet, such as schoolchildren use to communicate from one side of the classroom to the other. The letter
shapes make a strong visual impression on the deaf, who are no
more likely to confuse them than we confuse the various sounds
we hear.

Next we write (I say "we" because with my deaf pupils I often
have assistants) on a blackboard the words "the door," and show
them the door. The pupils immediately fingerspell each letter of the
word five or six times, impressing on their memory the number and

order of the letters. Once they have done this, they erase the word, and taking the chalk themselves, write it out, no matter how well- or ill-formed the letters. Then they write it out each time you show them the same object.

They do the same with everything else that is pointed out, the name being written down beforehand, first in large letters on the blackboard, then in normal-sized letters on different cards. When these cards are handed to the pupils, they take pleasure in examining each other's proficiency and in ridiculing errors. Experience has shown that a deaf person of normal intelligence will, with this procedure, acquire upwards of eighty words in less than three days.

Take some card with the appropriate letters, and give them one by one to your pupil. He will point successively to each part of his body corresponding to the word on the card. Shuffle the cards as you like, and he will never make a mistake. Or if you write one of these words on the board, you will see him point to each object named, proving that he understands the meaning of the name.

With this procedure the pupil will in just a few days learn all the words for the different parts of the body, from head to foot, as well as the words for various objects in the environment, as you point to names written on the board or on cards in his hand.

Even at this early stage, however, we do not limit ourselves to just this one type of instruction, entertaining as it is to the pupils. From the very first day or so, we write out the indicative present of the verb "carry" and explain it by signs as follows.

With several pupils seated around a table, I place a new pupil on my right. I put the index finger of my left hand on the word "I," and explain it in signs: pointing to myself with my right index finger, I give my breast two or three gentle taps. Then, with my left index finger on the word "carry," I pick up a large book and carry it under my arm, in the skirts of my soutane, on my head, on my shoulder, on my back, walking about with the expression of someone carrying a heavy burden. None of these actions escapes the pupil's notice.

I return to the blackboard. To explain the second-person singular, I put my left index finger on the word "you," and with my right index finger on the pupil's breast, I give it a few gentle taps, getting him to notice that I am looking at him and he at me. Next I put my finger on the second-person "carry" and handing him the book, I make signs for him to imitate my action. He laughs, takes the book, and performs the action indicated.

Then comes the third-person singular. I put my left index finger on the word "he," and with my right point to someone nearby, making it evident that I am not looking at him (for I am speaking *about* him, not *to* him). I give him the book without looking at him; he carries it about in the various ways described and lays it back down on the table. Then I draw a line under the three singular persons, the explanation of them complete.

We proceed to the plural. I put my left index finger on the word "we," and with my right point first to me, then to everyone around the table, and finally back to me again, showing that no one has been left out. Then we lift the table, and carry it about.

Then comes the second-person plural. Putting my left index finger on the word "you," I use my right to point to the person on my left and, in succession, all the pupils around the table up to and including the new pupil at my right. Instead of indicating myself, however, I withdraw a few paces from the group; the other pupils then lift the table and carry it about. It is evident that I myself am not involved in this action.

We now come to the third-person plural. Returning to the table, I put my left index finger on the word "they," and with my right point to everyone around the table, beginning with the person on my left and ending with the person to the right of my new pupil, whom I then take aside. He and I remain idle while the others lift and carry the table.

Needless to say, the new pupil is delighted with this activity. Still, we have to anticipate a minor difficulty. I have the new pupil do everything he has seen me do with the first, second, and third persons, singular and plural. He begins, and right at the start (through no fault of his) he makes a mistake. With his left index finger on "I," he puts his right on *my* breast, thinking that "I" was *my* name, as he had seen me several times apply this word to myself.

To correct this mistake, I immediately call on five or six of the pupils who were part of the "we," "you," and "they" to join us. Each of these pupils points first to himself, with one finger on the "I," then to someone he is looking at and to whom he turns, with a finger on "you," and finally to a third person, without looking at him or turning toward him, having an index finger on "he." So our student learns to call himself "I" as others do, and there is no further problem.

To avoid losing time, we use a language that means something right at the start. The pupil necessarily understands us, if he is not as devoid of intelligence as a horse or mule; and he henceforth understands what he is writing when, on the model of "carry," he conjugates "I pull, you pull," and so on, or "I drag, you drag," and so on.

In short, he understands in a day or two every sentence made up of one of the six persons of the present-tense transitive verb with its object (e.g., "I pull the table; you drag the chair; he offers an armchair; we are looking at the mirror; you close the door; they shut the window"). All these verbs express actions whose signs are immediately understood, and the pupil can see with his own eyes that this sign refers to these activities going on.

It would be premature to go into a detailed explanation of verbs. What we have shown with the present indicative of "carry" is merely a sort of anticipation, useful because it develops the mental faculties of the deaf better than the usual way of beginning with the declension of nouns or pronouns. Furthermore, the pupils have more fun with it because of the number of short sentences they thereby acquire which is a major consideration in teaching people who must be attracted to study by the pleasure of applying it. Although we confine ourselves to these preliminaries, our pupils, with the help of the teachers they live with and from their recreational scribbling when they are together, gradually learn the other tenses of this first verb. So without realizing it, they lay a valuable foundation on which we can build.

Chapter 2. How to Proceed with the Education of the Deaf

With the method just described, the pupils soon acquire the idea of a number of nouns. They see the article *la* or *le* or *l'* in front of each one. So it is appropriate to give them a sample declension, and to get them to practice it.

This exercise is considerably less entertaining than the two previous ones. But since our deaf student has developed respect and affection for his teacher, he is easily induced to try his best with whatever is offered for his instruction.

The Declension of Nouns: Articles and Their Signs

To teach declension we get our pupils to note the different articles, cases, numbers, and genders, giving him at the same time signs for these features of nouns.

Here is our procedure. We get our pupil to observe the joints of our fingers, hands, wrist, elbow, and so on, and we call them articles or joints. We then inform him by writing on the blackboard that articles [le, la, du, de la, des] connect words the way our joints connect our bones (grammarians must forgive the divergence of my definition from theirs). After this, the right index finger bent two or three times in the form of a hook becomes the general sign of an article.

Gender is explained by putting the hand to the hat, for the masculine article le, or to the ear, the part to which a female's bonnet extends, for the feminine article la.

The plural article les is expressed with the repetition of this movement for the four fingers of one or both hands in the form of a hook.

The apostrophe is shown by drawing an apostrophe in the air with the right index finger. If the apostrophe is followed by a masculine noun, we add the sign for the masculine, and for a feminine noun, the sign for the feminine.

Du and de la are articles of the second or possessive case. To the sign of the article we add the sign for the second case, and so on, as well as the sign for singular or plural, for masculine or feminine. We are careful to observe that de, du, and des of the ablative are not articles, but prepositions, each with its own particular sign depending on its use.

The Signs for Case, Number, and Gender

In learning declensions the pupil clearly sees the distinction between cases, in both the singular and the plural. I use fingerspelling to teach him the terms "nominative," "genitive," "dative," and so on. For the moment we need not give the etymologies of these terms, but we do give each an appropriate sign: "first," "second," "third" and so forth, descending from the first or nominative case to the sixth or ablative case. These are more understandable names than any others we could apply to these terms, even after defining them. We shall show later how "first," "second," "third," and so on, are distinguished from "one," "two," "three," and so on.

The following is a sign for the term "case": we twirl two fingers round each other while declining, that is, while descending from the first to the sixth case. Raising the right thumb designates the singular; the wiggling of several fingers, the plural. We ensure that our pupils notice that a plural generally ends in s.

We distinguish the two genders by moving the hand to the place of the hat or mobcap, as mentioned earlier.

The Difference Between Nouns and Adjectives and Their Corresponding Signs

To differentiate between nouns and adjectives, we take nine cards or nine pieces of paper. On one of them we write down the word "Pierre," and place it on our left. On each of the others we write an adjective such as "tall," "short," "rich," "poor," "weak," "learned," "ignorant," and place them on our right.

Pierre enters, and we see that he is a person of some stature. We take the card with "tall" on it, and place it above his name. He came in a coach, and is richly dressed. So we take the card with "rich" on it, and put it too above his name. We do the same with the cards with "strong" and "learned" on them. for Pierre appears to be strong, and he is said to be learned. The noun "Pierre" names a substance underlying these four qualities (*stat sub*), and this is the true idea of a noun to which we add the appropriate qualities. An adjective expresses a quality added to the noun. The general sign for a noun is the left hand under the right, and then the right hand becomes the sign for an adjective in general.

Because adjectives are added to both masculine and feminine nouns, they too have two genders, masculine and feminine. The deaf pupil is given some model, and told to decline the adjective using these models. He or she learns that the masculine noun is always modified by a masculine adjective, a feminine noun by a feminine adjective, and that the adjective always takes the same number, singular or plural, as the noun.

Adjectives Ending in -able and -ible and Their Corresponding Signs

Adjectives ending in *-able* and *-ible*, and derived from verbs, designate a quality that should or may, respectively, be attributed to an object. For *-able* we add to the sign for the quality a sign for necessity, and for *-ible* a sign for possibility. When these adjectives are expressed in Latin by the future passive particle ending in *andus-a-um* or *endus-a-um*, they refer to a quality that must be attributed to the object in question, and the following three signs are used. The first sign expresses the action mentioned in the verb, as with "love," "adore," and "respect." A second sign indicates that the word is an adjective. A third sign tells us that the adjective necessarily refers to the subject of the sentence. "Adore," for example, is the action of a verb; "adored" is the adjectival form, but "adorable" is an adjective that necessarily applies to God, the subject of the sentence.

When these adjectives are translated into Latin as words ending in -*bilis, is, e,* they generally refer to a quality which may, though not necessarily, apply to its subject. Then a first sign expresses the action of the verb "elect," for example. A second sign indicates the adjectival form "elected," but a third sign, representing mere possibility, gives the word "eligible."

To express necessity, we make several forceful taps with our index finger on the table, an action natural to everyone asserting something to be his right. To express possibility, we turn our head to the right, a "yes," and to the left, a "no"—which, we cannot tell; we shall know only from the event.

When adjectives ending in -*able* are not dervied from a verb, but from a noun, like "charitable," they express neither necessity nor possibility, but merely a quality inherent in the subject of which we are speaking.

Positive, Comparative, Superlative, and Excessive Adjectives and Their Corresponding Signs

Adjectives are positive, like "tall"; comparative, like "taller"; superlative, like "tallest"; and excessive, like "too tall."

To express "tall" I bring my hand up to a certain height, and make our established sign for an adjective. If I meant "taller," then after momentarily holding my hand at the preceding height, I raise it slightly higher. Thus I indicate the comparative. When I mean "tallest," I pause twice, once at the height of the positive, another at the height of the comparative; then I raise it even farther. And for the excessive, I make a final sign expressing my dissatisfaction and impatience at this fourth degree of tallness.

Nouns Made from Adjectives, Called Abstract Qualities, and Their Signs

Names of qualities such as "good," "great," "wise," and "learned" necessarily imply nouns to which they apply, but if we consider only the qualities expressed, without reference to a noun, then these qualities have other qualities applied to them, and themselves become nouns, like "goodness," "greatness," "wisdom," and "learning."

We express these strong, substantified adjectives as follows. To dictate the word "greatness," for instance, we first make the sign for "great," an adjective, and then add the sign for a noun, which signals that the adjective is a substantive and so modifiable by other adjectives. I present several examples, and then the pupil makes no mistake, either in reading or in writing from dictation.

Numbers and Their Signs

Nouns for numbers are divided into cardinal and ordinal, each type with its distinctive sign. For "three," we hold up three fingers vertically. For "third," however, we hold the fingers horizontally and move them forward in the order of procession or battle, thus indicating that "third" is in a row with the others, and specifies its rank. A cardinal number takes just the former sign, but an ordinal number also includes the latter sign. Our pupil need not notice that it is an adjective, however, as the thing speaks for itself.

CHAPTER 3. INDICATIVE TENSES OF "BE"

Once our pupil has an adequate understanding of the difference between adjectives and nouns, we show him how the verb forms "I am," "you are," "he is," and so on, unite a noun with an adjective when they go together, and how the addition of a negative to this verb separates them when they do not properly go together. We give him several examples and have him memorize all the tenses of the indicative of this verb so as to increase his stock of phrases before he has a thorough enough knowledge of verbs and the other parts of speech for his instruction to proceed unhampered.

The sign for the verb "be" is perfectly natural. We designate the person—first, second, third, singular or plural—and then by arranging the two hands, we predicate a bodily position: standing, sitting, kneeling, and so forth.

CHAPTER 4. PRONOUNS

To show in sign what a pronoun is, we draw a circle on the table and in it we set a snuffbox; then we push it ouside the circle, and substitute something else.

A pronoun is a word used in place of a noun. The general sign for all pronouns is the action just described, though each pronoun has its particular sign depending on its particular meaning.

Personal, Objective, and Possessive Pronouns and Their Signs

The pronouns "I," "me," "my," and "mine" each has its distinctive sign; without them the deaf could not write, *currente calamo*, anything dictated in methodical signs.

Public speakers, when speaking of themselves, frequently make a kind of half-circle by drawing the hand toward their breast as they exclaim, "I think," "I desire," and the like. This action we adopt as the sign for "I." But in order to say, "this thing belongs to me" or "is for me," we lay one hand on our breast like a priest delivering a sermon on justice, and press gently on the breast two or three times. We all do this naturally when, in dividing up something, we say, "this is for *you*, and this is for *me*." Although both these pronouns are personal, the second one focuses attention on the speaker.

We use the same sign for [the French] *me*, but place the right index finger on the left one, meaning that the pronoun is objective, always accompanying a verb of which it is the direct or indirect object.

"My" and "mine" are possessive pronouns and in reality adjectives. They are expressed by indicating oneself with one hand, and with the other the noun modified, that is, the thing we are asserting to be ours. We add the sign for an adjective, as well as signs for number and gender.

The signs for *le mien, la mienne, les miens,* and *les miennes* differ from the signs for *mon, ma,* and *mes* in that the articles preceding them, which make them pronouns rather than adjectives, never occur with the noun to which they refer. So we make the sign for the article and then the sign for *mon, ma,* or *mes*. This explanation makes clear the signs for all other pronouns, whether personal or objective or possessive.

The personal pronouns *tu* and *toi* indicate the second person or person being addressed. By adding to the general sign for personal pronouns signs for the objective or possessive, plus signs for the appropriate number and gender, we have signs that are perfectly clear for *te, ton, ta, tes, le tien, la tienne, les tiens,* and *les tiennes*.

The personal pronouns *il* and *elle* indicate the third person, the person of whom we are speaking. By adding to the general sign for personal pronouns the signs for the objective or possessive, for number and gender, we have clear signs for *se, son, sa, ses, le sien, la sienne, les siens,* and *les siennes.*

The personal pronouns *lui* and *soi* also serve as objective pronouns: *Je lui donnerai* [I will give him or her]; *on doit s'aimer soi-même d'un amour réglé* [We ought to love ourselves with restraint]. It is the same with the pronouns *nous* and *vous: nous vous donnerons* [we will give you], *vous nous donnerez* [you will give us]. In the first sentence *nous* is personal, and *vous* objective; in the second, *vous* is the personal and *nous* objective. To explain these sorts of sentences, we first write: *nous donnerons à vous* and *vous donnerez à nous.* Later, however, we put these two datives in their proper French order: *nous vous donnerons* and *vous nous donnerez.*

Ils, elles, and *eux* are personal pronouns of the third-person plural. *Leur* is objective, as in the sentence: *je leur donnerai,* meaning "I will give to them," but it is possessive in: *ils mangent leur pain sec* [they eat their bread unbuttered].

The possessive pronoun *leur* is singular when the thing loved, possessed, and so forth, by several agents is single, as in this example: *les parisiens aiment leur roi et leur archevêque* [Parisians love their king and their archbishop], but we use the plural *leurs* when there are several objects loved, possessed, and so on, by several agents, as in the following: *les parisiens aiment leurs curés* [Parisians love their priests]. In the former case we indicate the plurality of possessors by waving our hand in front of them, then making the sign for the possessive, and then adding the sign for the singular. In the latter case, after the sign for the possessive we add the sign for the plural.

Le, la, and *les* are articles when they precede nouns, but objective pronouns when they are direct or indirect objects and can be translated as *lui, elle, eux,* or *elles,* as in: *je le connais, je la respecte, je les estime,* and *je les honore.* A first sign indicates the persons being spoken about, a second sign expresses the conjunction with the verb of which they are the object.

Demonstrative Pronouns and Their Signs

Demonstrative pronouns are signaled by bringing the tip of one's finger close to the object referred to, or by pointing to the object without approaching it. *Ce* goes with a masculine noun beginning with a consonant; but when the noun begins with a vowel or *h,* we use *cet. Cette* goes with a singular feminine noun, and *ces* with plural nouns of both genders. *Ceci* means "this thing"; *cela* means "that thing," but when both words occur in the same sentence, *ceci* means simply "the thing that I am showing first," and *cela* means "the other thing that I am showing second." Sometimes they mean quite the opposite, because *ceci* usually refers to the closer or latter term, *cela* to the remote or former term.

Interrogative and Relative Pronouns and Their Signs

The interrogative or relative pronouns *qui, que, quel, quelle, lequel, laquelle, lesquels,* and *lesquelles* each has a distinct sign.

They are interrogative when preceded by a *d*, signifying *demande* [question], or when followed by a question mark. Then the word *qui* means "which person?" I look at everyone present, and ask with an interrogative gesture such as we all naturally use on similar occasions: "which is the person who has done or said whatever?"

Que means "which thing?" We look at things in general, and ask with an interrogative gesture: which is the thing (present or absent) that the answer will be about? *Quoi* also means "which thing?" *Quel* goes with a masculine singular noun. So we make the interrogative gesture and add to it the sign for masculine and the sign of the singular. With this example, *quel?, quelle?, quels?,* and *quelles?* need no explanation. *Lequel, laquelle, lesquels,* and *lesquelles* followed by a question mark are used in the same way, but are preceded by the sign for an article, and because they express the need for a choice between two or more objects just mentioned, we must inspect all the objects to determine our answer.

When these pronouns are merely relative, we put our right index finger on them, and then immediately put it on the noun, or the pronoun standing in for the noun to which they refer . . .

When *que* is merely a conjunction between two verbs, it is represented by hooking the two index fingers together in a clasp. We then inform our pupils that this conjunction governs (that is, requires after it) sometimes the indicative, sometimes the subjunctive, and of course we proceed to explain which of these two modes to choose in transcribing what we dictate by signs.

Que between two verbs governs the subjunctive when the action expressed by the first verb somehow influences the action expressed by the second, as in the example, *"Je veux que vous appreniez votre leçon"* [I want you to learn your lesson]. Here it is evident that my will has a causal influence on your learning your lesson. But *que* takes the indicative when the action expressed by the first verb has no influence on the action expressed by the second, as in *Pierre dit que vous apprenez votre leçon* [Pierre says that you are learning your lesson]. The action of Pierre's telling me you are learning does not influence the action of your learning; it simply declares it.

Therefore, in dictating to our pupil, if we must put the second verb in the subjunctive, as in the first example, we make the sign for the conjunctive *que*, the pronominal sign for *vous*, and the sign for *apprenniez* made up from (1) the general sign for the verb *apprendre*, (2) the sign for the present; (3) the sign for the subjunctive mode. But if the second verb must be indicative, as in the second example, then by making no sign after the sign for the present (there being no sign for the indicative mode), the pupil immediately understands that the verb must be indicative . . .

Improper Pronouns and Their Signs

The words "some," "many," and "all" constantly appear in our lessons and dictations. We use the following explanation in signs.

From a sack we take out one, two, three, four, eight, ten, and twelve tokens in succession, counting them each time. Then we take out a few, one by one, without counting. We call this "some." After this operation, we take out a large handful, and call it "many" or "much." Last we empty all the tokens into a hat or another sack, and call them "all." It is not usually necessary to repeat this operation more than once. We are also constantly coming across "nothing," "none," "not one," "each," and "each one."

To explain "nothing," we put several things into a hat, then take them all out again, one by one. We show our pupil that not a single one is left. We then inform him that the words "there is not a single thing in the hat," and "there is nothing in the hat" mean exactly the same.

Every Frenchman knows the sign for "nothing." We take the tips of two teeth between two fingers, and quickly draw the fingers away. The deaf all understand this sign even before they come to us. To say "none," we make the sign for "nothing," to which we add the sign for a masculine [*aucun*] or feminine [*aucune*] adjective.

"Each" is represented in this way. Fifty pupils are present; we call on them one after another to answer some question by signs. The action of all, one after the other without exception, is the sign for "each." Being satisfied with everyone, I give *each one*, after his answer, four chestnuts. This is the sign for "each one," to which we add the masculine [chacun] or feminine [chacune] gender. If the reader is surprised at the triviality of our examples, I remind him that our students are deaf-mutes.

CHAPTER 5. VERBS

Our pupils, as we have seen, have learned by heart the different tenses of the verb "carry," but are still ignorant of their meaning. Now we must acquaint them with the metaphysics of verbs. Without this knowledge their education would be markedly incomplete. This enterprise appears difficult, but its realization is simple.

Verbs are made up of persons, numbers, tenses, and modes. The present indicative of "carry" has already given us signs for the different persons and numbers; the only thing still required is to lend a bit of help to the language of signs that is natural to the deaf from childhood, by making the signs designate tenses and modes.

The Application of Signs to Tenses

Although deaf, our pupil had, like us, an idea of the past, present, and future before he came to us, as well as signs for indicating the difference.

To express a present action, he made a sign prompted by nature, unconsciously as we all do in similar situations, which consists in appealing to observers to pay attention to our operation. But if the action was occurring out of sight, he laid his hand flat on the table, tapping several times, as we all tend to do on similar occasions. These are the signs he relearns, in our lesson, to indicate the present tense of a verb.

Did he mean that an action is past? He moved his hand negligently two or three times over one shoulder. We have him use the same sign for the past tense of a verb.

Finally, when he meant a future action, he moved his right hand straight in front of him. Here again we have him use this sign for the future of a verb.

It is now time to call on art to assist nature. Having previously taught him to write the days of the week, one directly under the other, we want him to set them down in that order, and we put, on each side of his writing, what follows before and after the same words under different heads.

Today—Sunday—I am arranging nothing.	PRESENT
Yesterday—Saturday—I was arranging my books.	IMPERFECT
The day before yesterday—Friday—I arranged my room.	PERFECT
Three days ago—Thursday—I had arranged my closet.	PAST PERFECT
Tomorrow—Monday—I shall arrange my papers.	FUTURE
Day after tomorrow—Tuesday—I shall arrange my drawers.	FUTURE
Three days from now—Wednesday—I shall arrange my cupboards.	FUTURE

"Yesterday," "day before yesterday," and "three days ago" are explained by the number of times we have slept since the day we are talking about. "Tomorrow," "day after tomorrow," and "three days hence" are explained by the number of times we shall sleep until the day in question arrives . . .

We take special care to get our pupil to notice the different verb endings in different tenses, indicating these variations with his finger. We get him to take note of the eight different tenses of the indicative mode in French; we write them down in a horizontal order with their respective names on a table that is divided into eight equal unerasable squares.

We show him that four of the eight tenses are called perfect—first, second, third, and fourth perfect, as, for instance, *j'ai aimé*, *j'aimai, j'ai eu aimé, j'eus aimé* [I loved, I was loving, I had loved, I had loved].

The signs expressing these tenses naturally present themselves: after bringing the hand to the shoulder—the general sign for a past—we make the sign for first, second, third, or fourth perfect by the method given for signs for numbers, and so indicate which perfect we are dictating to our pupil. We find that he is never mistaken.

We do not leave him in ignorance about the use of these different perfects, some expressing a definite, some an indefinite past, and others a definite or indefinite past prior to another past event . . .

The Application of Signs to the Modes of Verbs

"Mode" refers to the manner of conjugating a verb. The modes are the indicative, imperative, subjunctive, and infinitive. To them we add the participle, for it has a present, past, and future, as do other modes.

To avoid a needless proliferation of signs, we give no sign to the indicative, for the absence of a sign for a mode suffices to tell us that the verb under consideration is in this one.

The pupil has noted the signs made with the hands and the eyes, and that he has sometimes made himself, to issue a command. We keep this sign to indicate the imperative. To make a polite request, however, the two hands are clasped, indicating the supplicative.

In discourse we often come across two verbs joined by the particle *que*, the first verb expressing a mode of being or acting with a direct or indirect influence on the action expressed by the second verb. The first mentions a cause, the second expresses the effect. This connection of cause and effect, expressed in French by the conjunction *que*, and in other languages by corresponding terms, produces a mode, that is, a different manner of conjugating, from that for simple affirmation. In French this mode has only four tenses—present, imperfect, perfect, pluperfect—all of whose personal pronouns are preceded by *que* and each with its own ending for each person.

But we should observe that the verb preceding *que* always expresses an absolute or conditional future, as in the following examples: *Pour bien répondre le jour de votre exercice publique, il faudrait que vous apprisiez bien*, or *il faudra que vous ayez bien appris*, or *il aurait fallu que vous eussiez bien appris les cahiers qu'on vous a mis entre les mains*. ["In order to do well on the day of your public exercise, it is necessary that you learn thoroughly," or "it will be necessary that you have learned," or "it would have been necessary for you to have learned thoroughly the texts given to you"]. In all three examples, it is obvious that the action of learning must precede the good effect that it will produce or would produce or might have produced, assuming the condition fulfilled.

It is easy to indicate the signs for dictating or expressing the grammatical persons of this mode. For example, *je veux que vous écriviez*. [I want you to write]. For the word *que* we make the general sign for a conjunction; for the word *vous*, the sign for that personal pronoun; and for the word *écriviez*, (1) the general sign for all parts of the verb *écrire*; (2) the sign for the present tense; (3) the hooking of the two index fingers immediately after the sign for the present tense means not a simple conjunction, but a conjunctive mode.

There are in French three other nonsubjunctive tenses called by Restaut the future past, the conditional present, and the conditional past, which we nevertheless put under the subjunctive so that we may parse them like the Latin grammar that places them there. The Latin *amarem* means "I would love" and "I would have loved."

Noting that they are not really subjunctive in French, we characterize them by their own particular signs.

We use the following method to explain them. I write on the table: *Je pars de l'endroit où est la fenêtre et je vais à la porte. Lorsque je serai à la porte, j'aurai donné à Monsieur qui est au milieu entre les deux, cette tabatière que je tiens en ma main* [I move from the window and I go to the door; when I am at the door, *I shall have given* to the person standing between them the snuffbox I have in my hand]. When I set out, the giving is future; it becomes present when I am giving, but is past when I get to the door. So we make the sign for giving, then the sign for the future, and then the sign for the past, omitting a sign for the present as superfluous (common sense dictates that between the future and the past there must have been a present).

We give the sign for the future imperfect tense to what Restaut calls the conditional present. The reason for doing so is clarified as follows: having assigned some homework to a pupil, I told him that I would return in two hours to quiz him and promised to give him a book if he did well. I return with the book in my hand and show it to the other pupils, telling them that I shall give it to the pupil if he has learned the lesson. On examining him I find that he has not learned the lesson at all. I show him the book and then ostentatiously pocket it, telling him he cannot have it because he is a lazybones. My desire to give is repressed by the unfulfilled condition, and it appears to me that the brake stopping me, which is prior to my expression, must take the sign of the imperfect.

For the same reason we give the sign of a future pluperfect to the tense called by Restaut a conditional past (I would have given), because there was a similar eventual or conditional future when I set out with the intention of giving if I found the condition fulfilled; in fact, if it had been fulfilled, the giving would already be in the past perfect while I was talking about it after performing other actions following my pupil's idleness, which prevented me from giving him the conditionally promised book.

The pupil often sees the action signified by a verb expressed with no mention of the [acting] subject. The action of looking for without finding the person or persons who act or ought to act becomes the sign of the infinitive, or better, the indefinitive, which has no person before it, neither singular nor plural . . .

By making as if I were drawing out a thread or bit of stuff from each side of my habit, I express a participle, which is partly a verb (*partem capit*) and partly a noun. It is actually an adjectival noun because it expresses a quality applicable to a noun while at the same time having the same objects as the verb it is taken from, whose action it expresses.

Active, Passive, Intransitive, and Reflexive Verbs

The active verb represents the subject as acting overtly. The passive verb represents a subject not as acting, but as receiving the action of another. To make our pupils aware of this difference, we carry one of them about on a chair. Our action is evident, and we get them to note it. The child being carried does not move; his arms, hands, legs, and feet are hanging and remain immobile as though paralyzed; with these two signs we distinguish these two species of verbs.

The explanation of intransitive and reflexive verbs is more difficult in signs. We give it here so that teachers may use it with pupils sufficiently advanced to grasp the grammatical application. But we omit it at first, and confine ourselves within certain limits for the pupils unacquainted with the parts of speech . . .

The general sign for intransitive verbs represents them as neither active nor passive; the sign for negation is made to the right and the left, meaning that the operation does not emanate outward from the subject, nor does the subject receive it from an external source, but goes on in and is confined to the subject.

Here is an example. If I want to explain by signs the words "I tremble," I must make: (1) the sign for *I* (the first-person singular), (2) the movement of someone trembling, (3) the sign for the present-tense verb, (4) the sign for a negation to the right and left, *neither active nor passive.* (I think appropriate here to repeat my observation that all these signs take only an instant.)

Reflexive verbs have the personal pronouns *je, tu, il* followed by their reflexive pronouns *me, te, se* in the singular, and *nous, vous, ils* followed by their reflexive pronouns *nous, vous, se* in the plural, before the appropriate form of the verb, as in *je me promène, tu te repose, il se délasse, nous nous promenons* (the second *nous* is a reflexive pronoun), *vous vous reposez* (the second *vous* is also reflexive), and *ils se délassent.* The particular sign for each of these verbs is found in the *Dictionary of Verbs for the Use of the Deaf.* The signs common to all are those we have given to the personal and conjunctive pronouns, both singular and plural. (Note that reflexive verbs are conjugated in the past tense not with the auxiliary *avoir*, but with *être*.)

Since we do not attempt to make the common run of deaf pupils into grammarians, we call all verbs active if they express an action or operation—whether internal or external, mental or corporeal, in short, every operation that is not totally passive (produced in or on us by an external agent).

The Object of Verbs

This section is likely to confuse the deaf, and requires special attention by the teacher when dictating and explaining lessons to them. We call objects of verbs the grammatical cases for nouns or pronouns which, after personal pronouns, go with the verb to make up a complete sentence. There are two kinds of objects, namely, direct and indirect. A direct object is a noun or pronoun to which the action refers and in which it terminates and that, together with the personal pronoun and the verb, suffices to make up a complete sentence. Thus, in the sentence, "I respect virtue," the personal pronoun is "I," "respect" is the verb, and "virtue" the direct object, that is, the noun to which the action expressed by the verb refers and in which it is terminated. It is exactly the same in the sentence, "I hate vice."

In these two examples "virtue" and "vice," the direct objects of the verbs preceding them, are in the accusative, that is, the fourth grammatical case. Every active verb requires the noun to which the action refers and in which it is terminated to be in the accusative. Now here is the source of confusion for our pupils.

When the direct object is a noun, it comes after the verb as in the two examples above. When the direct object is a relative or reflexive pronoun, however, it has to come before the verb as in *je vous honore* [I respect you] and *ils nous regardent* [they are looking at us]. Since the pronouns *nous* and *vous* are before the verb, we must be careful to get the pupil to see that these two pronouns are not personal pronouns, or he will write *je vous honorez* [I you respect] and *ils nous regardons* [they we are looking at]—neither of whichs makes sense. But if in dictating we make the sign for the objective pronouns for these two words, he will understand that the two personal pronouns are the ones preceding *nous* and *vous* and he will then write *Je vous honore* and *Ils nous regardent*. To avoid confusion in explaining these matters, the teacher always puts his pointer on (1) the personal pronoun *je*, (2) on the verb *honore*, (3) on the objective pronoun *vous*, as if it were *je honore vous*, and similarly for the second sentence.

The indirect object is even more difficult. We call an indirect object a noun or pronoun by which we express something to which the action designated by the verb does not refer directly. It is a secondary idea added to the primary one, for the sentence would be complete without the indirect object.

The indirect object is never in the accusative because the action designated by the verb does not refer to it directly. It occurs before the verb (except in the imperative) and so presents the same problem as the direct object, as in *Je vous présente le livre*, if we do not make the sign for conjunction with the *vous*. We must, moreover, indicate that it is not the direct object of the verb, and to do this we must add the sign of the dative, that is to say the third case. In French we dispense with the preposition *à* in this case, but in sign language it must not be omitted, neither in dictating nor in teaching. In explaining this case, the pointer should be used on the sentence as if it contained an *à*, which must not be omitted.

IV

JEAN MASSIEU

ONE DAY IN 1785, on a country lane in southwestern France, a passerby came across a young boy standing watch over a flock of sheep. The man found out that the boy was deaf, befriended the thirteen-year-old, and decided to bring him to the newly opened school for the deaf directed by the abbé Roch-Ambroise Sicard in nearby Bordeaux. In this way the benevolent M. de Puymorin—little other than his name is now known about him—set in motion a train of events that led an illiterate shepherd boy to become the first deaf person to enter the teaching profession.

In the following autobiographical extract Massieu tells of his poor farming family (his father worked in a vineyard), and of the poignant frustration he suffered of his desire to learn reading and writing. Although Massieu was able to use "home sign" to communicate with his five deaf brothers and sisters, he reports despair and isolation as a child. During his education, however, his intelligence and passion for learning written French soon made him Sicard's star pupil and chief performer in the priest's public demonstrations of his method.

After some three-and-a-half years with Sicard in Bordeaux, Massieu accompanied him to Paris when the priest succeeded the abbé de l'Epée as director of the National Institute for the Deaf. Shortly thereafter Massieu was appointed to the post of teaching assistant, a post he held for thirty-two years. In the course of his career he taught French to the young Laurent Clerc, and sign language to Thomas Gallaudet; these two would later found the education of the deaf in America.

Massieu's loyalty to the politically improvident Sicard several times rescued the priest from difficulties; the pupil even saved the teacher's life by addressing the revolutionary National Assembly, asking that the "father of the deaf" be spared from the Reign of Terror. Massieu's ability to read and to write with eloquence enabled him to impress the political authorities with the good achieved by Sicard.

Massieu's numerous personal eccentricities and general unworldliness caused great amusement to all who knew him. At court he pleaded on behalf of a thief who had stolen his wallet: "I beg you not to have him beheaded, for he has not killed anyone. Condemn him only to be a galley slave." His customary attire included a voluminous riding-coat that reached to his ankles. In its deep pockets he always carried books and chalk, and several watches, for which he had a passion and which he would display at every opportunity.

Nearly fifty at the time of Sicard's death, Massieu was the natural choice to be appointed the priest's successor. The administrative board of the school, however, saw fit to deny him the position and in fact forced him into retirement. After a few years living at his original home, he was called to the southern town of Rodez as teacher of a small school for the deaf. There he married a young hearing woman, the couple had a son, and in time Massieu became the director of the school. In 1834 the couple moved from Rodez to the northern city of Lille, where they founded a school for the deaf with Massieu the director and his wife the matron. It was in Lille, in August 1846, that Massieu—known in Europe and America as a symbol of the educated deaf—died at the age of seventy-four.

Massieu prepared his autobiographical sketch in 1798 at the request of Louis Jauffret, the permanent secretary of the Society of Observers of Man—the first anthropological society; Jauffret later published it in a collection of essays entitled *La Corbeille des fleurs et le panier de fruits* (Paris, 1829, v. 2, pp. 72-86), one of the two sources for this translation. When the address was read to the Society a member of the audience was moved to send Massieu a letter containing many questions about his early upbringing and ideas. Massieu answered those questions before the Society at its next meeting; the abbé Sicard published the autobiography and questions and answers in the appendix to his *Théorie des signes* (Paris: Imprimerie de l'Institution des Sourds-Muets, 1808).

Dessiné d'après nature et Gravé par Roy en 1803

J.ᴬⁿ MASSIEU,

Sourd-Muet de naissance

Né à Semens près de Cadillac Dépar.ᵗ de la Gironde

Premier répétiteur à l'Institution nationale des Sourds-Muets de Paris

Au défaut de l'oreille, au défaut de la voix
Il a l'expression et des yeux et des doigts;
Un plus intelligent sera long-tems à naitre:
Miraculeux élève, a son tour il est maitre.

Guichard

A Paris, chez M.ᵉ Duvernai Artiste, rue Beaurepaire N.ᵒ 21 et 22.

Déposée à la Biblioth.ᵉ Nation.ˡᵉ

Jean Massieu

AUTOBIOGRAPHY OF JEAN MASSIEU

I was born at Semens in the Cadillac district of the canton of
Saint-Macaire in the Gironde. My father died in January 1791; my
mother is still living. There were six deaf-mutes in our family, three
boys and three girls. The eldest boy died. I, the second son, am in
Paris. The third one is in Bordeaux, learning to read and write. The
eldest daughter knows how to read and write; she is in Cadillac.
The second daughter died; she was my twin. The third daughter also
knows how to write; she is at home. Until the age of thirteen years
and nine months, I remained at home without ever receiving any
education. I was totally unlettered. I expressed my ideas by manual
signs or gestures. At that time the signs I used to express my ideas
to my family were quite different from the signs of educated deaf-
mutes. Strangers did not understand us when we expressed our ideas
with signs, but the neighbors did. I saw cattle, horses, donkeys, pigs,
dogs, cats, vegetables, houses, fields, grapevines, and after seeing all
these things, I remembered them well. Before my education, when
I was a child, I did not know how to read or write. I wanted to read
and write. Often I saw boys and girls going to school; I wanted to
follow them and I was very envious of them. With tears in my eyes
I asked for permission to go to school. I took a book and opened it
upside-down to show my ignorance; I put it under my arm as if to
leave for school, but my father refused to give me this permission,
signing that I could never learn anything, for I was a deaf-mute.
Then I wept. I again took up his books to read them, but I did not
understand any letters, words, or sentences. In desperation I put my
fingers to my ears and impatiently asked my father to clean them
out for me. He answered that there was no remedy. I was discon-
solate.

I left my father's house and went to school without telling him.
I presented myself to the teacher and asked him with gestures to
teach me to read and write. He sternly refused and sent me away.
This made me cry a great deal but did not discourage me. I often
thought about reading and writing. I was twelve at the time. I tried
on my own to form the letters of the alphabet with a quill.

When I was a child, my father made me pray morning and evening
with gestures: I got on my knees, clasped my hands, and moved my
lips, imitating speaking people when they prayed to God. Today I

know there is a God, the creator of heaven and earth. But as a child I worshipped the sky, not God. I did not see God, I saw the sky. I did not know whether I had been created or had created myself. I was growing up but if I had not known my teacher, the abbé Sicard, my mind would not have grown like my body, for my mind was impoverished. I would have gone on, as I grew, believing that God was the sky.

Children my own age would not play with me; they looked down on me; I was like a dog. I passed the time alone playing with a top or a mallet and ball, or walking on stilts. Before my education I did know how to count; my fingers had taught me. I did not know numbers; I counted on my fingers, and when the count went beyond ten I made notches on a stick.

When I was a child my parents sometimes had me watch over their flock of sheep, and sometimes people happening by took pity and gave me a little money. One day a passerby took a liking to me and invited me to his house to eat and drink. Later, when he went to Bordeaux, he spoke about me to Abbé Sicard, who agreed to take charge of my education. This man wrote to my father, who showed me the letter, but I couldn't read it. My relatives and neighbors told me its contents: they informed me that I would be going to Bordeaux; they thought the reason was to learn to be a barrelmaker. My father told me the reason was to learn to read and write. I made my way with him to the city. On our arrival I found the houses very beautiful. We went to visit the abbé Sicard, whom I found extremely thin.

I began my education tracing the letters of the alphabet with my fingers. Within several days I could write a few words. In a space of three months I knew how to write many words; in six months, I knew how to write some sentences. In one year's time I wrote fairly well. In a year and some months I wrote even better and gave good answers to questions. I had been with Abbé Sicard three and a half years when I left with him for Paris. In four years I became like people who hear and speak. I would have made even greater progress, however, had not a deaf-mute instilled me with a terrible fear that still leaves me miserable. He told me, on the authority of a doctor friend, that people who are well from birth die young but that people who have often been ill can live to old age. Recalling that I had never been seriously ill since birth, I long thought that I could not live to be an old man, and that I would never be thirty-five or forty or forty-five or fifty.

Those of my brothers and sisters who had never been ill from birth died when they became ill as adults. But my other brothers and sisters, who had often been ill, recovered.

Had I not always been healthy and so convinced that I would die young, I would have studied more, becoming as schooled as a veritable hearing-speaking person. Had I never known that deaf man, I would not fear death and would always be happy, I would believe that I would live to old age, I would be well educated, I would write well, I would always be happy.

"My dear Massieu, before your education began, what did you make of people who moved their lips in each other's presence?"

"I thought they were expressing ideas," he replied.

"Why did you think that?"

"Because I remembered that someone had spoken to my father about me and that he had threatened to punish me," Massieu said.

"So you thought that lip movements were a way to communicate ideas?"

"Yes," he replied.

"Why didn't you move *your* lips to communicate *your* thoughts?" I asked.

"Because I hadn't looked enough at the lips of people speaking and I was told that the noises I made were disagreeable. Since I had been told that my infirmity was in my ears, I took some brandy and poured it into my ears and stopped them up with cotton."

"Did you know what hearing was?"

"Yes," he said.

"How did you learn about it?" we asked.

"One of my hearing relatives who lived in our house had told me that she 'saw with her ears' someone whom she could not see with her eyes when he came to see my father. Hearing people 'see with their ears' when someone is walking about at night. Nightwalkers have a gait that is different for different people, and their step tells hearing people their name."

"What is a sense?" Massieu was asked.

"An idea-carrier," he answered.

"What is hearing?" asked some people, trying to disconcert him.

"Hearing is auricular sight."

"What is gratitude?" asked the abbé Sicard.

"Gratitude is the memory of the heart," Massieu answered him.

"What is God?"

"The necessary Being—the sun of eternity."

"What is eternity?" someone asked.

"A day without yesterday or tomorrow," Massieu immediately replied.

"What were you thinking about," we asked Massieu, "while your father had you stay on your knees?"

"About the sky," he answered.

"What were you trying to accomplish by praying to the sky?" we asked.

"To make the night come down to earth so the plants I had planted would grow and so the sick would be restored to health."

"Were your prayers in ideas, words, feelings?"

"It was my heart that prayed. I did not yet understand words or their meaning," replied Massieu.

"What did you feel in your heart?" we asked.

"Joy, when I found the plants and fruits growing; pain, when I saw them damaged by the hail and when my sick relatives remained sick," said Massieu. With these words he made signs expressing anger and threats.

"Were you cursing the sky?" we asked him in surprise.

"Yes," he replied. We asked him the reason for his curses.

"Because I thought that I could not reach to give it a beating and kill it for causing all these disasters and for not healing my sick relatives."

"Weren't you afraid of provoking it and of being punished?"

"I didn't then know my good teacher Sicard and I didn't know that it was only the sky. It was only after a year of education that I became afraid of being punished by it."

"Did you imagine that this sky had a shape or form?"

"My father had shown me a large statue in the church near our home. It represented an old man with a long beard and in his hand he held a globe. I thought he lived above the sun."

"Did you know who had made the cow or the horse or other animals?" we asked.

"No, but I was very curious to see a birth. I often went and hid in a ditch to see the sky descend to earth to make things grow. I wanted very much to see it."

"What did you think when Abbé Sicard first had you trace words with the letters of the alphabet?"

"I thought that words were images of the objects I saw around me. I memorized words with great enthusiasm. When I read the word 'God' and had written it in chalk on the blackboard, I thought that God caused death and I was afraid of death."

"So what idea did you have of death?" we asked.

"I thought death was the cessation of movement, of sensation, of ingestion, of the sensitivity of the skin and flesh."

"How did you get that idea?"

"I had seen a dead person," he said.

"Did you think that you would live forever?" we asked.

"I believed that there was a heavenly land and that the body was eternal," Massieu replied.

V

ROCH-AMBROISE SICARD

Roch-Ambroise Sicard was born in 1742 in a village of the Languedoc region. He studied for the priesthood in the Congregation of the Christian Doctrine. At the age of twenty-eight he was ordained and assigned to the cathedral at Bordeaux. His archibishop, Champion de Cicé, had visited the school for the deaf founded by the abbé de l'Epée and decided to found a similar school in his own diocese, calling on Sicard to direct it. Sicard, now forty-three, spent a year studying Epée's teaching methods in Paris, one of dozens of disciples who had come from throughout Europe. Returning to open his school in Bordeaux, Sicard was seconded by Jean Saint-Sernin, who by all accounts did the actual teaching of the deaf pupils, while the priest presided at public demonstrations of their achievements, acquired with the abbé de l'Epée's "methodical signs."

On the death of the abbé de l'Epée in 1789, Sicard published a memoir critical of Epée's methods which, he claimed, made the deaf pupils into automatic copyists of signed French into written French without any understanding of what they were writing. To replace Epée, Sicard suggested a public competition of teachers of the deaf. Sicard won the contest, with his famous pupil, Jean Massieu, as his prize exhibit.

Sicard proved to be a zealous and highly visible spokesman for the cause of the deaf: as a member of the French Academy, where he helped initiate their dictionary, and as a faculty member of the National Teacher Training College, where he gave courses in deaf education and philosophy of language. Sicard guided the national school for the deaf through great adversity in the tumultuous years of the French Revolution; on more than one occasion it nearly cost him his life. As a cleric he was unsympathetic to the popular overthrow of the established order, maintaining a secret correspondence with the deposed royal family, as well as publishing a politico-religious newspaper. As a result of these activities, the government ordered him deported to Guiana in 1800 and he went into hiding in the outskirts of Paris.

Sicard took advantage of his retreat to write an extended account of how he educated Jean Massieu, published as *Cours d'instruction d'un sourd-muet de naissance*, 2nd ed. (Paris: Le Clère, 1803). It is the first comprehensive textbook ever written for educating the deaf. We translate here the first four chapters, which set forth and illustrate the method and its principles. Sicard published several more works concerning deaf education and collected several more titles, among them the Legion of Honor, before his long career ended in 1822. The great teacher of the deaf who made their education as a class a practical reality was laid in state in the cathedral of Notre Dame and all the bells of the city rang for hours

Abbé Sicard

COURSE OF INSTRUCTION
FOR A CONGENITALLY DEAF PERSON

PREAMBLE

Is it possible to educate the congenitally deaf? If so, how much instruction is needed for the benefit of these unfortunates and society? Is this extraordinary and hitherto unknown art less a matter of public utility than a mere curiosity or an ingenious invention?

I am aware that the impossibility of educating the deaf is generally assumed by persons who, never having attended my classes, have never given much thought to the various means of communication that people establish among themselves. As these persons are acquainted only with the rapid method of speech, they seem convinced that nothing else could take its place and that some insurmountable obstacle keeps those deprived of speech forever separated from other men. People born deaf and who are consequently mute are regarded as an irredeemably inferior species, condemned to vegetate like animals without reason or intelligence. In nearly everyone's eyes these unfortunates are mere organized machines, good only for rendering minor assistance, like the domestic animals trained to serve man. Hence nothing compares to the surprise of certain spectators when they first attend classes in which the deaf show signs of intelligence. These observers would be no less amazed to see a statue come to life. They hardly believe their eyes and find it hard to accept that they are not being deceived.

Up to a point, this prejudice is shared even by people with greater knowledge about communication without speech. While they may not regard the deaf as simple automatons, these people refuse to believe that the deaf can profit from even the most elementary education. No doubt, these skeptics say, with patience and care we can acquaint them with common things, the concrete things present to the senses, those that we can first show them and then designate with the sign indicating their use and shapes. But how can we get abstract or metaphysical ideas into their minds? How can we depict them so as to make them perceptible? What can be the analogy between material signs and the intellectual operations and affections of the soul, that is, everything that is pure understanding? I shall deal further on with this problem. For the moment it is enough to say to those people: why allow yourselves to be biased by deceptive appearances? Why should you proceed to explain nature without first questioning it, why marshall arguments against facts that were readily verifiable before the arguments were formulated? A school for the deaf exists right in your midst. Suspend your judgment. Silence your doubts for a moment, then pose your problems. Interrogate my pupils: their answers will eliminate your uncertainties by showing you the whole truth without undue enticement.

The deaf, who deserve only friends, have enemies. These enemies say that most deaf persons are born to the lower classes and usually become plowmen, vine tenders, gardeners. People in these occupations learn no grammar or metaphysics, but they are no less able workers. Why then single out a few of them? What is the good of teaching these privileged deaf persons a grammar created especially for them, a grammar that at every step poses problems that would be knotty for even a creative genius or subtle metaphysican? Will the deaf be made any fitter for the labors for which their birth has destined them?

People who are unfamiliar with the totally uneducated deaf person, and so confuse him with the normal child, might find this objection appealing . . . but only because they are considering the education of the deaf in itself, abstractly, without relation to this unfamiliar class of unfortunates.

First, it is a grave mistake to lump the deaf together with normal children or to think that deaf children need no special training to do what normal children can.

Indeed, how can we characterize the congenitally deaf person before any training has begun to connect him, by whatever bond, with the great family to which, by his external form, he belongs? In society he is a perfect nonentity, a living automaton, a statue like the one described by Charles Bonnet and later Condillac; we must activate and direct the senses of this statue, one after another, to compensate for the one he unfortunately lacks. Restricted to mere physical movements before we tear open the envelope in which his reason is enshrouded, the deaf person lacks even that unfailing instinct directing animals destined to have that as their only guide.

But why, we are asked, is the uneducated deaf person isolated in nature and unable to communicate with other men? Why is he reduced to this state of imbecility? Does his biological constitution differ from ours? Does he not have everything he needs for having sensations, acquiring ideas, and combining them to do everything we do? Doesn't he get sensory impressions from objects as we do? As with us, isn't the sensory impression the occasional cause of the mind's sensations and its acquired ideas? Why is it then that the deaf person remains stupid while we become intelligent?

Certainly the deaf person is in every respect just like other men, except for his hearing. But that cruel exception is the very source of an extraordinary difference between him and them. All ideas come to us either directly from the senses, or mediately through our different combinations of them (giving us all our ideas of nonsensory things). We express these ideas with spoken sounds and evoke them in the minds of others by impressions on their hearing; we combine ideas and fix them in our minds by means of words. Now because no sound can affect the deaf person's hearing (he has none) and because he consequently has no symbols for fixing and combining his ideas, it is evident that no original idea can remain in his mind and that no unfamiliar idea can reach him. Hence the total communication gap between him and other people—there he is alone in nature with no possible use for his intellectual faculties, which remain inactive and lifeless unless some kindly hand happens to pluck him from this deathlike sleep.

Up to this point the deaf person is a mere ambulatory machine whose constitution (as regards his behavior) is inferior to that of animals. In saying that he is primitive, we are still underestimating his pitifulness, for he is not even the equal of primitive man in morality or in communication. Primitive man hears the poorly articulated sounds of people around him. These sounds become his means for recollecting ideas that proliferate as needed and set up a communication channel of reciprocal thoughts between him and his fellows. However incomplete, these speech signals become fixed in the mind and serve as a standard of comparison for producing combined ideas, judgments, and logical reasoning.

But as the deaf person knows no speech signals and hence has no means of communication, his sensory impressions must all be transitory and his mental images fleeting. Nothing remains in his mind to which he can relate what is happening in him and which he can use as a basis for comparison. So all his ideas must be immediate and none can be the product of reflection. And because he can never combine two ideas at a time (he has no signs for retaining them), even the simplest sort of reasoning is impossible for him. Reduced to an awful solitude, he is surrounded by an endless, omnipresent, and profound silence. He cannot ask anyone a question. Does he even know what a question is? Does he know whether other people communicate with each other—whether they are not, like him, alone in the midst of their peers?

As for morality, it is the combined product of so many elements, all so remote from the deaf person that we must doubt whether he even suspects their existence. To refer everything to himself, to act on all his natural needs with a violent impulsiveness unmoderated by any rational consideration, to satisfy all appetites no matter what, to know no limit to them other than his inability to satisfy them always, to become enraged at obstacles, to thrash at them furiously, to knock over everything standing in the way of his pleasures, with no check by the incomprehended rights of others or by incomprehended laws or by the punishments that he has not experienced—that is the sum of this unfortunate creature's morality. Moreover, as he consults only his own tastes, I suspect that no affection for anything outside himself ever enters his mind, not even the love for one's progenitors engraved by nature in animals. Do I even know whether the deaf child's heart is reached by those sweet demonstrations of maternal tenderness to which other children are so sensitive? This unfortunate will perhaps never know a mother's loving responses to filial devotion or the delightful exchange of tenderness and gratitude that creates the indescribable bond between parents and children. Imprisoned within his sensations, he is happy if they are pleasant, unhappy if they are annoying. And because someone with no knowledge of how to anticipate his own needs or to change his own environment has more unpleasant sensations than pleasant ones, we could say that his commonest mental state is one of unhappiness. Accustomed to divining none of the causes producing the effects he observes, he is mistaken about everything. He has eyes only for the physical world in which objects impinge on his senses. And what poor eyes! Because he looks at nothing, he takes no interest in anything he sees. For him the moral world does not exist, and virtues, like vices, are without reality.

This is the deaf person in his natural state; that is how my longstanding habit of observation in living with him prompts me to portray him. We must remove him from this sad, deplorable state before we can think of transforming him into a plowman, a vine tender, a worker in whatever occupation. We must give this mere animate automaton a new being, establish some communicative link between him and other men. We must pacify this beast, humanize this savage, teach him that he is not alone in nature, that not everything refers to him, that there are bonds connecting men and making them interdependent, that there is property to be respected—in short, we must teach him that he is a man and what are the rights and, above all, the duties of man.

It may be claimed that the deaf children seen at my school are different from this description. They have been seen to be merry, communicative, sensitive, and even honest—similar in every respect to other children. That is because the observer was seeing the more or less educated deaf child already communicating with me and with his other companions in misfortune, whereas I have been describing the uneducated deaf person. The child was seen with his teacher and the other pupils behaving as other children behave among themselves. The day-to-day instruction of this deaf child proceeds in gradual steps; nothing of the kind happens to the uninstructed deaf child and he is as I have described.

So it is a great mistake to confuse the deaf child with normal children, or to think that he, like the normal child, can be cast into society and without special instruction engage in some mechanical trade. Allow me once again to emphasize this error so as to disabuse anyone still inclined to believe it.

The education of hearing children begins at birth, so to speak, and develops in their constant use of everything around them. The first gazes at these infants, the first signs made to them, the first caresses lavished on them all make ineradicable impressions on their minds. Just like seeds cast on fertile ground, they begin at the proper time to sprout. Gradually, everything conduces to scatter the seed and bring it to flower: the first games of a nanny babbling and frolicking with her charge; the tender sounds of a mother's voice which penetrate to the child's heart, surprising him, evoking the first and weakest indications of sentiment and reaching his soul inside the envelope, as it were, that still encloses it; his first childhood playmates whose movements he tries to imitate and with whom he stammers out the spoken sounds that they repeat to him.

All this is lost on the deaf child. In his first days, before we learn his sad fate, we lavish the same care on him, but vain caresses and futile care; the ground that was watered and sown was barren; no seed could sprout there—everything is dead. So when this unfortunate creature is first presented to his teacher, everything has to be done, everything has to be begun. The child is like a newborn baby—his physiognomy is vacuous, his eyes lack-lustre, his manner stupid; since his birth his life has been a kind of comatose sleep. Only at this instant will anything begin for him—the world, successive generations, duration, life, time.

Philosophers attempting to determine the original forms of human language—to specify the steps by which man has succeeded in expressing his ideas—have been frightened off by the complexity of the problem. This interesting topic just sets them stammering. The most sensible ones have concluded—correctly, in fact—that any attempt to create language by trial and error would have been impossible and utterly unproductive, and so God created man with speech. Observing children makes the matter much more readily comprehensible. From the moment of birth they hear everyone around them speaking; they imitate the tongue and lip movements that they see others making; and by trials to which something is added every day, they eventually manage to make speech sounds. But everything that happens gradually and as if without design for the hearing child must, for the deaf child, be carried out systematically and by means of a reasoned analysis. We confront the great problem of creating a language for the person without one, and presenting it to stupid individuals—to overgrown children—for whom everything is covered with a heavy veil.

For the teacher of the deaf a major obstacle is the assumption that the deaf person sees things as we do, that he attaches the same ideas to words as we do, and that he takes the words he has learned and connects them to form sentences. This was, as I claim further on, an error inevitably committed by the celebrated inventor of the sublime art of teaching language to the deaf. Here we must proceed with the greatest caution, mistrust our own ease of speech and comprehension, analyze all the words to be taught, distinguish carefully between literal and figurative meaning, between derived words and primitive words, between the compound sentence and the simple sentence, and between the dependent clause and the main clause.

We take the grammatical and metaphysical approach not in order to turn the deaf person into a grammarian, metaphysician, or scholar, but because these methods are absolutely necessary to raise him to the level at which hearing people can communicate with their peers without such assistance. True enough, the instruction of the deaf will produce better-educated young people than most of the same age, but they will owe this advantage to the misfortune of being born deaf. Indeed, most children learn by rote to make themselves understood; deaf children learn by analysis. Hearing children spend a great deal of time uttering words without attaching any idea to them and often continue this habit all their lives; the deaf use a sign only when they have an idea to express. Hearing children have only vague notions picked up from first, frequently erroneous impressions; as the deaf are unable to get any notions from the people around them, they always present their teacher with an ever-fresh mind, known as a *tabula rasa*, with no admixture of heterogenous ideas previously communicated.

The teacher can conveniently trace in this mind the characters that he wants to impress on it. He can eventually fill their minds, like perfectly clear, flawless, pristine vases, with the most accurate and uncorrupt ideas.

Hearing people have little understanding of the correctness or the rules of the language they speak, or even of any law of logic. The deaf, with their signs, become good grammarians and precise logicians. We could compare hearing people to persons born to wealth who enjoy their money without knowing its value or its employment for their own well-being. We can compare the deaf to poor people born to indigence and total destitution who have learned that intelligence and work will amass a fortune whose value they appreciate and which they know how to put to good use.

When the deaf person has completed his education, he is truly a man fitted for society. Then we can consider a profession for him, and settle him in one suitable for his resources, preferences, and aptitude. Before this new life, the happy effect of his education, he was good for nothing; he was a ferocious, maleficent animal. Today he is a rational creature, ready for anything and capable of anything—not just mechanical work requiring a strong arm, but any occupation requiring his highest capabilities and knowledge. Of all the human faculties, the only one he still lacks is speech; even so, he has magnificent resources to compensate for this lack and to communicate with us! So the deaf person is no longer a lower animal on that account; he is inferior only because of the difficulty he has in displaying his intelligence and because of the isolation to which this state reduces him.

Could there not be in some corner of the world a whole society of deaf people? Well then! Would we think that these individuals were inferior, that they were unintelligent and lacked communication? They would certainly have a sign language, perhaps a language even richer than ours. This language would at least be unambiguous, always giving an accurate picture of the mind's affections. So why would this people be uncivilized? Why wouldn't they in fact have laws, government, police less mistrustful than our own?

But what can we expect of one or two deaf persons scattered among families that regard them as a calamity and a source of shame? What can we expect of a deaf person left to vegetate, without culture, on the other side of the river separating him from us, with no boat or skiff or dinghy to get him across and bring him over to our side?

Alas! What a dreadful future is being prepared for this unhappy victim of this unpardonable abandonment! Suppose one of these creatures is an orphan. The law does prescribe a guardian, but in appointing one, is it giving him a father? And if his guardian is, like so many, an avid profiteer, who then can protect this child against injustices and oppression by one whose tyranny is unavoidable and whose authority is unshakeable? And to whom could the child complain of his guardian's violence? Would the child even realize that it *is* violence, and that his miserable state is not his natural one? How can the unfortunate ever claim his rights without understanding their legitimacy or their extent? What am I saying? Can he even know whether he has any rights, or whether the few rights granted by this rapacious, barbarous bloodsucker do not amount to a favor? In losing his parents, did the child perhaps think that he must also lose forever any holdings that, in their tenderness, they used to keep him alive? Can he understand the right of inheritance?

This supposition is no idle dream: the parents of every deaf child, who go to their final resting place before having him educated, must fear that the misfortune described here will be only too real some day.

And under the reign of law, when the sacred words "liberty" and "fraternity" appear everywhere, there would be persons condemned to oppression merely because of a birth defect!

Be comforted, you unhappy ones! Your rights will no longer go unrecognized. You yourselves can get them respected, for you will no longer be uneducated, and one day you can, if need be, go before the courts to fight injustice, as my pupil Massieu, deaf like yourselves, has done. Educated as he was, you will one day demand the reform of this humiliating law that condemns you all to live and die without ever exercising your rights. Be consoled; your misfortune will end.[1]

The barrier between the deaf and the hearing person, which one lone man had the courage and talent to break down, will be no more.

Man in nature and man in society are finally together and united. Receive our highest homage, creator of the art that has produced such an astonishing marvel! How dear must be the name of that sainted priest, that friend of humanity who, rightly believing himself called by Providence to a valuable and difficult apostleship, devoted himself entirely to that work so worthy of the tender piety that guided his whole life. Let the name of de l'Epée be dear to the many unfortunates to whom he gave new being and new life! They will forever bless him like a father, and a grateful posterity will unite with them to honor his memory and commend him to the respect and devotion of all generations.

As for me, I who have the honor to be Epée's direct successor, who was a witness to his zeal and whom the dying priest charged with propagating his work, if I have added to these happy endeavors, if I have understood and improved upon this sublime discovery, if I have made it into a complete system, a theory whose principles are now fixed, I must claim to have worked only for the glory of a justly celebrated teacher who gets credit for everything useful in this book. Here is the spirit of those lessons that I received from his lips in friendship. In publishing them, I am merely discharging my sacred debt as his sole heir. Enough for me is the magnificent title of disciple of that prodigious genius who had no guide or model, whose first masterpieces amazed both the city of their birth and the scholars of Europe who proclaimed their glory.

As nothing in the history of an important discovery is irrelevant, I think it appropriate to go to the beginning and relate how in the eighteenth century, after attempts made in the preceding centuries seemed to thwart any hope of success, this art arose which one philanthropist defined as that of "speaking with the hands, hearing with the eyes."

Here is how it happened. Two deaf girls were living in their father's home on the rue des Fossés-Saint-Victor in Paris, directly across from the house of the Fathers of the Christian Doctrine. At an age at which people begin to think of their futures, the two sisters took lessons from a Doctrinarian priest (Father Vanin) who tried, without any particular method, to replace the faculties of speech and hearing. Shortly after achieving some measure of success, this charitable tutor was lost to them. The two unfortunates were greatly distressed by their loss, and their mother grieved even more. She had seen all her hopes of communicating with her daughters vanish in an instant. The abbé de l'Epée has occasion to visit the household: he finds the mother out; he asks if he can await her return; he is invited in. The two deaf women receive him with the alert and interested manner characteristic of young people, their ingenuous charm further accentuated by their silence, which is yet quite unlike the silence of someone who is condemned never to break it. The abbé asks some questions; the young women remain immobile and show no sign of interest, their eyes fixed on their work. Again he speaks, still they do not reply: he does not know that the two sisters are unfortunately doomed forever to silence. The mother arrives and explains all; the good abbé mingles his tears with hers and withdraws, not without thinking to find a replacement for Father Vanin and giving, if possible, speech and hearing to these young women.

A great man's idea is an ever-fecund seed. Every language, says Condillac, is just a collection of signs, the way a series of natural history drawings is a collection of images, a representation of a great many objects. We can represent everything with gestures just as we can paint everything with colors and name everything with words. Objects have shapes, we can imitate them; physical movements strike our gaze, we ought to be able to depict and describe them with imitative gestures. Words are just conventional signs; why not also gestures? Thus there could be a gestural language, an action language, as there is a language of sounds, a spoken language.

Filled with these productive ideas, Epée soon returned to this household where the finest conception of the human mind had taken root in his thought. Never had his ardent soul expected that adversity would call for his aid; he vowed to offer it—he was welcomed with great delight! He begins, he tries his hand, he plans, he imitates, he gropes, he writes, he erases, he has them write. He thinks that here there is only a language to present, whereas there are two minds to create. He gives them the letters of the alphabet; and the young women copy them, but they do not get the point. Everything is reduced for them to the simple mechanism of Father Vanin. Epée writes words and in turn shows objects, but words are not images, and he is not yet understood.

How difficult the inventor's first steps were! And what assistance did he have along a road so bristling with difficulties and in which the first steps were so uncertain? He admitted to me that his only help in this unusual undertaking was Restaut's *Grammar*. But that grammar was written for people who could already understand the language; no matter how valuable it was for hearing people, of what use could it be to people ignorant even of simple signs for their mind's first perceptions? Why couldn't Epée see that no one ever learned a foreign language with a grammar written in that language? But the overcautious, overmodest great man did not dare to give flight to his genius by creating a grammar for the deaf as he dared to create their language. And he thought he had achieved his goal when the deaf eventually learned by heart the pure mechanics of this *Grammar*. How sweet it was for this good, tender, sensitive soul to delude himself! Without intending to, he caused his admirers to do the same, by presenting them with pupils who appeared to be intelligent grammarians. What might he have done if he had been as fortunate as I and had been the second to pursue this new career; if instead of making this first discovery, he had been its inheritor; if in this endeavor he could have profited from the mistakes of others and appreciated their first insights! Instead of being a first approximation, his theory would have been complete, and he would have left to his successor the credit for following in his steps by faithfully reproducing his procedures. But where is there a discovery whose inventor brought it to perfection?

The art of educating the congenitally deaf required too much knowledge and talent for any single individual to think he could invent and carry it to such perfection that his successors would have nothing left to do. I, who am entrusted with all the inventor's secrets, can pay him no better tribute than to show what he did and what still remained to be done when death took him from us. After taking lessons from him, working with him, and reflecting a good deal about his method (which is illuminated by the beacon of a sound metaphysics, and frequently corrected by experience), I could appreciate the whole extent of that art whose invention brought him glory.

I had always thought that every language had two essential parts that make up the whole and render it suitable for representing thought: the catalogue of words making up its lexicon, and the relative value of the words which constitutes its phrasing and syntax. The catalogue of words is independent of the syntax, but a language with only words would contain isolated images without linkage or sequence. Each word would indeed depict an object, but we would be lacking that other kind of word whose absence deprives the successive written words of the life-giving color that makes all these words into a complete sentence. Both these features had to be found in the language of the deaf. To be satisfied with the individual words and leave the syntax untouched would be like stopping in the middle of a race. Epée found the equivalent of all ideas in the various combinations of signs. Thus all French words had their counterparts in the language of the deaf. Nothing was easier than to parade words and signs simultaneously before their memory, and even to imprint them there. Only normal attention was required for this task, as each gesture was paired with the combination of letters making up the corresponding word, and for the deaf pupil the sign was what the word is for you. Once the pupils had learned the lexicon, they had no trouble writing words for signs or making signs for words. They copied entire pages of the most abstract books from the simple dictation of signs. But did they understand the meaning of what they were writing, any more than schoolchildren could understand the meaning of a passage from Tacitus, given only the bare, isolated meaning of each word? The deaf should have been taught the structure of French sentences, the particular syntactical role of each word—especially the verb (required in every sentence, for only the verb expresses affirmation). They should have been taught to decompose the adjectival verbs and shown that each is a combination of an active quality and the verb "be." They should have been told the secret of inversions in French to prevent them from making the mistakes made by people acquainted only with the direct order; they should have been given a purely mechanical method for identifying each part of speech; above all they should have been trained to compose simple sentences and to decompose compound sentences, and shown that all sentences are reducible to the form: "The earth is round." They would have given real meaning only to words that actually have one. Finally, actions should have been performed in front of them and the pupils trained to write out descriptions of these actions.

That is what was missing from Epée's discoveries and what needed to be sought by the one who had the perilous honor of succeeding him and the difficult task of replacing him.

But how, I shall doubtless be asked, did Epée fail to spot these inadequacies in his methods?

The fact is that, gratified by his astounding initial successes and intimidated by what still remained to be done, his heart had need to rejoice after its arduous search and to enjoy some repose at this happy point in his journey. I may also be asked how it is that observers of his teaching did not uncover what was missing from his method? The fact is that because they rarely attended more than one lesson, his admirers saw only his results, and the sudden admiration and respect demanded by the sight of a venerable old man surrounded by a crowd of idolizing unfortunates paralyzed all tongues and stifled even the slightest doubts that could moderate their almost religious enthusiasm. Who among those attending Epée's lessons for the first time could be safe from the illusion this unique wonder created, even among philosophers? Far from formulating objections, people blamed themselves for not understanding enough to admire him even more.

It was different when one or another of Epée's disciples repeated his lessons. In 1785 newspaper reports described a public demonstration by the abbé Storck in Vienna, where all observers were thrilled to see deaf pupils writing whatever was dictated to them in sign. A certain M. Nicolai of the Academy of Berlin, who did not share the general enthusiasm, proposed to perform some action himself while a deaf pupil wrote out a description of it without dictation. The challenge is accepted. Nicolai strikes his breast. The designated pupil immediately writes the words "hand" and "breast." Nicolai has no further questions. Convinced, as he had supposed, that Storck's whole method consists entirely of simple naming of objects, Nicolai departs and publishes his criticism in a newspaper; these criticisms were reprinted in a Paris newspaper.[2]

I will also be asked to explain why Epée never suspected that he was not understood. It is because he so much wanted to be understood, because his pupils had an air of seeming to do so, because one word written after another often determined the meaning of the first one, a third one determined the meaning of the second, and a few "approximatelys" were enough to yield an understanding of a few simple sentences.

But why did he not train the pupils to compose sentences by themselves? Why did he always dictate both questions and answers? Because he assumed that no other kind of work could be demanded of them. "One can understand a foreign language without being able to speak it," he replied when I raised this objection. "I understand Italian," he added, "but I cannot write in Italian. The deaf understand French, for they translate it into sign and that is enough for me."[3]

"Yes," I might have said, "but these signs that you believe are their language, it is you who have given them to your pupils. This language is no more theirs than the one they are translating." This would have been my rejoinder. But would it have been seemly for a disciple to mount a full attack on his mentor, especially when he told me continually that his successes pleased all of Europe and that such great glory had to be sufficient for his imitators? He made the following modest confession: "After all, I found the glass; you are destined to make the spectacles."

This is the reply to the laments of parents who, on being reunited with their children after their training, believed they could communicate with them in writing, and who got only a "yes" or "no," without their children asking a question themselves or answering questions with more than one word. This is the explanation for those long demonstrations in several languages where everything was an effect of memory that had no more trouble retaining words in Latin, English, Spanish, or Italian than words in French, because the total meaning of any sentence was not understood and the pupils' intelligence was going untapped . . .

Has everything that was missing from this kind of training now been discovered? Do we now have a complete system of this instruction? Does this book which I am publishing—the product of a retreat seemingly provided by Providence for me to do this writing, which required profound meditation—include all the procedures that should have been added to the ones already found? I dare think so, and I can prove it with the pupil whose story this is. He exists, he is present to all eyes, the coach of his schoolfellows, each day inventing new ways to enhance my pupils' performance.

But what order was I to follow in this difficult exposition? The goal of the book itself made it clear to me; it was not to write a systematic and purely speculative treatise, a mere scholarly account of an ingenious theory, nor a metaphysical discussion of the subtlest operations of the human mind, nor a cold and dry grammatical analysis of all the parts of speech. Rather, the order was to follow the education of a savage, an education put into action, in which the teacher—profiting from the few elements known about the grammar of this man of nature—creates with him, so to speak, the grammar of social man which will always be born of necessity.

Hence this book cannot follow the plan of most other elementary texts. In this plan of instruction each element of the sentence will in turn take the place assigned to it by need. If I had followed the usual order, the education of the deaf would still be a secret, my secret. But I thought that this book ought not contain just an indication of the road I traveled, but the road itself. So I am always viewed on stage with my pupil whose complete education is a better justification of my theory than any discourse.

Following the final chapter, you will find the applications of the means of communication discussed in the preceding ones, along with a few model lessons.

As for signs—as yet unmentioned and not, as might be thought, the most essential part of this sort of teaching—I am presently collecting and will publish the theory of all the signs for words, classified in the order I followed in the great dictionary whose tables have already been prepared. It will be a kind of dictionary of the language of the deaf, a companion volume to the present one. It is not for me to invent these signs; I merely set forth the background theory as dictated by their true inventors whose language these signs are. The deaf create the signs; I merely say how they do it. Signs must be taken from the nature of the objects they represent. Only signs given by the deaf person himself concerning actions he has observed and objects he has seen can replace spoken language. This figurative language even has a definite advantage over spoken language, for it is not restricted to any one dialect. It is a kind of universal language that, if well articulated, is understandable to people of every nationality. I do not even know whether Leibniz's *specieum*—the universal language that so long concerned him—was not based on this pantomime. At least we know that the ancients, particularly the Romans, made extensive use of it and even performed plays in it in which, without uttering a single word, they captured the attention of the audience that followed them with as much or perhaps even more pleasure than if they had used spoken language. Now suppose people always expressed themselves this way, and you will agree that the deaf would no longer be a race apart and that their education would proceed exactly like other people's.

Man undeniably possessed, in fact, two ways to express his ideas, gesture and speech; one limited to concrete objects, the other encompassing the physical world in its entirety. Actually, gesture could not imitate sound, nor was speech any the more capable of assuming the shape of objects. So what then was man's choice between these two means, supposing that he had a choice and that speech was no more natural to him than gesture?

All expressible ideas are related to three chief faculties: the body, including all sensory processes; the heart, including all the affections; the mind, including all intellectual operations. Now what relation do we find between the affections of the soul and the sounds of the voice? What words will depict fear, love, hate, or hope? Will the sounds selected by one people be understood by another? It must be acknowledged that spoken language is consistently recalcitrant to the expression of the emotions, whereas that is the triumph of sign language. And indeed, in what nation is there no understanding of eyes expressing hate and the lust for revenge, fear or hope, sadness or joy, indifference or love? For the affections of the soul, spoken language is all local convention, whereas the gestural language is their veritable portrait; it alone possesses their eloquent accents.

If we go on to consider ideas of objects that are particularly striking, either because of their diverse shapes or because of their brilliant colors, if we consider our own physical acts, what relation do we find between spoken sounds and these shapes, colors, and acts? Where is the people who choose their words so well that they are understood by all others? Beyond its own territorial limits, every nation is mute, but the nation using gesture is nowhere mute. For this language is the language of nature and is to some degree spoken everywhere. At the very least it is the language of sensory and intellectual ideas.

But is gestural language also the language of ideas specifically called abstract which belong to pure understanding? Probably yes, if this language (as I attempt to prove in one of my methods of communication) borrows its forms from the language of physical objects and actions. For if a particular word from the physical language enters by extension and metaphor into the domain of metaphysical language, why could not its exact translational equivalent in sign also enter into the metaphysical domain? So even for the expression of metaphysical ideas, gestural language could be preferable to spoken language. And if it were judged preferable, this language would not have its rival's uncertain fate. It would not have to seal itself against the corrosive effect of time; and becoming the one universal language, it would make all people into one great family in which the ancient virtues were preserved along with the first signs constantly recalling their comforting memory.

The difference in communicating ideas with signs or with spoken sounds is that sounds get their meaning only from convention while signs have real meaning by themselves. So sign language (I must be forgiven for not concealing any of its advantages) is truer, richer, and imitatively more accurate. Why not then use sign language as a favor to the people to whom it especially belongs and who have been excluded from general communication by the choice of a means which they cannot use?

Do we have to repudiate all means of communication with the deaf because they lack the one hitherto used by other people? Is spoken language the only means of communication? Observing the deaf person, we soon realize that another means, which is equally reliable though admittedly not as rapid, is always available to him. We listen to the noise of sonorous objects, and we imitate it with sounds. A multiplicity of root words found in all languages leaves no room for doubt about this primitive imitation. The deaf person considers the shapes of objects and imitates them with a probably clearer and less ambiguous pantomime. Analogy has led hearing people to assume resemblances between sonorous objects and other objects, and thereupon other combined sounds have enriched their vocabulary. Why wouldn't the same analogy eventually enrich the mimic vocabulary of the deaf? If hearing people thought they could use sounds to express things beyond the realm of the sensory, why could not the deaf person express the same things with gestures? Would vocal inflections be more natural than other conventional signs?

But . . . if among the exceptions of nature or among its distressing mutilations we came across someone who was both deaf and blind, what would our means of communication be? This cruelly diminished creature would find himself greatly estranged from other people! How hard it would be to close the gap between him and us! What teacher can we provide for this afflicted child? The teacher of the deaf? But his art is restricted making thought visible, to representing the operations of the intellectual eye to the organ of physical sight and the unfortunate person lacks the use of his sight. Would we entrust his education to someone whose purely mechanical talent, instead of just training blind people's hands for easy tasks, would merely teach them useless feats of skill and so make of them mere jugglers or street musicians?[4] But what could he teach a deaf [and blind] person? . . . What can the teacher's hand do on the pupil's hand when the tongue can express no sound, when the ear cannot hear any, when the face also keeps silent?

I think it proven that from the beginning man had two ways to express his ideas, that instead of sonorous imitation he could have decided in favor of manual signs. Why don't these signs come to our aid in this case? For if we lack eyes for seeing these signs, don't we have hands for touching them? And if the dark of night still allows Massieu to use his hands to see what I am expressing with mine, would not the daylight, which is the deepest night for our deaf-blind person, likewise allow him to see my message?

Oh, if the experiment I would like to perform were successful, if

I managed, as I have done for the deaf, to give such a person a mind, this triumph would make me even happier than its subject.

My illustrious predecessor dared to believe this possible. He did not hesitate to publish, in the newspapers of the time, a proposal for an education that had always seemed impossible even after his successes had accustomed people to faith in the greatest wonders. Here are the methods he communicated to me.

Epée planned to use an alphabet of polished iron letters to form the vocabulary for physical objects and actions identifiable by touch. He hoped to familiarize his pupil's hands with these letters, getting the hands to do the work of the eyes. The pupil was to touch the object with one hand and to spell its name with the other. Epée's creative genius would probably have invented the rest as he went along.

I fully appreciate the difficulties arising at each step. For how, without ever seeing or hearing each other, do we agree on a sign to establish a connection between the object and its name? I would think we should stimulate instinct. I would give the pupil some interesting object, whose name he was willing to make an effort to remember, and have him make the sign and combine the letters. This first step might be followed by a second—discrimination of the qualities or modes of the objects. Of course we realize that colors and sounds would not enter into our reckoning, but the basis for the new metaphysics and the first objects in this training would be the shapes of tangible objects. Because the visual qualities have led the deaf by analogy to the discovery of purely abstract moral and intellectual qualities, why would not the tactile sense lead us to the same kind of discovery? The procedures outlined in this book need only be presented in relief for the deaf-blind pupil. Necessity would dictate the changes required. The deaf-blind pupil would become, as the deaf one frequently was, his teacher's teacher. At every point the pupil's cumulative progress would indicate the next step. Instead of speaking to the eyes, the teacher would have to speak to the hands.

Would that this instructional system were just of purely speculative interest and that its application never became a necessity! Would that no child was born so unfortunate as to have only the hands for eyes and ears! But because this delinquency of nature is only too possible, let us think in advance of a method for rectifying it. To restore a person to society and family and himself, and to restore society and comrades and family to him is too sweet a gratification and too precious a conquest for us to give up hope.

CHAPTER 1. THE FIRST METHOD OF COMMUNICATION

Comparison of Common Objects and Drawings

Because the education of the congenitally deaf requires special procedures, I should be only half-fulfilling the important task imposed on me by the privilege of being the chosen replacement of my illustrious teacher, the renowned abbé de l'Epée, if, as the sole trustee of his secret, I restricted this book to a simple theory of French grammar. People would inquire how I ever managed to get someone who had never heard sounds to understand the meaning of the words of any language. How was I able to give words a precise meaning for persons who had only manual signs for presenting their ideas? How was I able to ascertain whether the minds of deaf people, which seem to be outside the sphere of normal intelligence, did not ascribe to written words a broader or a narrower range of meaning than we do? Finally, how was I able to establish a perfect correspondence between the deaf and the hearing person; how were physical signs able to transmit abstract ideas to the deaf person, and how was this correspondence established and this education begun?

I can answer all these questions by reviewing my repertory of methods. To satisfy public demand, the best procedure would seem to be for me to recapitulate the lessons of one of my pupils, Jean Massieu. Each day his educational progress substantiates the advantages of the method that he and I have devised.

This book will therefore be a review of my methods, a sort of diary of my lessons at which the reader will be present as judge. It is a form best suited to reveal all the secrets of a precious discovery. These secrets are within the reach and as if in the hands of anyone who wants to exploit them. Such should be the goal of inventors of practical methods: in passing on these methods, the inventors outlive their own precarious existence, and after they are gone, they continue to deserve humanity's gratitude ...

It was in June, 1786, some months after the archbishop Champion de Cicé founded the still-extant School for the Deaf in Bordeaux, that I was presented with the pupil whose amazing progress I shall relate.[5] He was about fourteen years of age, from an impoverished family, with two brothers and two sisters, all deaf. He was accompanied by his mother and his elder sister who I also took as a pupil. The mother had no expectation of my taking on brother and sister both ...

We can easily get an idea of young Massieu's personality and manners when we learn that he was born in a humble cottage six leagues from Bordeaux and had never seen anyone but his family who never took the trouble to communicate even purely physical ideas to him. He spent his whole childhood tending a flock of sheep, and all his ideas were confined to the circle of objects at which he happened to glance. He was a boor with the habits of an animal, startled and frightened by everything. Coming to Bordeaux, he thought he was merely changing residence and imagined that he would be placed in charge of another flock of sheep. He longed to return to the scene of his first childhood games. Everything he saw seemed frightening, to every movement he responded as if to a trap. How far was this simple child from the realization that he was coming to Bordeaux to learn, to become human, for he regarded himself as no better than the animals he tended! His bland and impassive physiognomy, his shy and mistrustful gaze, his inane and suspicious manner, his difficulty in assuming that steady uprightness without which the mind wanders and cannot weigh and compare ideas—everything seemed to portend Massieu's ineducability. But he was not long in raising fonder hopes.

The subject of the first lesson was the alphabet. I had not yet realized the inadequacy of this procedure which, from the first, ran counter to the analytic behavior Massieu needed to learn in order to become something more than an automaton. Indeed I have since asked myself: how can a sequence of abstract and meaningless characters, in no particular order and with no equivalent in nature, inform one's reason? But that is how my illustrious mentor began, and for me all his methods were sacred.

Massieu learned the alphabet in less than two days. I printed the letters on the blackboard, and he imitated them by writing and by making various handshapes . . . It would probably have been more reasonable and quicker to begin his instruction the way I have subsequently devised it: on the bench supporting the blackboard I place several objects and have Massieu draw them on the board. The objects are common everyday items always at hand, such as a scissors, knife, key, penknife, pen, snuff-box, and the like. The deaf person need only glance at the object and at the sketch of it to see immediately the resemblance between them. I get him to note this likeness, and from the object he indicates the corresponding drawing, or from inspection of the drawing he presents me with the corresponding object.

How, without this initial reversible exercise, would the deaf pupil acquire an interest in the words we would like to present him with, and particularly in the individual letters that he is later to see one by one? Discouraged by his failure to find the reason for these characters, the need for a particular number of them, and a motive for combining them, the bewildered pupil is tormented in these first lessons. It was Massieu himself who revealed this problem to me.

At the beginning of his education, the hearing child experiences none of these difficulties. Before he or she even suspects that we communicate by writing, before learning about words and letters, the hearing child understands spoken signs or, if you will, articulate sounds functioning as signs for recalling objects. He already has a nomenclature in his head, and all he need do is draw it on paper. He utters sounds which have to be converted into written words; these words have to be decomposed—and that we do by naming the constituent elements, the letters. The deaf-mute child can utter nothing. Like other children he doubtless has a series of images held in the same reservoir, drawn on the same canvas, but he has only manual signs, not letters or words, for recalling their shapes. The hearing child paints, as it were, the sounds he utters, and by uttering words, he in his fashion draws the objects for which these words are signs. The deaf child also has objects to paint, but he does not have the same means available to him. The hearing child draws with his pen, his marks are wholly conventional; the deaf child draws with his pencil without calling on some unneeded convention for which he still has no signs. So in this first lesson the deaf pupil's words are object shapes in the way that we could say that, for readers, printed words are object shapes. We speak to a hearing person's ears; we speak to a deaf person's eyes. Because we speak to both persons, our goal is the same. The only difference is sense modality: hearing for one, sight for the other.

So in this first lesson we use a pencil to talk to the deaf pupil the way a nanny speaks to a hearing child; in both cases we present him with the object to be named, either by sounds or by shape. I daresay the hearing pupil has no advantage here over my deaf pupil, and this first lesson is no harder to give to the deaf child than to the hearing child. We could say that the deaf child's ears are in his eyes and that the hearing child's eyes are in his ears, for images transmit to the deaf child's mind what words transmit to the hearing child's.

Therefore one should not be surprised to find a perfect analogy between my instructional procedures and the ones used with normal children, for their minds are quite similar, and the difference in their senses is practically negligible. Let the teacher then assume the obligation to surround his deaf pupil with all the things found in the environment of the hearing child, for these surroundings have a teaching function. Everything is of value to the education of the newcomer. The reader must already realize that the only blunder in the education of the deaf is to skip a link in the chain of ideas and, instead of connecting all things up in their proper order, to assume the pupil knows something that, in fact, has yet to be shown. A sign or word must never be presented until the pupil has seen the object to be recalled by word or signs.

Thus the first lesson concerns neither words nor letters. We devote the time to getting the pupil to compare objects with sketches of them, and to invent for himself a handier, more efficient way of expressing his ideas and of fixing the image of these objects in his memory.

The designated objects are then set on a table. I show the pupil the drawing of the knife; he immediately goes looking for the object. I show him the drawing of the key; he gets the key. I do the same for all the drawings, and he understands me perfectly. I in turn pick up each object, signing to the pupil to show me its drawing. This second exercise has the same success as the first one. So far it is evident that I am being understood; like a mother pronouncing the names of objects she is showing her child, so is the drawing the name of the object for the deaf pupil and me, and I am assured that we have established the first means of communication.

The pupil finds this initial success encouraging. Eager to name everything within sight, he tries his hand at drawing everything that meets his gaze, and he urges me to show him every object he draws. As he sees that he has been understood when, going by the crude shapes made by his still-novice pencil, I present him with the objects he has named by drawing them, his delight is extreme. Can I express my own great joy when this trial-run promised more intimate communications to come? The gap hitherto separating me from my pupil was going to be closed . . . Massieu was going to become human; he was beginning to communicate, and it was to me that he owed this dawning of happiness.

Massieu wanted to know if I could also draw the external parts of his body. He showed me his eyes, forehead, nose, mouth, cheeks, ears, temples, chin, his whole head. Without suspecting it, Massieu was already training himself in the great art of analysis to which we owe so many wonders in the mind's development. He continued the analysis of his body, not overlooking any of his limbs. He tried drawings of his own, but totally unacquainted with proportion or perspective, the attempt was discouraging for him. This was not unintentional on my part. We needed quicker and easier ways to draw. For the moment, I had to give Massieu a distaste for this first method of communication, and get him to desire a better one which became the subject of a second lesson.

CHAPTER 2. SECOND METHOD OF COMMUNICATION

A New Application of the First Procedure. Vocabulary.
Classification of the Objects of This Vocabulary.

On the same bench I place the objects whose drawings had served the day before to open up the doors of Massieu's intelligence for the first time. As in the first lesson, sketches of these objects were drawn on the blackboard set on the bench. Massieu thought I was going to repeat our first exercise. But to his surprise, he saw me trace around each drawing the characters he had already learned to discriminate and whose shapes he had learned to imitate but whose purpose or meaning he still did not know! In a corner of the blackboard I wrote all the letters of the French alphabet. I got him to notice that these new characters drawn around each figure had their analogues in the corner of the blackboard. He was puzzled by these marks depicting and representing nothing, and constituting an apparently aimless pencil game. In his eyes, in his whole physiognomy, I read both surprise and curiosity. I have him count the characters; our first numbers were on our fingers, each one equal to one unit. I have him note the shape of each letter and I attempt to explain with my signs that he merely had to retain them, that I am presently going to erase the figure, and that it will be replaced by these letters. I was some-what unsure of being understood, but it was easy to carry out the attempt on the spot and so to make certain. Besides, the illusion was already so comforting! Then, as I had said I would, I erased the drawing of the knife. That is when I saw how people ignorant of sign language are deluded in thinking they are being understood when they randomly make signs that, without a counterpart in na-ture and without any conventional meaning, depicting nothing to the eyes, say nothing to the mind. Massieu had not understood me;

I had merely increased his surprise. I had to draw the object anew and write the letters on the drawing itself, not around it. In erasing, I had to be careful to leave out only the part between the letters. Finally the letters covered the whole length of the drawing. The letters almost outlined the knife. I brought the knife close to this strange, ill-formed shape (but one easier to trace than the drawing), and to show Massieu that this way of drawing objects was not so peculiar, I called on an observer who knew how to read, showed him this handwriting, and the observer immediately took the knife and held it up to view. Massieu was utterly mystified. He had no idea how lines that did not appear to picture anything could function as an image for objects and represent them with such accuracy and speed. Once again, I had him count the letters; I did not write around the shape of the knife but along a horizontal line, the way we write normally. He tried imitating me and, hard though it is to believe, he needed only two lessons to manage it. Imagine my delight when a stranger, erasing the letters that I had traced and leaving only Massieu's, presented me with the same object from the inspection of Massieu's letters which were still rudimentary but accurate enough to be recognized as the object's name! I hasten to show him the palette of these new colors—the alphabet at the corner of the blackboard. Massieu appeared intimidated by the difficulty of combining and remembering these shapes. But he became even more alarmed when I showed our stranger various combinations of the seven letters [couteau] used to draw the knife, and got Massieu to realize that only a single correct combination would do, that only one of them could represent the knife, that a letter more or a letter less, a displacement of even one letter and the slightest error in their arrangement made the whole combination useless. So he had to resign himself not only to learning the number of all the letters taking the place of the picture and representing objects, but also never to be mistaken about their particular and relative position. At that moment Massieu learned the whole advantage and difficulty of writing, although he still didn't know the name for this marvelous invention. Each object to be drawn with these new characters seemed to him a great science to master and a huge effort; he fell into a profound despondency. I tried to raise his spirits by explaining—as best I could in these first attempts at communication—that there was a sort of canvas in his head where, one by one and without any effort on his part, pictures would take shape of all the objects he had seen. I made him see his eyes as mirrors constantly reflecting objects that then passed from these mirrors to the canvas. I explained that these characters passed onto this canvas in this way, arranged themselves and were preserved there without any effort. I used comparative signs to tell him that the habit of seeing these characters together in a fixed combination would connect them in his head, and that they would remain as closely connected as they were on the board where he saw them written.

In fact, Massieu's untrained intelligence did not quite grasp what I was telling him; some of it was lost on him. But I am certain that my signed explanation gave him some consolation. His energy seemed to revive and his spirits to be rekindled, his eyes seeming to tell me that fear was yielding to hope and despair to delight.

From that moment on, the drawing was banished; we replaced it with writing. You understand, of course, that even in these early stages we avoided writing the alphabet where isolated letters do not make up a word and occur without order. Of what interest to Massieu was a row of meaningless letters? We continued to "draw" objects with these new marks that needed no name. So we were writing words, but without realizing that they were made up of letters and even less that the letters were consonants or vowels. And it was as yet immaterial to us to know the name of these assemblages of letters called "words." How could we be learning grammar and its technical terms when we had no set language, when we barely had a few fleeting ideas to fix and express?

At first we wanted to express everything, to name everything, write everything. Massieu presented me with everything he saw, even things he went looking for. He wanted to know everything, and I had to write the name of everything. This newcomer to earth was a stranger on his own estates, which were being restored to him as he learned their names. Oh, how great was his pleasure as his vocabulary grew and I enriched his ample memory with new names! Not a day passed in which he did not learn more than fifty names, nor a single day which he did not in turn teach me the signs for the same objects whose names I had had him write. Thus, in a felicitous exchange, while I was teaching Massieu the written signs of French, he was teaching me the mimic signs of his language. That is how we readied ourselves to converse some day, in this pantomime in which I was becoming more fluent as my pupil revealed its roots with his gestures.

Indeed, it must be confessed that neither I nor my illustrious teacher Epée was the inventor of the language of the deaf. As a

Frenchman cannot be taught French by a foreigner, a hearing person has no business meddling with the invention of signs, giving them abstract values.

By now Massieu knew the name of nearly everything he saw. He compiled a sort of portable dictionary with the shape and name of every object he came across in the classroom or dining hall or dormitory or garden. It was now time to decompose these objects and to teach him that each part, like the whole, has a name distinguishing it from every other part. The upper part of the human body, for example, has a name that distinguishes it from the lower part; the two limbs that he stands on, that take him from one place to another, have a particular name, as do his arms and hands. I had to teach him to decompose the head where the most delicate organs, the highest senses, were. Because everything in the head is of interest, each part of it warrants a name to prevent confusion with any other part. What a new treasurehouse for this child who, knowing only the names of objects considered as wholes, saw each object appear in a multiplicity of forms seeming to proliferate the objects themselves by making each into a little universe!

Massieu and I analyzed the head. I got him to note the cranium, which the Creator formed of a fairly hard matter to make it invulnerable, as it were, having made the roofing or covering of the softer substance in which all the nerves terminate. But the time had not yet come to tell Massieu about all its dignity and excellence; I would not have been understood. I talked only about what he saw; I withheld for a more propitious moment the revelation about what he had once been condemned never to know. Massieu learned the name of that noble feature on which all human majesty is unfurled, which no animal has, for no beast has a brow like his. Of his own accord and before giving me the chance to suggest the question to him, Massieu asked for the name of this mirror of the soul and its privileged seat, of the eye; because for the deaf it is in the eye that the soul lives and will forever remain. On our blackboard I decomposed all the parts of the eye, not omitting the eyebrows or eyelashes or any part of the pupil. I made a drawing of all these parts within a brace at the point of which I wrote "eye," which then became the model for all words of the same kind that we would later write about the body, whose many wonders still remained to be admired.

We also analyzed the ear. I did not dare, alas, reveal all the miracles of this organ whose remarkable function he could never understand fully. I did not describe the auditory nerve or the tympanum, which

doubtless was nonexistent or paralyzed in him. As with the eyes, I
enclosed the parts in a brace under the name "ear"; likewise for the
mouth, an organ that will sadly be forever fastened shut, never to
express the deaf person's thought in any of life's circumstances and
never to affect a friend with the entrancing charms of tender sounds.
To Massieu, the mouth could be described only as an organ involving
taste, like the palate. I listed its constituents: teeth and their different types, gums, tongue, palate, throat, and so on. All these organs
took the name "mouth," and each part had its own specific name.
I wrote the name "hair," "chin," "cheeks," and so forth; everything
on the surface of the head—all these parts forming particular wholes
within a general whole enclosed in a large brace . . .

I beg the reader's indulgence for these details; they will help him
understand or even invent similar procedures that I shall later merely
mention.

We decomposed all the parts susceptible of decomposition. This
way Massieu learned the names of all the parts denoted by the
collective name "human body." You can already see that the sign
for the body was a collection of the signs for its principal parts.

Massieu saw at once that any creature or thing in nature could
be decomposed, just as his body had been, and realized that there
were as many names to learn as an object had parts. He became
interested in identifying body parts with specific functions, and this
scientific curiosity made him more observant. It was a great victory
for me just to stimulate his mind, and cast into it that spark of
desire—the first blaze of imitation—without which I would have
been working alone, without him, for his own instruction. The reverse was required: he had always to be in front of me, to precede
me. Well! Would he ever have done so, would he ever have followed
me if he had not felt the need to increase the number of his first
pleasures? Although he had already risen to the dignity of hearing
people, he could not fully comprehend their means of communication and this afflicted his soul. He began, like them, to write down
his memories, to retrace them, and to recall all the objects he had
seen. But ever since the human body had presented him, under one
name, with so many objects, each with a particular name, he thought
he knew nothing, since he did not know the names of the parts of
objects of which he knew only the collective name.

So I had to indulge Massieu's impatient curiosity and analyze with
him all other natural objects. He obliged me to follow him anywhere
there were objects to decompose—into the classroom with its benches,

windows, doors, stoves. He had to be told the name of every object
and of any part of it with a particular name. He continually divided
and subdivided, asking the name of the divisions and subdivisions.

That is how he unintentionally essayed the great art of analysis,
and how he trained himself for the classification of knowledge to
come. Could it be? Massieu, who seemed to be learning just words,
was mastering the analytical science of things, inasmuch as true
science consists less in knowing a great deal than in knowing it
well, that is, in properly classifying what is learned!

Massieu had a general idea of all natural entities. Now all he had
to do was to divide them into classes, and we could not postpone
classification any longer. So on to genera, species, and individuals.
We went into the countryside. We had to begin with the first class
of entities, those on the lowest rung of the ladder. We had to find
mines, and to question nature in the deep, immense arsenals where
it silently works forming the metals that have existed since the
world began and whose ample veins cannot be exhausted by the
passage of centuries. But we could find only quarries. We went down
into them and saw, as though in their wombs, stones awaiting a
skilled hand to rip them out for the construction of buildings and
the adornment of cities. I had brought along some samples of iron,
copper, lead, gold, silver. I tried explaining that these substances
also grew, or rather increased, in the bowels of the earth; that peb-
bles, stones, and types of marble came from there, that the earth
was the mother common to many families, and that this deep hab-
itation was the source of the common name "mineral," meaning
deep. In the same way that the term "body" applied to all body parts,
the name "mineral" applied to all the members of this mineral body,
or rather kind. Massieu's manual sign—the sign common to all metals—was the same as the one for *deep*. He acted out the movement
of someone digging for these hidden substances, going down into
these enormous storehouses, finding the substances, collecting them,
and taking them out. We needed a sign for each kind of mineral.
Massieu had seen men working with iron, copper, lead, silver, and
gold. The first part of the sign for each kind of metal was the sign
common to them all, as Massieu had just made it and as I have just
described. Then came the sign for the forging process that each kind
underwent. To act out iron, Massieu imitated a person blowing on
the hearth and giving the red-hot iron a shape by blows with a
hammer and anvil. He beat the copper and polished it, melted the
lead and poured it into imaginary little molds from which he re-

moved the lead as bullets and cannonballs. For him, silver was distinguished from gold by its whitish color. (In the final chapter we see his general sign for colors.) The sign common to these two metals was that of value or price which he gave them by acting out the movement of someone counting out crown pieces and gold coins.

We returned to the earth's surface. There, in wonder at the variety of objects adorning it and nourishing its inhabitants, we also gave names to those other organisms that, feet implanted in the earth, receive the sap that nourishes their limbs and bodies. We called their feet "roots"; we named their arms "branches," and their body "trunk." With these analogies we penetrated the Creator's secret, and beginning to form some idea of His existence without yet knowing it, we admired in His works the Being who must have produced them . . . We considered them as making up a single entity or body which we called "vegetable."

Each species was considered as a part of this great whole. When we had isolated the species, it in turn became a body of which each individual was just a part. All of them were plants that could be torn out of the earth at the cost of hastening their destruction and death. We called them "plants." I had noticed that Massieu more readily gave the same name, a common noun, to several individuals in which he saw similarities; individual names presupposed differences that it was not yet time for him to observe.

We saw many different classes during our useful strolls. Many families populated the fertile fields we crossed. The study of distinctive names for each had taken up too much time, and we were not yet doing a course of natural history and botany. We were content to distinguish the principal genera and species. We began with the most interesting ones, the source of our daily sustenance . . . Massieu learned the names for cabbages, lettuce, parsley, carrots, leeks, onions, chervil, white beets, and eventually all the garden vegetables.

We visited an orchard to name all the fruits. We went into a woods to distinguish the oak from the elm; to the edges of brooks to identify the willow and the poplar, eventually all the other inhabitants of those majestic, solitary cities inviting profound meditation. Massieu's visits were those of a landowner seeing his rich domain for the first time.

He didn't have enough tablets and pencils for all the names with which I filled his dictionary, while his soul seemed to expand and grow with these innumerable denominations. Oh, how great and proud these prodigies of nature appeared to him! He classified garden plants, fruit trees, and the trees in the forest. Each genus had its own page, each series its own column, like the names of so many creatures with which he was eager to form a connection (which would last as long as the sense modality noting their similarities and differences). The names he wrote down and the various shapes he drew were guarantees that he would never forget them.

But whatever interest these things had for our young observer, they were not the only or even the most interesting things. I took him to a farm where I showed him all the features that contributed to its richness and charm. The shed where the animals rest from their daily labors, man's fellow workers who nourish him with their flesh and their milk during their lives and even serve him afterward: the ewes whose fleece covers him, kids, lambs which are the hope of the sheepfolds, the poultry yard where for everyday meals we find chicken eggs and for holidays more succulent foods. Massieu took down the name of all the various classes; all of them enriched his vocabulary, and the generic name for all these creatures was the word "domestic" added to the word "living" or "animal."

I shall relate elsewhere how we invented signs for all these objects.[6]

The earth is populated with other animals. Massieu had seen a great many, but far from most. So we went into their solitary haunts to visit those other creatures for most of whom man is an enemy and who flee at his approach. The war of extermination had not yet been declared on all their kind, and it was easy to find and name the timid hare, the destructive rabbit, the swift stag and buck, the trusting woodcock, the quail and the partridge. We took note of all the species of birds that play about in the open air, and we added their names to our already copious lists.

We returned to town and visited workshops. Artists and workmen gave us an enthusiastic welcome and answered our questions with great kindness. The artists would show and name their supplies for us, the workmen, their tools. All of them allowed us to examine their handiwork and told us the names of everything . . .

So passed the first months of instruction without our yet tackling the first problems of the grammar we needed to express our thoughts. We were collecting various materials that already were contributing to our mental development. I informed the abbé de l'Epée of this initial work. He criticized its slowness.[7]

But I was vindicated by the felicitous results I had obtained. "I do not yet control the instrument of thought," I told him. "I do not yet conjugate verbs." But does a mother begin her child's education with the theory of conjugations? Isn't it important to store up useful provisions, to enrich an untrained memory with the names of objects? Indeed, what could the objects for a deaf person's judgments be if we didn't lift the veil covering the spectacle of nature? Continually frustrated in our education by an ignorance of the signs to represent objects, we would always remain strangers in our own country, knowing nothing and consequently unable to discuss anything. All education begins with vocabulary, and children know the names of everything around them before they know how to construct a sentence. Any instruction for a deaf person that does not begin this way will be lacking a foundation. So, much as I may respect someone holding a contrary opinion, I knew I had to check an impatient desire to produce fruits before the season of flowers.

Chapter 3. The Third Method of Communication

Learning the Words Être, Chose, *and* Objet. *The Origin of the Adjective. Invention of a Pronoun and of the Verb* Être.

By now Massieu believed himself deeply knowledgeable; indeed nature had opened all its stores for him, as the artists and workmen had opened their studios and workshops. He had some knowledge of both genera and species in all three kingdoms though he did not quite know what a kingdom or genus or species was. He also had some knowledge of products, that is, the results of human labor. Together we tried to divide and classify all objects, but we did so without verbs or pronouns. Let the reader follow along with patience and good humor, however, and he will be persuaded that we didn't yet need them.

The reader must already have noted that with the second method of communication Massieu had grasped not only the names of individuals, but also collective names and even the names of species. So there could be no difficulty teaching him generic names, and here is how I proceeded to do so. Massieu knew the names of various metals and minerals as well as a large number of living things. He was acquainted with living creatures and inanimate objects, rest and movement, sleep and wakefulness, life and death. A glance at a pebble and a plant, a rod and a tree branch, a ewe's fleece and the ewe itself gave him an on-the-spot idea of organism and object without his having seen the words for these categories. So all that remained was to evoke these ideas in him, for they were there, and I did so by bringing together these organisms and objects and by questioning him with my eyes and by using one hand to indicate an organism and the other hand to indicate an object. But can this manner of questioning be shown? Can it be described? A hundred times I have called on observers in my lessons for the deaf. But when I try to state the theory here, the right words for describing this method elude even these observers, for whom the language of the eyes is a foreign idiom. I saw Massieu grasp the difference between the organic and the inorganic, between a ball and a living tree trunk, his gaze alternating between *boule* [ball] and *arbre* [tree], and I wrote it directly inside each of these words, as in the following example.

B c O h U o L s E e A ê R t B r R e E

By writing the word *chose* [thing] in *boule* this way, and *être* [being, creature] in *arbre*, I avoided giving *chose* and *être* independent and individual existence, removing them from the class of modifiers. So Massieu was getting his first lesson in the sublime art of thinking. I directed his mind back to the simple idea, and this return of his mind, so justly called reflection, made it into a thought—that was a new piece of work. In this lesson the word *être* was written within the name of all the objects we had found increasing in the earth's entrails or growing in its bosom and rising above its surface or breathing, moving, and going from one place to another. We wrote the word *chose* to express something that did not increase or grow or live—in short, everything produced by human labor. So "creatures" were things not humanly fabricated, and "things" were everything that we had, or could have, seen made. We went a step further, and with a similar procedure we gave creatures and things the even more general name "object." That was how we began our training in generalization.

But not all creatures and things, not all objects had the same mode of being, not even things of the same kind; they had, for example, different shapes or different colors. These differences could be noted only by bringing these objects together, comparing them, and observing that one of them lacked what the other had. But once we had grasped this difference, what sign did we have for keeping it in mind? Should we use two signs or two words, one for the object, the other for its color? But two words . . . would seem for my pupil to presuppose two objects where there was only one. So how do we teach a deaf person to distinguish a quality from an object of which the quality is merely an accident and not be confused with the object? How to keep Massieu clear of the trap set by two words for an object when the quality and object are not separated in nature?

Here I encountered in full force the problem of abstractions, and the only way to avoid a mistake was, I thought, to repeat with adjectives the procedure just used successfully for generic words. This way was to imitate nature, as it were, which did not separate from objects the qualities that are their substrata or supports. It is this completely original procedure, later found highly successful, which let me progress so confidently where there was nothing else to guide my teaching.

I used seven sheets of paper, each with one white side and the other painted with one of the seven primary colors. First, I set them on our exercise table with only the white side visible, thus making them all look alike. On the blackboard I wrote the word *papier* [paper], with spaces between all the letters.

I turned the first sheet over and had it compared with the six others. Massieu readily observed that this sheet was different from the others. It was red, the others white. I filled in the spaces with the word *rouge* [red]; I did the same with the other sheets. The color name for each appears written in the spaces between the letters forming the word *papier*; these two intercalated words formed a single word but a double or twofold word simultaneously presenting both substance and quality, object and modification, noun and adjective united as they were in the object itself. Again I turned over the red sheet, which now appeared white. I erased *rouge* and substituted *blanc* [white]. Massieu understood that the first word, the one not erased, was the name of the object and that the second one was the name of the quality.

I applied the same procedure to the shapes of objects by replacing the colored sheets with objects of different shapes. This also worked. I tried the same procedure with flavors. I went on to the names of people, always inserting in the open spaces the qualities corresponding to each name; Massieu never made a mistake. I thought this the best way to represent the inseparable connection between quality and object, and hence the best way to express the affirmation or pronouncement of a judgment. This was our first way of stating our judgments, our thoughts; this was our first proposition, our first sentence.

PrAoPuIgEeR

How hard it was to bridge the gap between the object and the quality affirmed! We had just distinguished between them; now we had to abstract the distinction. Here is how I was able to do this.

I took a handkerchief, and spread it out in front of Massieu. I got him to notice the four sides by tracing four lines in the air, each as long as a side of the handkerchief, which Massieu was holding with one hand and I with the other. Beforehand I had written the word "handkerchief" in our new way. I wrote the word "square" in the spaces, after tracing the handkerchief's four sides in the air.

I made the shape of the handkerchief disappear in a sort of ball and immediately erased the word "square." I returned the handkerchief to its original shape, and restored the word for this shape. I hid the handkerchief, but immediately outlined its shape in the air as if it were still spread out and I were holding it by one corner and Massieu by another. I then erased "handkerchief," but without touching the letters expressing its quality. I had Massieu consider the word "square"; in the air he described the shape, as if he had the handkerchief in front of him.

In this way the shape remained with him, separated from its object, this shape to which I was trying to give a kind of being without support! So abstraction has been achieved! Another step! What a giant step for someone who had never compared anything and had never done any thinking! Henceforth we can expect everything of him, ask everything, try everything! The greatest difficulties have been overcome. Massieu understands abstractions, Massieu is a thinking creature!

But we are dissatisfied with this experiment. Our success could be doubted. The step was too difficult not to arouse legitimate suspicion even though we believe the difficulty overcome. Let Massieu himself perform the abstraction; let it become clear to him; let him take away, as it were, a quality from an object; let him trace the path that he will make this quality take; let him perceive the full course that it will run; and let the eye move from the object and come to rest on the quality, and from the quality back to the object. Then we will no longer doubt whether Massieu knows how to abstract or whether in his mind the quality remains distinct from its object.

Here is the procedure I used or, rather, had Massieu carry out.

$$P \quad A \quad P \quad I \quad E \quad R$$
$$\cdot \quad \cdot \quad \cdot \quad \cdot \quad \cdot$$
$$\cdot \quad \cdot \quad \cdot \quad \cdot \quad \cdot$$
$$r \quad o \quad u \quad g \quad e$$

I carefully wrote the letters for the quality on little strips of card-board, putting each in the place indicated by each vertical line. The separation between the quality and its object was therefore physically apparent, as were the distinction and the procedure. To show that he understood this demonstration, the pupil had put his hand over his eyes. Then, with the other hand he mimes taking the quality away from its object, as if he were getting the quality under the object to take the direction shown by the vertical line.

The proposition was just a few steps away. We took the now easy steps using the following overall procedure.

$$P \, r \, A \, o \, P \, u \, I \, g \, E \, e \, R$$
$$\cdot \quad \cdot \quad \cdot \quad \cdot \quad \cdot$$
$$P \quad A \quad P \quad I \quad E \quad R$$
$$\cdot \quad \cdot \quad \cdot \quad \cdot \quad \cdot$$
$$\cdot \quad \cdot \quad \cdot \quad \cdot \quad \cdot$$
$$r \quad o \quad u \quad g \quad e$$
$$PAPIER \; rouge$$

The path was the same, if a bit longer; there had been one additional step. Still another step remained:

$$..P..A..P..I..E..R.....R..O..U..G..E..$$

Here the line, as we see it, is the connection between the object and the quality. The line brings to mind all the lines indicating abstraction. In the following procedure it will become shorter and undergo a kind of ellipsis:

$$PAPIER.....ROUGE$$

Here we finally have arrived at that universally recognized phrase, that important word translating and replacing our connecting line: the word that is, as it were, by itself speech, verb, and thought, the word that is all alone and the elliptical utterance of a complete judgment, the "yes" of the mind, which distinguishes man from beast, intelligent man from the man of unreason; the word that cannot be applied randomly for it expresses the applicability or non-applicability of a quality that must be considered in an object or separated from it; finally, this word so necessary to language that we cannot think or speak or write without it; the word that must consequently be found everywhere, and for the understanding of which we will agree that we could not make too great an effort or generate too many procedures.[8]

But this important word is or will be understood because its sign is understood. We merely have to couple the word with the connecting line for the line to give it its meaning. The word can now stand alone. The word recalls the meaning of all the lines traced to yield the true understanding of them.

> PAPIER est rouge   PAPIER . . . est . . . rouge

This is the formulation of the inner judgment made by everyone giving even the slightest attention to a sheet of red paper. So this is a picture of what occurs in an attentive mind. But . . . the statement contains three words . . . As our procedures had accustomed Massieu to giving a real meaning to each word, could he not think, when he saw three words here, that there were three ideas? How do we keep him from making this mistake? By making these words into a single sign, by making into one sign the two words expressing the substance and the way of being or modification. This is what I had been doing in the preceding procedures when I translated the connecting line into the verb être, thereby making this word lose any possible meaning representative of an image. In the end, the proposition, and the sentence which is its material embodiment, had to be reduced to a simplicity of judgment such as we might find in a newly created people who, without communication with other peoples, could have only words, double words, word-sentences, or word-thoughts for the expression of its judgments as we have simple words to express our ideas.

But if everything in nature is an object or a quality, if around us there are only objects and their ways of being, then thought can only be concerned with objects and their modifications. The only strictly necessary things in the linguistic expression of thought would be nouns, adjectives, and the word connecting them—only these three kinds of words would be important. The deaf person's grammatical studies could end here, for Massieu understood the use of these three parts of speech, the only ones needed for any judgment. Indeed, once Massieu was acquainted with the magic of the word that the Romans called verb or word par excellence, he continually applied it to all the objects whose qualities he noticed.

I must include an important observation about the intention of the word *être*, an observation justifying what I said about the origin of adjectives in my *Elements of General Grammar* (vol. 1, p. 89). To express the various visual qualities continually meeting his gaze, Massieu did not wait for the adjectives, but made use of names of objects in which he found the salient quality that he wanted to affirm of another object. For example, to express the swiftness of one of his comrades in a race, he said: "Albert is *bird*." To express strength, he said: "Paul is *lion*"; for gentleness, he said: "Desylons is *lamb*" . . . He thought he was saying something nice about a friend by saying: "Col is my *dog*," and something highly insulting about another friend, who was making slow progress, in saying: "Letertre is *turtle*."

He took some of his qualities from our flowerbeds. He said of a deaf girl who seemed to him quieter than the other girls (this was, I must say, his sister's personality): "Blanche is *violet*." In speaking of another girl's complexion, he said: "Queney is *lily*," "Chabon is *rose*."

As yet Massieu had no inkling of the richness of French expressions that leave nothing without sign or image, and he thought that French contained only the names of objects. Because I had not realized this initial error of his (if indeed it was one), I had a good deal of trouble ascribing the meaning of the various ways of being of these objects to words that are not the sign of any object. Perhaps instead of inserting the word *rouge* in the noun *papier*, it would have been better to insert a noun in a noun: *sang* [blood], in *papier*, as Massieu was used to doing. In a short time I would have substituted the adjective for the noun, the word *rouge* for the word *sang*, and *vert* [green] for *gazon* [grass]; the words replaced would thereby have acquired a real meaning from their replacements.

For some time I let Massieu express himself with his own images, which called to mind ancient memories taking us back to the cradle of the world, that happy age in which people worked, by frequent communications, at improving the language whose roots and chief forms were a gift of the Creator. Reluctantly, I substituted the adjectives "gentle" and "sweet" for the nouns "lamb" and "turtle-dove," "white" for "snow" and "red" for "rose." But Massieu eventually had to begin using the same language as other people, for between him and them there had to be set up communication that would never have existed without my procedures. I consoled him for the goods that I had stolen from him; with our agreed-upon sign of equality I explained that the additional words I was giving him were much the same as those I was demanding that he abandon, that mine were newer and his old-fashioned, that in the future he would often have occasion to see a shocking preference given to novelty.

A new vocabulary was required for the foreign invaders of the territory of qualities, who had just driven out the original land-owners. This was a new task, but similar to the one for naming objects. The signs for the adjectives were easy. They were familiar; my pupil merely lacked the words that were their written imitation. (A supplement to the present volume will set forth the theory).

Chapter 4. Fourth Method of Communication

Active and passive qualities. Theory of the proposition.

As yet we had no pronouns or conjugations. Nevertheless, affirming the qualities of objects—during the utterance or before it or afterward—was going to require pronouns and conjugations. We were finally at the point of needing to express the past, the present, and the future. How to give Massieu the idea of these three tenses forming the long, endless chain of duration? All we had for expressing them were manual signs. But what sign would convey future or past? How could I make these two time periods clear to him? What would set the stage? The sheet of red paper seemed to have a continuous existence, so it was existed in a kind of continuous present. I realized that time could be measured only in active qualities. Like time, only the successive existence of the qualities could serve as a measure of their duration. An action has not always existed, and when it was yet to happen, it was future. It can be talked about when it is occurring, and then it is present. It can also be discussed when it no longer exists, and then it is past. With the day before, the current one, and the day following the current one I had the material for explaining the three major time periods.

"Yesterday," "today," and "tomorrow": these were the written signs for the three tenses to be clarified by three unmistakable actions. Here is the procedure I used.

Unfortunately, French lacks the English present continuous: "I am walking," "you are walking," "he or she is walking," and so on. French has only the form: *je porte, tu portes, il porte,* and the like.

How can we find a complete proposition [attribution of some quality to a subject] in the two words *il porte*? That is what we had to do before all else, before thinking about the theory of tenses.

Here I realized that I should have marked each element of a sentence with a symbol, for we would be using a word containing in itself two sentence-elements.

Here one of our worst difficulties cropped up. We no longer had, as in the purely enunciative proposition, words similar to adjectives for expressing active qualities or for forming the active sentence. Here we had the verb and the quality both together in a single word. So before proceeding any further, we needed to go back to our original sentences mentioning permanent qualities.

We took the following sentences as examples: "The sky is blue. The air is calm."

We put the numeral 1 above the word "sky," the subject of the first sentence. We also put the numeral 1 above the word "blue" (the sentence attribute) and the numeral 2 above the word "is" (the link between these two words). We did the same with the words in the second sentence: the numeral 1 above the subject and the quality to show that these two words are not distinct signs for two distinct and separate objects, and the numeral 2 above the linking word or verb to show that the word was in a different category from the two others. I got Massieu to note that for every liaison, and consequently every affirmation, the numeral 2 had to be written above the connective word, that for every sentence subject, the numeral 1 had to be found, and that the same numeral also necessarily indicated the quality or what was affirmed of the subject.

When I had specified the three numerical signs for the enunciative proposition—the simplest kind of proposition—I thought it necessary to use a new procedure to emphasize the need for a connection between the subject and the quality, and to ensure that Massieu would give the verb "be" (the sign for this connection) only the meaning that I had just assigned it. This procedure, which must come first because it can only be used when the need for this connection is understood, seemed to me indispensable.

The reader has already noted I had used the dotted line to connect the name of the quality abstracted. So the line had become an agreed-upon sign of connection, similar to the deaf person's verb "be." It was possible that although Massieu grasped this meaning, the other pupils did not, and it would have been too unsafe for us to continue along this route without our making sure of their understanding. So I believed I again had to use this line but in another way, which would ensure that its true meaning was perfectly understood.

The following table shows this procedure:

Hat	long
Handkerchief	green
Ball	red
Tree	black
Blood	white
Bench	sharp
Knife	round

Examination of this table may not reveal why it contains a total lack of correspondence between the object names and the quality names they are paired with. This disorder is, however, intentional. The pupil was forced to endeavor to establish the missing correspondence, which he did by drawing a line from each [appropriate] quality to each object named.

I then wrote the verb "is" on each line. After this I wrote out a new table, placing each quality after its corresponding object, and a third one, with the verb "is" between each object and quality:

Hat	is	black
Handkerchief	is	white
Ball	is	round
Tree	is	green
Blood	is	red
Bench	is	long
Knife	is	sharp

The reader is invited to judge whether these methods were the easiest, surest, and quickest way to inform the deaf person about the elements of a sentence. My, what success I had with this procedure! I hastened to communicate it to Epée, who never ceased worrying about the slowness of my operations. Again, the reader may judge whether "operations" was the proper term for this analytical procedure, which seemed long only because in the chain of mental operations, in the search for appropriate methods of expressing thought, no link had been overlooked, no intermediary skipped over, and no medium omitted. It is for my colleagues in this work, who walked along the same path and repeated my procedures, to report the success they themselves have obtained it.

It was not enough . . . we still needed to study the mechanism of the active sentence, whose elements also had numbers. So I prepared Massieu also to identify, not a subject, but an active quality at every place in the same group of letters where he saw both the numeral 1 in the first part of the word and the numeral 2 in the second part or word ending. This was to tell him that there were words that the connecting verb "be"—whose necessity and importance I had already explained—always accompanied.

All was ready for the explanation of the active sentence; we could henceforth pass on to it without risk. The reader will see this theory worked out in the procedure following these reflections.

We had for some time been feeling the need for pronouns. To do without them, we had constantly to repeat the subject. Repeating the same word this way became not just annoying, but liable to make our sentences ambiguous and obscure. It was time to invent the pronoun. I say "invent"—that is the surest and perhaps the only way to learn what is not yet known.

$$\begin{matrix} 1 & 2 & 1 & & 1 & 2 & 1 \\ \text{Albert} & \text{is} & \text{deaf.} & & \text{Albert} & \text{is} & \text{good.} \end{matrix}$$

I showed that in two sentences with the same subject, the subject necessarily had to be repeated in the second sentence unless another word with the same meaning was substituted for the word beginning the sentence. The actual choice of the word to be invented is arbitrary, so for men the substitute was "he" and for women "she," and we rewrote the two sentences as follows:

$$\begin{matrix} 1 & 2 & 1 & & 1 & 2 & 1 \\ \text{Albert} & \text{is} & \text{deaf.} & & \text{He} & \text{is} & \text{good.} \end{matrix}$$

We made sure to give this new word the subject-number when it replaced the word. We turned this new invention to account by constructing many similar sentences about the various objects within view. It was a little hard to get Massieu to apply the new word to anything other than Albert. He thought he had to invent a like word for every object—how difficult it is for natural man to generalize ideas! He only sees individuals. Massieu succumbed to another error. He thought that "he" was a name, and so could be the name of any object; not only did he use it as the subject in the second sentence, but also wanted to use it in the first sentence and for both sentences.

So instead of writing the name Albert in the first sentence, he re-wrote the two sentences, construing them as follows:

1 2 1   1 2 1
He is deaf.   He is good.

Using signs, I asked him of whom he was affirming these two qualities. He showed me Albert. But, I tell him, "he" is said of an already understood subject. In the second place, "he" applies to all the deaf individuals here. I was still talking with signs, signs lacking the precision that words can give our judgments. My signs still had all the irregularities of the first language of the deaf, but I was understood and that was enough. This was an instance of teaching Massieu that just by itself "he" does not identify any particular individual, but only the name mentioned in a preceding sentence. Writing on our blackboard, I explained a large number of twofold or compound sentences of which the subject of the first sentence was always the name of an individual. Then he saw that "he" is common and has only the meaning given it by a preceding noun to which the pronoun refers. At the same time he learned that "he" applies only to the person being talked about and not to the person addressed, and that the speaker never says it of himself. So without a lesson in grammar Massieu learned by repeated applications that "he" is a personal pronoun, applied only to a single individual of the third person, and never to more than one individual.

We were too far along not to attempt a second trial, which was destined to succeed. I wrote the following two sentences:

Albert est sourd-muet. [Albert is deaf.]
Col est sourd-muet. [Col is deaf.]

This was to give the idea of the plural of verbs and qualities:

Albert   *est sourd-muet* ⎱
                        sont sourds-muets
Col   *est sourd-muet* ⎰

I got Massieu to notice that a single word was sufficient to connect the two subjects to a common quality, and that a single word could also affirm the same quality of two subjects. I showed him that the two letters *-nt* indicated the plural verb, and that the letter *-s* at the end of a quality also indicated plurality. Then our two sentences could be made into a single one, and we wrote:

Albert, Col, sont sourds-muets.
Ils   *sont*   *bons.*

It was then that I began to believe that I could broach the conjugation of the three absolute tenses, for we had the necessary pronoun. But this required an object or complement for the active sentence; how were we to connect this complement with the rest of the sentence?

I reflected for quite a while. Before undertaking to teach the theory of conjugation, I had to find a solution to this problem.

There is no action in nature without an object affected by this action or, in other words, no active subject without a passive object and therefore no active sentence that does not presuppose a passive sentence . . . Hence there are two forms for expressing any action: an active form and a passive form. We can consider the object of an active sentence the recipient of the action mentioned. This object, expressed by a noun, receives and suffers the action; when the sentence is active, we call the object of the action the *souffrant*, the "patient." But if instead of expressing it in the active form, we express it in the passive form, this object becomes the subject of the passive sentence.

With these considerations I constructed an active sentence mentioning an action to be performed in our presence.

Albert frappe Col.   [Albert hits Col.]

I showed Massieu that Albert was the acting subject because his name was connected with the active quality forming the first part of the word *frappe*. I had already shown him that the ending *-e* was a residuum of the word *être*. We shall shortly see how Massieu grasped this element. I also showed him that at the same time that Albert had acted in hitting Col, the latter had remained motionless and inactive—I called this state passive. He demonstrated an impressive grasp of the need for the two names, Albert and Col, seeing that one was hitting and the other was being hit, that one was giving and the other receiving. For the sake of greater clarity I then wrote the two sentences applicable to the same action and placed them side by side.

Albert est frappant. Col est frappé.
[Albert is hitting. Col is hit.]

In these two sentences everything takes place simultaneously, both the subject performing the action with the active quality being affirmed, and the patient, sufferer, complement, object receiving the action, direct object, or—if you will—the subject of the passive sentence. We even find the quality [*frappant*], as superfluous as it is, in the two sentences, for the passive form presupposes it. So we suppress the quality with its linking word. Here is the way of it.

1 2 1	1 2 1
Albert est frappant.	*Col est frappé.*
1 1 2	1 1 2
Albert frappant est.	*Col frappé est.*
1 1 2	1 1 2
Albert frapp est.	*Col frappé est.*
1 1 2	1 1 2
Albert frapp e.	*Col frappé.*
1 1 2	3
Albert frappe.	*Col.*
[Albert hits Col]	

Massieu fully grasped that the progression of changes in the verb *être* appeared only in the ending of the active verb, and that the active verb was a verb only because *être* was an essential part of it; he saw how the passive sentence as a whole—owing to the excision of everything presupposed by the active sentence—became reduced to the single word not expressed by the active sentence. He also saw why the 3 is written above the only remaining word of the passive sentence—because it includes both the quality (marked with the 1) and the verb (marked with the 2) which becomes superfluous, for the suppression of the quality leaves nothing to be connected. Massieu realized that the noun that replaces a whole sentence must represent its elements, and that it represents and recalls them with the number 3 in which we find both the number indicating the quality and the index number of the verb.[9]

The object of the active sentence, called the *case* in Latin grammars, will henceforth represent the passive sentence for a deaf person. It will be a kind of ellipsis for a whole sentence which the pupil can easily supply when he sees the 3.

From this moment on, and before proceeding to the explanation of tenses, all our various actions (and we proliferated them ad infinitum) were expressed only in the active and passive forms, one always accompanying the other. In this way Massieu became familiar with the two kind of sentences, until a knowledge of the preposition would allow him to give the complement of the passive much as he had just learned . . . to give the complement of the active proposition.

VI

ROCH-AMBROISE BEBIAN

Roch-Ambroise Bébian was born in the Caribbean colony of Guadeloupe in 1789, at the dawn of the French Revolution. His parents had been friends of the abbé Sicard, director of the National Institute for the Deaf, whom they designated as the boy's namesake and godfather; they entrusted their son to Sicard's care when the youth went to Paris to be educated at the prestigious Lycée Charlemagne. While living at the institute, Bébian took the opportunity to attend classes there, made friends with the students, particularly Laurent Clerc, and acquired fluency in sign language. Upon his graduation from the lycée, he was named instructor at the deaf school. The admiring Sicard credited Bébian with the fullest grasp of his own instructional methods.

At the age of twenty-eight, Bébian published the *Essai sur les sourds-muets et sur le langage naturel* (Paris: Dentu, 1817) translated in this volume, as well as a eulogy to the abbé de l'Epée in which he criticizes the teaching and use of "methodical sign." More than any other man, Bébian was responsible for ending the worldwide practice of teaching the deaf in a manual version of the national language rather than in their own sign language.

During Sicard's declining years Bébian's candid protests about the disorganized instruction and mismanaged finances of the school so displeased the board of directors that they forced him to resign. Nonetheless, the board recognized that the school's educational program was deficient in overall design; to obtain a manual for teachers, they applied to Bébian. The book he then wrote promulgated the use of sign language for instruction rather than spoken language. He also created a system of written characters for signs, naming it *mimography*. Bébian founded a journal devoted to the education of the deaf and blind.

After leaving the institute, Bébian opened a small school of his own in Paris, still hoping to remedy the ills of the national institute. His hopes were constantly frustrated and in 1825 he returned with his wife and son to Guadeloupe and set up yet another school for the deaf there. At the age of forty-five "the greatest hearing friend of the deaf" died in Pointe-à-Pitre.

Roch-Ambroise Bébian

ESSAY ON THE DEAF AND NATURAL LANGUAGE, OR INTRODUCTION TO A NATURAL CLASSIFICATION OF IDEAS WITH THEIR PROPER SIGNS

PREFACE

The observations contained in this essay were planned as the introduction to a book whose outline I give later in this work. I am publishing them as an appeal for the counsel of persons interested in the deaf.

This short book may have some value at a time when people everywhere are interested in increasing the number of educational institutions for these unfortunates, who have a twofold right, as subjects and as poor people, to royal protection.

In undertaking a systematic classification of ideas and determining the proper signs for them, I may incur criticism for drawing more on my boldness than my strengths. But what cannot assiduous, sustained work do for humanity! I will have reached my goal if readers find this book sufficiently well organized that, with no basic changes, every part of the original can later be improved. I would be delighted if it suggests to some clever person the means for doing what I myself was unable to do. At least, I hope that my intentions will excuse my rashness and cause this essay to meet with an indulgent reception.

It is hard not to become impassioned on a subject about which one has so long reflected, especially when the subject is vast, new, and immediately applicable.

In explicating the resources of the language of the deaf, I have been led to discuss the inadequacies of spoken languages, but I am far from agreeing with Vossius (whose opinion I cite) that we should renounce the use of speech and express ourselves solely by gestures. Spoken languages are the fruit of centuries and the combined efforts of the greatest minds. The words of great writers sing the praises of speech better than anything one could say.

Condillac said: "To regard the art of speaking merely as a means of communication would be to betray ignorance of its chief merit. I consider it an analytic method leading us from one idea to another, from one judgment to another, and from one piece of knowledge to another."

Precisely because speech is not just expression, but also the normal instrument of thought, imperfections in it have unfortunate consequences and call for philosophical consideration.

There is no need, I believe, to argue against the opinion that ideas are inseparable from the words representing them; too many demonstrable facts already militate against this error. Taking examples just from the deaf and without mentioning their considerable mental development before they have learned any language, I will mention the case of two deaf persons, one from Chartres and the other from England, who, upon the spontaneous recovery of their hearing, learned the language too quickly for us to suppose their ideas had been acquired just with words. The man from Chartres did not inform his parents about the happy change in his sense organs, but listening attentively to everything spoken around him and practicing in secret, he began one day to speak as others do—to his family's astonishment.

I could also mention all the deaf people coming to the institute who, after a few days, chat with their fellows as if they had long been living together. I have seen some eight, ten, or twelve-year-old children without any education who had enough mental acuity to recognize and describe the imprecision of some signs used in their homes.

It is incontestably true that deafness takes nothing away from the force or breadth of thought.[1] Moreover, it is unproven that complete ignorance is any further from true science than much knowledge riddled with errors and prejudices. And it is similarly unproven that we would not be gaining by losing everything we know, on the condition that we also lost everything that we merely think we know. Even so, I hope that I shall not be accused of placing the deaf in a higher condition than our own. Far be it from me to dispute the advantage of hearing or to undervalue this gift of the Creator. Even if hearing added nothing to one's intelligence, it is still a source of enjoyment. Its utility is evident at every moment, and the privation of hearing is a real calamity. All my wishes would come true if I could restore hearing to people afflicted with its absence.

DEDICATORY NOTE

To the Abbé Sicard, Director of the Royal Institute for the Deaf-Mutes of Paris, Member of the French Academy, the Legion of Honor,

Knight of the Order of Saint Vladimir of Russia and of the Order of Saint Wasa of Sweden.

My respected friend,

It is no longer possible to speak of the deaf without calling attention to your work and achievements. Your name finds a natural place at the beginning of a book about your adopted children.

In presenting you with this feeble essay, I am merely giving back what already belongs to you. The honor of your friendship since my childhood, our frequent discussions, and the example of your life have long led me to share your keen interest in this class, which is so interesting because of its misfortune and, overall, because of its great qualities of the heart, as if nature had wanted thereby to make restitution for a horrendous oversight.

You appreciate my arduous studies of the deaf. The bonds of friendship I formed with some of your pupils, particularly Laurent Clerc—called to the United States to acquaint his brothers in misfortune with the benefits of your method—familiarized me with the language of gestures, which the deaf learn without a teacher and which can be called man's natural language (for we carry its source within ourselves and circumstances unfold it according to our needs). I have been impressed with the richness of this language; with you I have often admired its potentialities for expressing intellectual ideas and for explaining acts of the understanding. In addition, we have sometimes desired the education of hearing children to adopt a method similar to the one used successfully with children deprived of hearing and speech.

As I began to understand the deaf better, I came to the bitter realization that only a few of the thousands of these unfortunates were restored by education to religion and society. This fact is particularly deplorable as the ignorance and inexperience of the many deaf without education, who are thus condemned to vegetate, make it easy to pervert their happy natural character. On the other hand, the deaf accepted for instruction cannot, as you know, do much studying by themselves, for they have no dictionary or elementary text, having as yet learned none of our languages.

This twofold disadvantage became the chief object of my reflections. I thought it could be righted if a way were found to get their signs on paper, as we do with speech. To this end I investigated the elements of gesture, which are few, and I gave each its own printed character. In view of the simplicity and ease of this procedure, its invention reflects no great merit of the author.

I submitted this book for your perusal; you recognized the fecundity of the principle and its potential benefits by putting the practice of your art within the reach of all teachers and parents wishing to instruct their children. You have engaged me to publish a few reflections on it, and I have acceded to your counsels. Published under your auspices, this essay will be received with greater indulgence. It is my impression that the book still leaves much to be desired, but I hope (and this is my intention in publishing it) that people interested in the deaf will enlighten me with their views. All observations will be received gratefully and I shall benefit from them with no other purpose than to make myself useful to these unfortunates by following in your footsteps.

Please accept, my respected friend, the tribute of my gratitude and deep veneration.

DEFINITIONS

The word "sign" has been taken to mean many different things. The *Dictionary of the French Academy* defines it as "the external indication of what one is thinking or willing." We can also say that a sign is the expression of an idea designed to evoke a similar idea in the mind of the person addressed.

In speaking of the deaf, we usually restrict the meaning of the word "sign" to the gestures they use to communicate their thoughts; a sign in this sense is one or more gestures expressing an idea.

Signs that have a direct and natural relation to ideas, and that by themselves and without prior convention recall ideas, can be called natural signs. The products of artistic design, for example, are the natural signs of the objects they represent.

Taking the expression in its strictest sense, we limit the name "natural signs" to signs directly evoking the idea, having been inspired by nature itself and produced without instruction or art. Examples are the facial expressions so candidly depicting all the affections of the soul and even the operations of the intellect, wherein all their gradations are reflected: pleasure, grief, joy, sadness, love, hate, compassion, anger, desire, horror, admiration, scorn, fright, surprise, attention, worry, meditativeness, and so forth. Other examples are the hand or body gestures accompanying these facial expressions and giving them more force and precision. The hand rejects with disdain or clasps with tenderness; it beckons, commands, begs, or threatens;

it brings together objects that the eye examines and compares; it shows their dimensions or shapes; indicates their movements, draws their outlines, and expresses all possible actions by imitating them. This is how the deaf understand each other and how primitive people, even speaking mutually incomprehensible languages, communicate their thoughts, plight their troths, and form alliances. This fact is supported by a number of reliable reports. Among others, we will later cite a curious excerpt appearing in the *American Philosophical Transactions*, using our own translation.

The totality of these signs, which are natural to all men in all places, forms a much richer language than is commonly supposed; it is adequate for all intellectual needs, and it merits the name "natural language." We shall return to this subject after a look at the history of deaf education.

Historical Summary of the Education of the Deaf

The deaf have long had the double misfortune of having their infirmity deprive them of human intercourse and of being lumped together with the retarded and the insane. The ancients regarded the deaf as victims of fate, struck down by the wrath of the gods. In some Asian lands, on the other hand, the deaf share general honor with persons deprived of reason, and are revered as chosen people.

The Romans, whose actors carried the gestural language (the natural language of the deaf) to a high degree of perfection, must have derived from it the idea and techniques for ameliorating the fate of these unfortunates; thus an art designed for the most frivolous pleasures became valuable for humane ends.

But the blessing of education for the deaf was reserved for the charitable spirit that descended to earth with the Christian religion. Even so, for a long time the fate of the deaf excited merely a sterile, impotent pity; only recently did their misfortune capture the attention of the noble souls who undertook to bring the deaf within the fold of religion and society.

The Instruction of the Deaf by Speech

Normally men transmit their thoughts by speech or writing (the visual depiction of speech). Because this means of communication is widespread, people have been led to regard it as the only one possible. It has even been believed—and this opinion has not yet been completely discredited—that speech is indispensable for the exercise of thought. Consequently one must seek to give the use of this faculty to the deaf before anything else.

The Benedictine Pedro de Ponce of the convent of Sahagún in the kingdom of León in Spain was apparently the first to attempt this, and his achievement surpassed his expectations, for reports have it that his pupils were able to take part in public discussions of various subjects. Vallès says: "Marvelous to tell, my friend Pedro de Ponce taught the congenitally deaf to speak, with no art other than to teach them first to write, and using his hand to indicate the objects designated by letters and then provoking the corresponding tongue movements . . . That is how the deaf can replace speech with writing and acquire a knowledge of divine matters by means of sight, as others do by means of hearing; I witnessed this with my friend's pupils."[2]

These pupils reason, it is said, about astronomy, physics, and logic, and they understood Greek, Italian, and Latin. Some of them, moreover, were able historians. "They are so distinguished in the sciences," says Pedro de Ponce, "that they would have passed for normal people, even in the eyes of Aristotle."[3]

The unanimous testimony of contemporaries leaves no doubt about Ponce's truly prodigious success, and can at most be suspected only of some slight exaggeration. It may be that in the wonder caused by an unheard-of phenomenon, some illusion was created. Persons familiar with the deaf know that it frequently happens that what is an effect of their memory is attributed to their intelligence, especially when the persons are accustomed to expressing themselves only with speech. However that may be, it appears that Ponce did not entrust a successor with his procedures, even less his skill. But even though his art died with him, his example was not lost for humanity.

In 1620, thirty-six years after Ponce's death, Juan Pablo Bonet[4] published, in Spanish, *The Art of Teaching the Deaf to Speak*.[5] He was the secretary to the constable de Velasco, whose deaf sister and two deaf brothers Ponce had instructed. Bonet necessarily had knowledge of Ponce's method, but nowhere appears to make mention of it. I cannot determine the facts for certain, or indeed say anything about his book which I have searched for without success.

Two other Spaniards, Emmanuel Ramirez de Cortone [de Carrion] and Pedro de Castro, followed honorably in Bonet's footsteps.

John Wallis, professor of mathematics at Oxford, having long meditated on the formation of speech sounds, about which he wrote an excellent treatise, found a way to correct all speech defects not due to congenital organic malformations, and even to teach the deaf to speak.[6] He is, in my opinion, one of the persons who best understood the art of educating the deaf. He instructed many of these unfortunates, teaching them to express their thoughts in speech and writing, and to read. "He had them distinctly articulate," he wrote, "words of the greatest difficulty, showing them the position and movements made in the throat, tongue, lips, and the rest of the vocal apparatus. The breath leaving the lungs always produces the desired sound, whether the speaker hears or not."[7] "That is the part of their education," Wallis adds, "that we most love to admire, but which nevertheless is the easiest and least important and which would be for them of little use without what remains to be done; for of what utility would it be in human intercourse to mouth words like parrots without understanding their meaning?" Thus he scorns teaching many of his pupils to speak. With the help of signs by which the deaf naturally express their thoughts, he soon succeeded in getting them to understand what they were reading and hence to acquire all the knowledge that can be transmitted by books.

Without any knowledge of the works of the three Spaniards or of Wallis's book, Conrad Amman, a Swiss physician, took up the same task and had similar success. His treatise, entitled *Surdus Loquens* (1692) reports the happy result of his investigations; the *Dissertation on Speech* (1700) which followed up the earlier work, contained the best explanation to date of the mechanism of the vocal apparatus and of the formation of sounds. In these two authors we find all the information we need for teaching the deaf to speak. Although Wallis's book is more specifically designed for the pronunciation of English and Amman's for German, only a little study is required to apply their principles to all languages.

To his precursors' practice the Portuguese Pereire, a contemporary of de l'Epée, added a manual alphabet which he had picked up in the Spanish colleges and which he adopted, improving and enriching it with many new signs indicating the pronunciation of the words and their intonations. I do not know whether this alphabet has been preserved anywhere in its entirety.

At about the same time the Doctrinarian Father Vanin, who was similarly concerned with the education of the deaf, communicated with them visually, by means of engravings representing the main features of biblical history.

Somewhat later the abbé Deschamps published *An Elementary Course of Education for the Deaf*. This work provided the impetus for an interesting booklet by a deaf man [Pierre Desloges], who believed that sign language should be defended from Deschamps's misunderstandings, and the booklet is itself a striking proof of the superiority of sign language for the unfolding of the intelligence.[8] With almost no help other than the employment of natural signs and the frequenting of some deaf people—most of them less educated than he—Pierre Desloges had acquired an intellectual acuity that could be the envy of many educated hearing people.

Moreover, the abbé Deschamps added nothing new. He concentrated more on getting his pupils to articulate words clearly than on acquainting them with their exact meaning, and he believed he had done everything for them and restored them to society by sending them back to their family, carrying in their notebooks, or memory, many questions and answers that they articulated distinctly enough, but nearly as impoverished in ideas as they were before. What he did not dare attempt on behalf of these children he believed that only they could do; that is, that with no help other than the words he had taught them to pronounce, they would in time be seen "to increase the sum of their ideas, rectify them, and combine them as do normal children with the advance of age." In vain had the abbé de l'Epée gone to the trouble of explaining the advantages of the procedures in his method for instruction by signs. Deschamps was impressed only with the defects in any new invention. Problems intimidated him, stopped him cold, in fact, before he sought to overcome them in an attempt to pave the way for his pupils.

To restore the mechanical faculty of speech to the deaf without teaching them to attach a precise idea to each term, without acquainting them with the absolute and relative meaning of words as well as their influence on each other in sentence construction, without eventually initiating them in all the secrets of spoken languages—is finally to provide them with small comfort indeed in misfortune, to fatigue their memories with no profit to their intelligence. This was the fundamental defect of Deschamps's method—the defect of any method with no principle for enlightening the mind and training the judgment.

If speech education for the deaf is still held in some favor, it is due to the genuine successes obtained by Pereire. But how few children find themselves in circumstances as happy as those of his pupil, Saboureux de Fontenay—in the constant presence of an excellent teacher, in the bosom of a family all of whose members and all of whose friends, as he himself tells us, contributed to his education with a compassionate interest which was increased by the novelty of the undertaking. What we can reasonably conclude from this is that the able instructor exclusively devoted to the training of one or two deaf persons will by dint of care, time, and patience triumph over all obstacles. But notice that for this education to be ultimately something other than parrot-like training, it must necessarily begin with the language of gestures—the only means of communication that in principle exists between the teacher and student because only signs are directly related to the idea. And we can dispense with gestures only when the deaf person is already advanced and has a large enough vocabulary to understand definitions of unfamiliar words.

Although this method—tedious for the teacher, irksome for the pupil, uncertain in its results—can be effective in private instruction, its use has unfortunate effects in a public institution where the teacher is obliged to divide his efforts among a great many pupils. The aim of education must be not the learning of words, but the accurate expression of ideas, not the training of a sense organ or a single faculty like memory, but the unfolding of the totality of the intellectual faculties to form correct and certain judgment.

The inestimable advantage of bringing the deaf together in a group, one incompatible with their instruction in speech, is to enrich each student with the ideas of every other student, to rouse their awareness by stimulating their attention, and to force them to give a sufficiently clear and precise form to all their ideas, making them communicable through gesture.

But instead of the fascinating spectacle of these assembled children, instead of the sprightly groups, of their vivacious pantomime, of their sparkling conversation, of the play of their physiognomy revealing, as in a vivid picture, all their souls' emotions, let us imagine a number of deaf persons that we would oblige to use only speech, forced to confine all their thoughts to the circle of a few half-understood words, taken up with the laborious reading of some meaningless sounds from lips whose uncertain movements were uncontrolled by hearing—boredom and distaste would then be merely the first and least hindrances of this tyrannical, defective procedure.

So the education of the deaf cannot be based on speech, but speech can and must complement this education. Ever present in human intercourse are circumstances where it will be advantageous for the deaf to have the ability to express their thought more or less like other people. Thus even the abbé de l'Epée, who, as he puts it, would have debased himself in the exclusive use of this [oral] method, which he compares to the blind rote method of schoolmasters, confesses that "the one way to bring [the deaf] totally into society is to teach them to hear with their eyes and to express themselves orally. In large part we are successful at this with our own pupils; there is nothing, absolutely nothing that they cannot write from oral dictation alone, with no sign made to them."[9] Moreover, it is something that takes little trouble or time once a deaf person has reached a certain level of education, learned to harness his attention, and is ready to understand the necessary demonstrations.[10] He then appreciates the benefit and feels the desire to be able to converse with other people; he understands the value of the lessons and redoubles his efforts to put them to good advantage. He already knows the words we are using, and every principle provides him with a great many applications that make the study both pleasant and useful. In a few days he will be able to pronounce all the letters and in two or three months, if he is well taught, he will be able to read and hence to speak, for he now knows how to write out his thoughts. His rapid progress becomes a pleasure, in contrast to a task that is repugnant when undertaken with untrained deaf pupils who barely understand you, who lack a clear idea of the goal, and often make strenuous objections to a laborious, seemingly bizarre, insufferably boring exercise with no prospective benefits. So is it not absurd to devote all of the instructional time to giving the deaf the use of speech when, a little later, we can do it in two or three months? Not that they will then speak like hearing people—that is impossible. Their speech will always be wearisomely monotonous, and in my experience all deaf people speak in heavy and disagreeable accents. I do not know how much a skilled teacher's diligent attention, even when encouraged by the pupil's happiest dispositions, could correct this fault: at the very least, it would require a great deal of time and unfailing patience, and the benefits derived would be far outweighed by the distress encountered. Deaf people with the ability to speak prefer to converse in gestures or even in writing. In addition, their skill in lipreading will never be great enough to enable them to understand sustained speech.

So the abbé de l'Epée is rightly regarded as the founder of deaf education. We are not attempting to conceal the fact that, before Epée, Wallis used the sign method of instruction (a fact that had not been previously remarked); Wallis simply mentions this without going into any more detail, as can be confirmed by reading his letter to Doctor Beverly (cited further on).

After Wallis, education with signs fell into disuse, where it still would be had it not been reinvented by the abbé de l'Epée. Epée tells us, and we cannot doubt his veracity, that he was unaware of Wallis's book. This happy convergence of two superior minds is unsurprising, for this method is the simplest and the most natural. Do we not, in fact, normally learn foreign languages with the help of our native language?

It is noteworthy that the English, who are so jealous of all their inventions, have so shamefully neglected Wallis's method, for the English deaf are still educated only by means of speech, which Wallis himself recognizes as inadequate.

If it were true, which we do not for a moment suppose, that the abbé de l'Epée had taken the initial idea for his method from Wallis's letter to Doctor Beverly, his glory would still be no less great or less pure. Surely no one will contest his title as "benefactor of humanity and father of the deaf." We know that he devoted to them not only his talent and care, but also his whole fortune—imposing the hardest privations on himself, even going without heat in the winter. It is Epée's example,[11] even more than his talent, that fixed public attention on the deaf; it is his zeal that set the public's hearts afire; so it is Epée to whom the deaf from every country are indebted for the schools based on his model being set up all over Europe and even in America, where one of Abbé Sicard's deaf students has just been called for this purpose.

When charity inspired the abbé de l'Epée with the plan of restoring the deaf to society, his genius—untrammeled by received opinion— soon discovered that speech is not the easiest or surest way to reach this goal, and he judged that speech could better be replaced with the sign language that his pupils offered him as a model.

EDUCATION OF THE DEAF BY MEANS OF SIGNS

In the mind, thought necessarily precedes whatever signs are designed to express it. The word by itself is unrelated to the idea; the word cannot give rise to the idea, but it does serve to recall it when some prior convention has connected the word with a previously understood idea. To establish this convention with the deaf, we must first know how to communicate with them. Before teaching them to express an idea with a word, we must make sure they possess this idea in some clear and precise way. If they do not, we must impress it on their minds. We cannot penetrate their intelligence and examine what goes on there, but the deaf easily can and do inform us about it, using signs that they themselves determine and that we understand without difficulty because the signs are taken from the very nature of the idea. The pupil's signs are carefully collected by the teacher, who uses them to recall the idea; from their common starting point the teacher proceeds ahead of the pupil and unfolds new ideas; these ideas give rise to new signs which are then replaced by the corresponding words in the language being learned.

A similar method secured the initial successes of the abbé de l'Epée and gave promise of many even more brilliant successes rewarding his zeal, if he had proceeded along the same lines to the very end. But we must tell the whole truth, and we can do so with no harm to his memory (the great man's glory is too firmly established and justly merited to fear any attack). De l'Epée lacked sufficient confidence in his method and did not realize the fertility of the principle he had discovered. He merely needed to continue what he had so happily begun; he had only one more step to take and he did not take it. When he entered the domain of abstractions, that bewildering labyrinth, he suddenly lost hold of the thread that had so happily guided him; he then resorted to dubious etymologies as a guide.

Instead of getting his signs from nature, Epée sought them in the physical decomposition, so to speak, of French words. He gave these signs to his pupils, rather than getting them from his pupils, or rather then getting the pupils to discover them through the analysis of thought. Ultimately, this was merely a kind of syllabic spelling of French words in gestures instead of the direct translation of thought and its living image. In this way, for example, for *comprendre* [understand] he made the signs for *prendre* [take] and for *avec* (Latin *cùm*) [with]; for *surprendre*, *prendre sur* [take over]; for *intelligence*, *lire intérieurement* (*intus legere* [read internally]). So the deaf, who could write down anything dictated to them with signs, could not express spontaneously even their simplest thoughts.

The abbé Sicard, whose virtues earned him a heritage of glory and beneficence, completed what Epée had begun, and perfected what his teacher had merely adumbrated. To Sicard we owe the theory of compound tenses of verbs; he has also shed new light on the meaning and use of conjunctions. No mention need be made of Sicard's achievements, for they are well-known and justly praised. We no longer doubt that the deaf person can be completely restored to society. With the benefit of education, the deaf person is not deaf to someone who can write, nor is he mute for someone who can read. We can put the deaf person in possession of all the treasures of the human mind; like us, he can enjoy works of genius, the enlightenment of the sciences, the wonders of art. He now need have no envy of other people. But regrettably few deaf people have been able to enjoy these benefits. Sicard's institution comprises only sixty-nine children of both sexes; there are thousands of others for whom there is no enlightenment and who are condemned to bear in brutish ignorance the burden of an existence useless to themselves and onerous to others! One consoling thought is that this method, which has enjoyed such brilliant success and is patronized by many sovereigns, is gaining ground every day, and establishments for reducing the number of these unfortunates are being founded in every country in Europe. Beginning teachers will get their guiding precepts from the works of the abbé Sicard, but there still remains a great obstacle in the education of the deaf—the extreme difficulty of initiating the new teachers in sign language, for it cannot be learned from a simple written description, which would often take entire pages for a sign performed in a fraction of a second.

Without some way to overcome this obstacle we cannot hope for a dictionary of signs, which is still needed, or to make a regular and complete system of signs, for how could we classify these signs, or fix them for comparison, or express the exact results of these comparisons? As the formation of signs is not determined by any principle and does not follow any fixed rule, the sign language—vulnerable to the ignorance and idiosyncratic methods of each teacher and to the inconsistency and caprice of each pupil—far from being perfected, will be further corrupted by the introduction of the forms and defects of spoken languages, and will lose its present advantage of transmitting thought directly.

These considerations set me wondering about the possibility of recording the gesture and of setting it down on paper, as we do speech.

At first I set about determining the physical elements of sign, and then assigned to each of these few elements a simple, easy character directly related to it. These characters are written down in the same order as the gestures. After a short while the deaf person is enabled to express his thought directly on paper, with as much clarity as with gesture, and with no need for a prior translation into spoken language, even without knowing a word of any other language.

MIMOGRAPHY

How Accurate Transcription of Gesture is Obtained

Considering the variety and extent of mimic language, one would think any attempt to put it on paper would meet with resistance, for such a great number of signs might seem to require an infinite number of characters. This multiplicity of signs is less intimidating when compared with the combined vocabularies of all the spoken languages of the world, and yet only a few characters suffice for writing down all the words of all these languages.

The Decomposition of Signs

Might not signs also contain elements to which we would assign particular characters, combinations of which would yield all possible signs, just as combinations of letters produce all words?

Every sign is made up of one or more gestures; the gesture is a movement of a part or whole of the body. So to write the sign, all we need do is to indicate the gesticulating organ and its movement.

The Characters Indicating Movements

The movements we can make are infinitely varied in direction, irregularity, speed, extent, and so on. Consider a universal character for movement—whether a portion of a wheel or the arc of a circle described by a swinging pendulum. This character, variously turned, and with a radius attached to it for greater precision, indicates the direction of the movement. The character is modified by six accents indicating whether the movement is slow or quick, brief or prolonged, and so forth.

Characters Indicating the Instruments of the Gesture

The organs involved in the gesture will be represented by schematic drawings of their essential features.

The chief instrument for gesture is the hand. Most signs involve just the hand and face; to represent the various positions of the hand alone, we need almost as many characters as for all the other organs combined.

It is an educational principle hallowed by experience that we have less need of teaching the deaf directly than of getting them to discover what we are trying to teach them. And nothing is easier than for them to discover these new characters for themselves. We sign to them to place a hand on the blackboard and to outline its shape with a piece of chalk. The outline becomes a prototype for the various handshapes.

In the same way we lead them to find in other parts of the drawing characters requiring no great effort of attention or memory, for these characters always are directly related to the thing signified.

The greatest hurdle is the representation of facial expression which plays such an important role in this language and requires special care. The means we adopted seems to combine clarity and precision.

Physiognomic Points

Everything tells us that man was created to live in society. He has a need to communicate with other men; he is inclined this way by the very essence of his thought, its tendency to radiate outward like light or heat. The first ray of thought is communicated by the face. The human face is like a faithful mirror reflecting everything going on in the mind; in society we learn with some hardship to disguise this too transparent surface with a veil, and the effort it costs us to suppress the play of the facial muscles and to prevent the physiognomy from revealing our secret sentiments prove (allow me to say in passing) that the lie is no less contrary to the physical make-up of man than to morality.

The instantaneous action of the mind on the body, of the mental on the physical, is clearly revealed not only in the face but also in the rest of the body, though less clearly: breathing becomes faster or slower, chest movements from breathing that provide the blood with its purest nourishment undergo a similar modification; similar changes occur in the respiratory passages, and the air passing in or out of the lungs produces the varied intonations which, independently of speech or even of any articulate sound, express pain or pity or fear—all the emotions in fact—and occur simultaneously with a corresponding facial expression.

In normal writing we have only two punctuation marks for these various emotional accents; the meaning of the sentence, and various short words that in each language are applied to particular emotions compensate for the inadequacy of these marks. But to represent the language of action, where physiognomy plays such an important role, it is important to indicate the chief facial expressions more precisely.

To try to represent all possible facial expressions would be absurd. The combination of the various passions agitating the mind at the same time produce such delicate gradations of facial expressions that the eye sometimes finds them hard to distinguish. To convey thought we need just the main expressions giving rise to all the others. It is enough to describe them; the gesture will do the rest.

To the question and exclamation marks, I add eight other physiognomic indexes. Though simple, each one stands for the part of the face primarily involved in the expression signified.

These new characters are formed like the exclamation and question marks, with a dot and a line in different shapes. The placement of the dot above or below the line indicates opposite expressions. One, two or three dots for each expression indicates the intensity of the mental state. With this double index, we use eight characters to represent forty-eight variations in facial expression.

I have classified these expressions in a table that is, if not rigorous, at least sufficiently exact to jog one's memory without giving any false impressions . . .

The Value of This Writing System for the Education of the Deaf

Before the deaf person begins his formal education, he has already acquired some knowledge on his own, sometimes more and sometimes less (depending on his age, natural disposition, and circumstances), but always a great deal more than is commonly supposed. When he joins his comrades in misfortune, the interchange of thoughts among them quickly develops his intelligence; his imperative need to communicate soon leads him to find signs for his ideas.

The teacher does not usually enter into this early education. During the initial lessons he teaches the pupil to identify the letters, to represent them by various finger positions (the manual alphabet), and then to form them with a pen or pencil. Then he begins teaching the pupil the vocabulary of common physical objects and everyday actions. Next to a drawing of some familiar object he writes the corresponding word; but more often he explains the word by signs.

The difficult thing for a deaf person is not just to get the meaning of a word substituted for signs he knows, but also to connect the word and the idea so closely together that later the one will always remind him of the other.

Words offer no purchase for the deaf person's memory—they depict nothing for him, because the sounds they stand for have no existence for him.[12] Furthermore, as words are made up of a small number of common elements, words are easily confused; the transposition of one letter often changes the whole meaning. The deaf person is all the more prone to error here, for he hears nothing and has nothing to indicate the order of the letters in a word. Even this first difficulty is minor in comparison with his difficulty in attaching a particular meaning to each expression.

When the teacher gives the meaning of some twenty words, the pupil will record these words in his notebook, but he cannot in the same way set down the ideas in them. Nor does he have a dictionary with signs for explaining the spoken expressions to be learned. What can the pupil do if he wants to study on his own and put the time between classes to good use? [13] If some of the ideas presented by the teacher are lost to the pupil, the material he studies cannot restore them, for the words in themselves have nothing that reminds him of the ideas. Even if he does remember everything in the lesson, he still runs the risk of relating a word to only one of the ideas used to explain it or—a more serious error still—he will confuse one word with another and give one word the meaning of another. Instead of making progress, he will backslide by replacing ignorance with error.

This twofold difficulty must have been even greater at the time of the institute's founding because the pupils, all ignorant, could not help each other; and these must surely have been the reasons that decided the judicious abbé de l'Epée to adopt, as a sort of mnemonic device, the ambiguous signs that recalled both the idea and the word, though most often merely the word.

The teacher must patiently pair the word with the idea until they are firmly united and deeply etched, one on the other as it were, in the pupil's memory. Any word omitted by the teacher or forgotten by the pupil is lost for some time to come. Only at the end of his education can a deaf person know enough French to appreciate a definition and to use a dictionary to find the meaning of an unfamiliar word. Even then, if he wants to state an idea that he can express perfectly in sign but not in French, what will he do? A child learning Latin would merely have to open his dictionary to find the Latin word he needs next to the French word. The only dictionary for the deaf pupil is his teacher; but this resource is sometimes unavailable, and is totally absent once the pupil's education is completed and he returns home. Each forgotten word is then lost until chance presents it anew and enables him to look up its meaning in a dictionary of French.

For more than three-quarters of a pupil's stay at the institute, he does his studying only in the teacher's presence and in class. The time between classes is lost for his advancement. In regular schools, on the other hand, the study time is the most valuable, for a person knows best what he has learned by himself; his attention is more sustained because he has a better or at least more satisfying grasp of the connections between his own thoughts than someone else's. Ideas that are interconnected become less transitory and form a solid, lasting whole. The mind becomes stronger; like the body, it becomes stronger only through exercise. Then the progress made and the knowledge acquired are the result of our own efforts; we treat them like a possession, a personal fortune that increases our self-esteem and for that reason becomes all the dearer to us. The deaf person, whose time is precious owing to his late-starting education, would no longer regret the loss of potentially profitable time if he could use it to study and train his mind. This homework, which is always so productive, is also the most satisfying; in it one acquires the habit and love of study.

To appreciate all the consequent benefits to the deaf, we must recognize how all-consuming is their desire to become educated. They have a sense of their deprivation, and they soon realize the need for study; nothing is more poignant than the ardor with which they pursue it. At Abbé Sicard's institute I have often seen children spend their whole recreation period in a corner of the courtyard, leaning on a post or windowsill and copying, for lack of anything better, jumbled lists of words collected at random and frequently misspelled and occasionally recalling some rough idea. The futility of this hard and tedious work barely dampens their eagerness. What good use we could make of this tireless enthusiasm by feeding their minds tastier nourishment!

We could do this, it seems to me, with written signs. A deaf person needs no more time to learn to read and write signs than we do to reach and write speech. Next to the known signs we put the corresponding French expressions or even short phrases that the signs would make clear. In this way the deaf person acquires a feeling for a great number of expressions and turns of phrase that only practice can make familiar. Everyone knows that, in learning languages especially, no theory is wonderful enough to replace practice. In use the word is so intimately conjoined with the idea that they seem to be one and nearly always occur together in the mind; with practice the dawning thought naturally takes the form of the language familiar to us, a fact we express by saying that we are thinking in that language.

The deaf person learning the previously elusive words can review the lesson and even go beyond it. The teacher, for his part, no longer suffers the boredom of going over the same words time and time again. The diligent pupil will no longer idle in the wake of the lazy one whom he has always had to wait for. Emulation will occur and progress will be rapid.

To leave nothing to be desired, we would also have to give the pupils a reasoned vocabulary, one with words and the corresponding signs methodically arranged according to the generation of our ideas, so that we can go naturally and effortlessly from one to the other. And as the position of each idea would be determined by the very nature of the idea, the deaf person could easily look for the needed word in the same way we find the name of a plant in a taxonomic table.

This kind of classification, which would be useful just by itself, will become even more valuable as the language of gesture reaches its highest peak of perfection, which will not take long. The similarity between the ideas found in the corresponding signs would lead from one idea to another; and the appropriateness of the sign would guarantee the appropriateness of the idea.

But as we have observed at the Institute for Deaf-Mutes, although the sign system is already extremely rich and in every way worthy of philosophical attention, it is at present far from being a perfect and regular whole.

I hasten to add that I am referring only to the familiar language of the deaf which no one teaches them and which is the direct and artless expression of their thought; it is different from the purely grammatical signs and from signs for recalling words that indicate ideas only secondarily by means of a presupposed knowledge of words.

The abbé de l'Epée gave a dazzling proof of his genius—and this alone would ensure his glory—by discovering in the signs of the deaf a way to lead them to the knowledge of a language that enabled them to communicate with hearing people. It was for this purpose alone that the signs were envisaged; for even while signs were used to aid in the development of thought, the goal was merely to clarify the meaning of certain words. Signs were considered only in relation to French, and great efforts were made to bend them to that language. But as sign language is quite different from all other languages, it had to be distorted to conform to French usage, and it was sometimes so disfigured as to become unintelligible. That is the result we observed of the attempt to mold signs to fit the composition and etymology of French words.

The forms of true sign language, as we will demonstrate further on, are extremely simple; it faithfully represents thought, and leaves out all inessentials. Sign language lacks the luxury of the different grammatical forms abounding in spoken languages where the expression of the same idea can in turn become a noun or adjective or adverb without any of the modifications changing the basic idea. But it is still imperative to make these forms known and understood so that the deaf can use them as we do. The signs taught for this purpose are not natural to the language of the deaf and are adapted to make it closer to French. Everything that French has that is not found in sign language must be supplied by methodical signs; they are designed to signal grammatical features that are not just extraneous to sign language, but sometimes utterly incompatible with it.

We know that despite these problems the abbé Sicard brought these signs to a quite satisfactory level of perfection. This kind of translation is a genuine, comprehensive grammatical analysis that reveals the categories of words as parts of speech, their composition, inflections, and interconnections forming the sentence.

But, one senses, the more profoundly these signs decompose the sentence—thus revealing the structure of French—the further they get away from the language of the deaf, from their intellectual capacities and style of thinking. That is why the deaf never make use of these signs among themselves; they use them in taking word-for-word dictation, but to explain the meaning of the text dictated, they go back to their familiar language.

An excessively literal translation is, as we know, often unintelligible, because of the difference in spirit of any two idioms. A literal translation in sign language is utterly incomprehensible, for in the absence of grammatical forms it inserts between the various parts of the sentence artificial, abstract signs that cancel out the relations and that make the scattered parts of the thought unrecognizable!

Constant attention and acumen are therefore needed to prevent the deaf person from writing what is in fact perfectly correct French, but still meaningless gibberish to him, much as a schoolchild writes Greek. The ideas dictated are not above their heads and could be perfectly understandable if stated in the schoolchild's native language or the deaf child's natural language.

The spirit and resources of sign language have not received enough study. In particular, there has not been sufficient appreciation of its independence of any other language. The tendency has been to fit the sign to the word rather than to the idea. Occasionally, the appropriateness of signs has counted for so little that some signs have been brought into use whose whole meaning depends on the finger shape indicating the initial letter of the word they recalled, such as *Vin, Tante, Oncle, Durant, Pendant, Jeu* and so forth. As this essay concerns only the natural language of the deaf, I shall not dwell on the kind of sign based on this silly gimmick. A number of signs have been introduced into the familiar usage of the deaf through corruption from spoken language; this is what prompted me to say previously that sign language was being altered rather than improved.

We can find many other defects in familiar usage, but it is surprising not to find even more, and not to find in the usage the effects of the ignorance and inexperience of the children who are its source.

Despite its present barbarity and primitiveness, sign language is graceful and forcible, and its present defects will eventually disappear as it becomes the object of intensive study. It repays our study in more than one respect: as the natural, direct expression of thought, it can shed light on the development of our intellectual faculties; as the normal language of the deaf, it is worth cultivating because the better it becomes, the better it fosters their intellectual development and facilitates their education.

Because the source of this language is inherent in our nature, we find it easy to master. By observing it in action, we should be able to deduce some rules for determining the characteristic sign of an idea and for identifying the meaning of a given sign. The formation of signs can provide fascinating insights. The syntax of signs, which people are scarcely aware of, will perhaps yield new and intriguing observations.

The Language of the Deaf

Few people have an exact idea of the language of the deaf. Some assume that it is the fingerspelling of words and sentences from spoken language; others recognize it as a genuine language, but think it is limited to the representation of concrete objects. What analogy can there be, they ask, between the gesture and the subtlety of a thought? What purchase will a crass pantomime give to the nuances of mental abstractions? In using it, will we constantly have to resort to metaphors that necessarily have the disadvantage of revealing the thought only through a partially transparent veil?

We shall not bother to combat this double error. Only the criticism concerning the need for metaphor warrants attention, but it is easy to demonstrate the contrary, that sign language has less need of metaphors than speech itself, for it is certain that all spoken languages contain not a single abstract word that did not originally designate a concrete object.[14]

Sign language is different. In it intellectual ideas are always expressed clearly and easily. This assertion may at first appear incredible, but actually nothing could be easier to understand. Even the simplest external object is still compound; our idea of it is a combination of the qualities through which it can affect our senses. The idea of a peach is composed of the idea of its shape, taste, aroma, color, and even the tree that produces it. All these features provide us with signs that will give a rather good description of the isolated idea of a peach but whose complexity would impede the flow of thought. So we must choose among these signs; and where there is choice, error is possible. It is true that the choice is not arbitrary and that we should prefer the signs that characterize the thing best. But this problem does not arise for signs concerning intellectual matters.

However complicated intellectual acts appear, they are rigorously interconnected. There is always one act that presupposes all the preceding acts, and that when named, implicitly recalls all the others. The truth of this quickly becomes clear if we take the trouble to examine ourselves without regard to the different names correctly or incorrectly applied to the operations of the understanding. We shall see that the signs of the deaf always correspond to the greater or lesser precision of their ideas. Now our ideas are what we know best. They make up, so to speak, our whole existence; and the faculty of expressing our thoughts is as natural to us as that of forming them. We merely have to let loose, so to speak, the impulse of our biological constitution to produce externally everything that happens internally.

In representing the impression that an object produces in us, the gesture first designates some essential feature of the object and then indicates its effect on a particular sense—the resting face livens up, becomes animated, and reflects the occurrence of the impression. Simultaneously, we see whether the sensation is pleasant or unpleasant.

The mental reaction we call *attention* is revealed in a more composed physiognomy, in a sense organ directed to the object, and in the accompanying gesture.

Attention alternating between two objects seemingly brought together by the two hands gives rise to *comparison*; we prefer one object and reject the other. The mutually reinforcing gesture and facial expression leave not even the densest person in the dark about these actions.

When the object causing the sensation is gone, the impression of it faithfully remains in the back of the mind, confided to memory, and able to reproduce the sensation.[15] Our eyes close, but the image remains as though in front of us—the hand outlining its shape seems to follow the image's contours as if it were still present. We perform the same operations with these images as we do with the objects themselves. We think, we judge, we reason: a deaf child would see the connection between all these acts sooner and more easily than would a hearing child.

So I think that sign language has a superior capacity for expressing mental operations. Discussions founder in the vagueness of words, and a definition cannot completely correct this (definitions being themselves made up of words that are sometimes just as vague). In discussions we go astray, we look for each other without success, each of us employs a different language, we speak to each other without mutual understanding, often without understanding ourselves. Hence the interminable quarrels that lead to doubts about man's ability to determine truth with any certainty. But if the question is asked in sign—the language that cannot deceive, for it is the voice of nature—it would, I think, frequently acquire a self-evident certainty or become a manifest absurdity to all.

The faculty of thinking is nothing other than the faculty of perceiving relations. In speaking, we usually express relations between objects that are already familiar. So it is superfluous to describe these objects; it is enough to designate them precisely. If we mentioned all their features we would obscure the thought by deflecting attention to things that are extraneous to the main idea.

The flow of thought is always rapid; to be clear, its expression must be precise. So, as we have said, we must choose between the possible signs for depicting an idea. To be exact, these signs must be taken from some essential and distinctive feature of the thing signified. For instance, the name of some chemical compound not only clearly designates a substance, but also indicates its composition, the constituent elements, and their respective proportions.

Only by bringing an object together with all similar objects, and comparing them in all respects, can we find out how the objects differ from all others. Only comparison yields precise ideas, only comparison produces precise signs. An idea is followed by a sign, like a shadow; a sign is an accurate representation of an idea.

But for both ideas and signs reliable precision presupposes extensive comparisons made with order and method. And that is what we cannot expect to find in most deaf people, all of whose knowledge is the product of their unassisted personal observation.

The first deaf people brought together by the abbé de l'Epée recognized each other as brothers in misfortune, and were able to act on the desire to communicate their sensations, memories, and thoughts to one another. Nature, which had instilled them with this need, soon provided them with the means of satisfying it, and enabled them to find this means chiefly in the tendency to imitate which is one of the marks of the human make-up.

When they had to represent an object for the first time, the feature that first struck them determined the sign. To determine whether this sign was distinctive and essential to the thing required knowledge as yet unavailable to them. So it sometimes happened that the feature was transitory and accidental, and when the same object was represented from a new angle or the idea had to be viewed differently, the initial sign was no longer appropriate, but it was preserved because it had already been adopted and was understood. What was needed to make a change was the authority of a teacher who realized that if the cause of imprecise signs is imprecise ideas, false signs in turn have an unfortunate influence on thought, and that the thought is rarely adequate when the signs are inadequate.

But, I repeat, no attention had been paid to the language that the deaf used among themselves. That is, however, where their minds acquire all the habits favoring or hindering their education, more so than with hearing children who can resort to reading, which the deaf child can begin to enjoy only toward the end of his education.

There is another, less important but still noteworthy source of imprecision in the language of the deaf. An event occurs before their eyes or is reported to them; by allusion the most salient feature is used to characterize all similar facts; tradition passes the sign from one generation to another; once the anecdote giving rise to the sign is forgotten, it becomes nearly impossible to grasp the thread of the analogy leading from the idea to the sign, and the sign appears purely arbitrary. We can compare these signs to the idiomatic expressions of all languages in frequent use by the common people. The deaf with good taste and education employ these kinds of signs as little as possible, not just because of their imprecision but because of their apparent triviality. They are to true sign language what high-school slang is to correct French. When a deaf person wants to make himself understood by a deaf foreigner, he realizes the need to forego these signs, which are not understood beyond the boundaries of their usage, and to take his expressions from nature and the very essence of the idea. If these pantomimic signs leave the idea somewhat obscure, he describes all the features needed to make it understood.

We will also notice another linguistic defect, in itself of minor importance, but warranting educational attention because it encourages a bad habit that carries over into French. I am referring to the tendency of the deaf to repeat a gesticulated idea over and over again, which frequently makes their thought diffuse and obscure. Because each part of the sentence is repeated several times in a rapid succession of gestures, we run the risk of confusing subject and object, the consequent with the antecedent, the active and the passive.

I have often had this problem in determining the syntax of signs. But some deaf people hardly ever commit this error, which is extraneous to sign language, and I think all the others could easily be discouraged from doing this. Their own experience could be cited to show them that thought is clearer and more easily expressed when we refrain from these tiresome repetitions on which the teacher could cast a bit of ridicule that the cleverer of them would appreciate and that all of them would constantly guard against . . .

It will be less easy to reform the imprecise signs, for they go back to this institution's founding, and long use has given them deep roots. This would not be a problem in a new institution. The teacher can satisfactorily mold the new pupils who arrive without preconceptions or bad habits. He will painlessly lead them to choose signs that are more satisfying because they are directly related to the thing. Once these signs are in use, the deaf will communicate with each other the way a limpid stream flows from a pure spring.

Before undertaking the hard job of educating the deaf, the prospective teacher should study the works of the abbé de l'Epée and of his worthy successor, the abbé Sicard. But this is not enough. A good teacher must familiarize himself with the natural language of the deaf. The first and most important thing is to know how to make oneself understood by them.

The establishment of a regular system of signs would require intensive preliminary study, constant attention, and assiduous care on the teacher's part. Then his pupils' progress will amply compensate him for his pains. This work has considerable charm for someone with a feel for it. Indeed, what is more fascinating than to observe nature at work in the development of moral and intellectual man? What spectacle is worthier of the philosopher than to be a witness, so to speak, to the formation of human intelligence, to see budding and unfolding the faculty that raises man above everything around him and places him between heaven and earth! . . .

We can learn a great deal by observing those children whom the privation of a sense has kept apart from society and from the burden of our prejudices.[16] If you want to guide the deaf person in the long run, you must for some time limit yourself to observing him and receiving his lessons. You will perhaps be surprised to learn truths from him that had been enshrouded in human dreams and had escaped the sagacity of deep thinkers. We must be circumspect in observing the deaf and studying their language to distinguish precisely between what is proper to them and what is the effect of some external influence. We should be most confident of the observations provided by the less educated deaf person. If his signs are inadequate to express his idea fully, we will almost always discover that the cause is his incomplete appreciation of all the implications of the idea, for, I repeat, the sign follows the thought step by step, like a shadow that takes on all its different shapes.

The educated deaf person can elaborate his ideas better. He furnishes us with fascinating information. But how can he himself distinguish what belongs to him alone from what is the result of suggestions from his teachers or even from the use of spoken languages? Are we ourselves always able to identify the sources of our opinions, hopes, fears, and resolutions? ...

On the Voice Considered in Relation to Natural Language

Up to this point we have discussed little but sign language, with barely a mention of the voice, which also enters into natural language. When we are aware of some sharp sensation owing to some sudden change in our state, the chest abruptly expands and contracts, the air passages undergo similar movements, and the air rapidly moving through them produces the strongly accented, broken sounds known as interjections, which differ from words by being similar in all languages and universally the signs of the same emotions, and thus characteristic of natural language.

It is important to make a distinction here: the voice was part of the natural language, but speech was not. In interjections, for example, the meaning depends not on the word, but wholly on the stress, and in place of interjections we often see other words which, in this case, lose their normal meaning and instead take on the meaning naturally connected with the stress for which they serve as a vehicle. It would be impossible to write out most interjections, for they are not articulated! Can we call them speech, or words? I think that sighs, groans, bursts of laughter, and the like have never been classified as words, for then we would have no reason to exclude vocal trills and other musical sounds. Everything we are saying about interjections necessarily applies to the vocal imitation of the various cries and noises of animals, a highly restricted sort of imitation. So, most often, the voice was a mere auxiliary in the original primitive language: interjections always correspond to facial movements expressing the same emotions, but with more force and variety. The gesture can, without any auxiliary, express both ideas and the relations between ideas; without a prior convention, the voice can provide only a few signs for expressing thought. The gesture takes from the external shape, from the typical way of being, features belonging to the very essence of things; it gets them from the facial expression reflecting, so to speak, the inner man; the only material for vocal imitation is the movement impressed on the air by the vibrations of sonorous objects, which produces on the auditory organs the sensation that we call noise or sound; except for some animal cries, there are few characteristic sounds. The sound itself is an accident, and does not strictly belong to the object that produces it—varying in the same object, often the same in different objects, hard to hear distinctly and even harder to imitate with the human voice. We are overawed by the marvelous edifice of languages erected on such a seemingly precarious foundation.

The Transition from Natural Language to Conventional Language

Beyond the interjections wrenched from us by a sudden sensation, lively and animated delivery requires that the voice be accompanied by gesture, because the chest and vocal apparatus are then part of the whole movement, as we can observe with the deaf who in gesticulating often make clearly articulated sounds. Frequently the sounds add nothing to the thought, but even more frequently they give more force, precision and variety to its expression and put the finishing touch to the picture for recalling cries and noises, for depicting rapid movement. Sounds that by themselves would express something only vaguely would have a precise meaning through gestures speifying the objects related to the sounds; and as the same sound often accompanies a particular gesture, the sound becomes the conventional sign and eventually evokes the same idea. These signs grew in number, at first maintained and explained by gestures but later replacing them. By analogy, the process extended from sonorous objects to noiseless objects, and there gradually emerged languages. From this perspective alone it can be claimed that this great achievement of the human mind originated in nature. But the same would have to be said of the arts, sciences, of all knowledge, and every invention. Man can make nothing from nothing, and when we say that he invents, we must understand that he finds the principle in nature, and works it out for application to the needs of society.

A quick and easy mechanism that stimulates attention; one that combines the advantage of bringing thought out of the shadows and over the obstacles to sight, with the equally precious advantage of requiring only the use of organs useless for other tasks—such a mechanism was surely preferable to any other means of communication, especially when the prolific human species no longer found adequate sustenance in nature, when man, to satisfy new needs resulting from the growth of civilization, was obliged to put his hand to constant labor and subdue arid soil which he irrigates with his own sweat to force it to produce . . .

The use of speech soon became nearly universal; its rapid development paralleled the development of the human mind. We see speech afford flashes of genius, follow the imagination in bold, brilliant flight, ponder together with philosophy the secrets of nature, and sound the depths of the understanding.

As speech improved, the natural language was abandoned. Furthermore, as each language increasingly realized its potentialities, fewer and fewer persons used the natural language. Neighboring peoples no longer understood each other, and speech, first designed to facilitate human communication, became itself the greatest obstacle of all.

Certain fortuitous circumstances, or (what amounts to the same thing) a tenuous and vague analogy, produced the first primitive words. The same source was often responsible for compound or derived words. But even if the formation of languages had been governed by the wisest philosophy, the continual variation undergone in the meaning of every word would soon have destroyed their harmony.

That is not all: each expression took on several different meanings, and in this the structure of things was not always consulted, not even a strict analogy. We often find the same word combining opposite ideas or, worse, utterly unrelated ideas. As children, utterly submissive and trusting, we accept these collections of ideas as finished products, and at a later age almost no one takes it into his head to examine the soundness of these first ideas that became the basis for all our judgments. We received them uncritically and continue to use them unreflectively and in total security. In speaking, when our attention alternates between this and that part of the collection, we affirm of one part what is correct only of another part, and it commonly happens that each isolated proposition has an appearance of truth although in fact these propositions lead to a completely false conclusion. We reason with words rather than ideas. This is the art of Sophists, and also the source of most of our errors, errors the more pernicious as we apply the love of truth the Creator put in our hearts to words that obscure the truth—whence such grave consequences! Crime, it has been said, is incorrect judgment, and the history of the French Revolution provides terrible evidence of this on every page. One wit, exaggerating the thought a trifle, added: "And the person presenting an invalid argument has something of the murderer about him."

So speech, which sets up so many obstacles to communication between peoples, also puts shackles on the progress of the mind; or sometimes offers a deceptive guide that leads it astray, the same way the will-o'-the-wisp glowing in the nocturnal dark, providing the uncertain traveler with a treacherous beacon, misleads him and trips him into the quagmire from which it came.

Thoughtful people must necessarily be struck by these major imperfections, and philosophers, deploring these serious drawbacks, have often expressed the desire for a systematic language more favorable to the development of thought and communication between peoples. We find this wish in Vossius, Scaliger, Hermann, and others. This idea did not escape Bacon, who sensed the necessity for recasting all human understanding. This idea was dear to Leibniz, and in his last years it was the constant subject of his meditations. Condillac thought the language could be based entirely on analogy, with the language of calculus as a model. The abbé de l'Epée thought that the language of the deaf could suit this purpose. Degérando, who better than anyone else described the benefits of a truly philosophical language (whose realization seemed to him impracticable), does not adopt Epée's idea. Degérando thought that the signs of the deaf had three disadvantages for this purpose: they are full of metaphors; they are not simple enough; they do not analyze thought with sufficient precision. Finally, as signs require the presence of interlocutors, they are of no use in communication between people who are far apart.

Our discussion of the nature of sign language and its improvement seems to meet these objections. They may be even more definitively resolved by the facts themselves that we will set forth when we speak of signs in particular.

Few of the books promoting the establishment of a universal language are worth much attention. We could single out that of Wilkins, which contains many bold and profound ideas on languages and general grammar. The more elementary book, *La Pasigraphie* by Maimieux is less systematic. Hourwitz's *La Polygraphie* was even less successful. Despite their authors' gifts, the basis for all these books is much too arbitrary for their intended purpose; we should be especially wary of the arbitrary in the expression of thought which is so free in nature.

The most appropriate vehicle for reaching the goal of a universal language appears to me, as it did to Vossius and the abbé de l'Epée, to be sign language. It already functions that way for the deaf; they all understand each other—that fact no longer needs proof. The authorities frequently called the abbé Sicard's pupils Massieu and Clerc to interpret for the deaf vagrants picked up in the streets of Paris.

Clerc was like a guardian angel to his uneducated brethren: they went to him to get work or help—it was he who drew up their petitions and wrote their letters, which they then had translated into their native language if they were foreigners. The barrier created by the diversity of languages does not exist for these children of nature. No matter what country a deaf person is born in, he is their brother in infirmity and their linguistic compatriot.

But the benefit of communicating in an unlearned language has not been granted just to the deaf. We have already spoken about the primitive peoples of South America who, though speaking different languages, understand each other by means of gestures. That, we can say, is humankind's proper language. And if it seems the prerogative of the deaf, the reason is that gesture is prompted by need while our customary artificial languages cause us to overlook sign. But we need only a little practice to become as fluent in sign as we are in speech.[17] We make a great many signs without thinking about it. What a host of ideas we each naturally express with gestures! Who could have any trouble making the signs for coming, going, sleeping, ordering? Who could confuse the expressions of sadness or joy, disdain or respect, threat or compassion? Who could not indicate whether an object is round or square, large or small, and the like? Once we have found the sign, we are in no danger of forgetting; the sign and the idea are so closely intertwined that they are one, though in spoken languages nothing is more usual than to confound them and take the sign for the thing meant. Without mentioning poetry, which thrives on images, the style of common parlance is full of this kind of figure, and very often the word expressing the gesture is also the only one for the corresponding idea.

If at first we have some difficulty expressing ourselves with signs, the reason is that despite ourselves and owing to our habit of speech, all our ideas are connected with words, and when we try to speak with gestures—or in some foreign language—we always tend to translate the word, which often is vague, rather than the idea, which should be always precise.

So the first point is to understand clearly what we mean, independently of the sounds we use. Far from tiring the mind, this labor gives it new vigor by releasing it from the shackles of verbal expression and from the problem of ambiguities, eventually delivering it from the influence of words. Words often give the full import of ideas only at the expense of accuracy, tend to encourage the mind's natural laziness, make it neglect the exercise of its forces by giving it artificial help, and often dispense with the labor of thought or at least present thought to the mind only partially digested, as to a stomach weakened by overrefined food and now intolerant of simple, substantial fare.

We could not in fact give each possible idea a simple sign immediately understandable to everyone. But the signs natural to us all suffice (as proven by the education of the deaf) to explain all combinations of ideas and consequently to determine clearly the sign appropriate for each one. So it should be possible to compile a sort of dictionary, with written signs and some illustrations providing the key, that would yield a precise understanding of all ideas without any assistance from spoken language, without even the assumption of prior knowledge. A book like that would have the virtue of a difficulty overcome. By adding explanations in French, we could make it both more understandable and more useful.

VII

FERDINAND BERTHIER

B EFORE LEAVING FRANCE to found the education of the deaf in America in 1816, Laurent Clerc declared that the thirteen-year-old Ferdinand Berthier, a student of his for the past five years, was the brightest pupil at the Paris Institute for the Deaf. Young Berthier in turn idolized Clerc and made a lifelong project of emulating Clerc's career as deaf teacher of the deaf. Born in 1803 in the town of Louhans in the province of Burgundy, the congenitally deaf Berthier entered the institute at the age of eight. After graduation he rose quickly through the teaching ranks, beginning with the post of monitor at sixteen and achieving full professorship at twenty-six. He was the leading figure in the signing community of Paris of the time.

With extraordinary proficiency in written French, Berthier wrote several books and numerous articles about the deaf, their education, and their legal rights, including biographies of the abbé de l'Epée, the abbé Sicard, and R. A. Bébian. The essay translated in this volume is *Les Sourds-muets avant et depuis l'abbé de l'Epée* (Paris: Ledoyen, 1840). Berthier's colleagues and students esteemed him highly and described him as ambitious, elegant, and possessed of great good humor. Among his prodigious activities on behalf of the deaf was the creation of the first social organization for the deaf, which promoted legal reform and adult education. Berthier was the first deaf person to receive the Legion of Honor.

Ferdinand Berthier

THE DEAF BEFORE AND SINCE THE ABBÉ DE L'EPÉE

You, the Fellows of the Society for the Moral Sciences, Letters, and Arts of Seine-et-Oise, propose the following as the subject for an anonymously offered prize: "To investigate what the social condition of the deaf was before the abbé de l'Epée, and what means were employed for their education; to use these two investigations to gain a proper appreciation of Epée's achievement as the founder of a new institution and as a benefactor of humanity."

Even though you desire to honor the memory of one of Versailles's most illustrious children, you also wish to avoid the platitudes and exaggeration usually accompanying a panegyric. So your request was not to make the abbé de l'Epée the chief subject of these efforts but merely the term in which they end. Thus my task is, first, to make a historical assessment of the improvement effected in the moral and social condition of the deaf through modern education, and then to give an impartial account of the glory and gratitude thereby redounding to France and to the abbé de l'Epée in particular by judging, the documents in hand, the debate occasioned by the well or ill-founded claims made by other countries or by other men.

Grace be yours, gentlemen. It was fitting for the learned society of Seine-et-Oise to pay this admiring tribute to the memory of one of the most illustrious sons of the town of Versailles, the Saint-Vincent-de-Paul of the deaf, the man to whom an entire class of unfortunates owed its intellectual emancipation.

God's grace be with you. You will provide more than one lover of humanity with an occasion for quenching his raging, consuming thirst by offering to the sad plight of this group of outcasts new sources of consolation and more powerful reasons yet, if possible, for hope!

As the weak instrument of the deaf, I convey to you their gratitude. Oh, if the honors were reserved for talent alone, I, an incomplete man, would not try my luck in combat, and would withdraw from an engagement perhaps closed to my fellows. I am certain, however, that you also will appreciate the unheralded devotion and the humble efforts of a deaf man who has labored for twenty years to improve the lot of his brethren.

May it please God that I never present myself with the deceptive appearance of modesty, like one of those charlatans who, to increase their apparent worthiness, depict in factitious colors the deaf condition before, and even after, their emancipation. Lover of the truth above all, and a scrupulous observer of the events that I have encountered in my long career, I shall recount everything I have seen and read, but *only* what I have seen or read. And, despite my great esteem for Epée, I shall not flinch from daring to point out his errors. Even were the truth not to demand it, the conclusions that ignorance and prejudice have drawn from these errors, to the detriment of my fellows, command me—like all men of good will—to silence my feelings and discharge this strict but painful duty.

First, let us examine the conditions in which the deaf lived before they came by the godsend of education. What was their position in society? What were they, really? The picture of the social class of these outcasts, as they were then disdainfully called, is so heartrending that we can contemplate it only with a shudder.

Until the middle of the sixteenth century, because of some absurd laws, the deaf were almost universally relegated to the class of idiots and madmen. The Lycurguses of this era of ignorance claimed to justify their rejection by consigning the education of these unfortunates to the realm of impossibility and idle fancies. Are we not rightly amazed to see princes of philosophy and theology, Aristotle[1] and Saint Augustine[2], living treasurehouses of enlightenment and dialectic—one plumbing the depths of matter and mind, the other glimpsing mysteries seemingly reserved for God—yield like weaklings to vulgar prejudice, and loftily declare the deaf incapable, through any effort of reason or faith, of bridging the great gap between creature and Creator? But a source of even greater wonderment is the silence maintained by the Roman writers: Pliny the Naturalist devotes a mere two or three lines to the deaf; throughout there is pompous praise for mute actors, for pantomimes. Nowhere is the least effort made to apply the marvelous effects achieved in mime to find a remedy for an infirmity that must surely have been as widespread then as now (if we can rely on the reports of physicians specializing in diseases of the ear, that vulnerable organ).

If you read the history of the Trappist monastery, the austere order in which, as everyone knows, to open one's mouth is a crime, you would find the language of gestures presiding at the foundation of the order. Nearby, among the monks of Cîteaux, you will be shown a dictionary of signs that has been kept from time immemorial.

Among some ancient peoples, parents—as ashamed as they were grief-stricken at the birth of a deaf child—concealed him or her from all eyes.

We hasten to add, however, that the Roman legal system made provision for people who were "deaf without being mute" or people who were "mute without being deaf." The emperor Justinian considered different kinds of deaf people, and then decreed the fate of each group. But the pathetic distinctions he established are highly advantageous for people to whom the double handicap is the result of some sudden accident, and highly disadvantageous for the people to whom it is natural! That is what caused Louis Vivès[3] to hesitate before admitting as probably true Rudolphus Agricola's claim that the deaf person could achieve mastery of the written word. One fifteenth-century writer even thought that a deaf person who could weave a fishnet was a genius.

While touching on the subject, I cannot contain my outrage at seeing that the laws of England still uphold a provision classifying the congenitally deaf among those individuals incompetent to leave their goods by will, and this in the nineteenth century, at a time when French law has long ago at least tacitly repealed these outdated edicts!

Still, in those distant times when nascent civilization, having just emerged from the chaos of barbarism, sought all over for a fulcrum to lever itself up, can it be believed that the laws of Lycurgus, of Solon, and of Numan condemned deaf children to undergo the fate reserved for the retarded or deformed. A father's glance at these poor creatures was a sentence with no appeal: it was all over for them if they saw written in his look: "I don't want you!" The unfortunate child was promptly smothered or had his throat slit or was thrown from a precipice into the waves. It was treasonable to spare a creature from whom the nation could anticipate nothing.

The abbé de l'Epée assures us that even in his time there were still countries where children who could not hear or speak by the age of three were put to death. Through public credulity these unfortunate children were classed with monsters. Oh, how much better was the Turkish sultan who, unsure what to do with the deaf in his domain, employed the most intelligent ones as pantomimes to charm away his royal cares!

Among the Egyptians, on the other hand, and especially among the Persians, the fate of the deaf was a matter of religious concern. Their handicap was regarded as a visible sign of heaven's favor.

But it remained for the Christian religion of brotherhood and good-heartedness, which has broken so many earthly bonds, to loosen the chains of the deaf and to efface the last vestiges of those atrocities that are as outrageous to reason as they are offensive to nature. At the appearance of this religion, the savage rulers of the world learned of the powerful voice of humanity; they then took pride in protecting the children of men, and the proverb *res sacra miser* became a universal truth . . .

Be that as it may, let us contemplate the moral degradation into which the deaf had fallen at the advent of the inspired man they gratefully proclaimed their Messiah! What revulsion, I would even say horror, was universally caused by the approach of these modern pariahs! If, as has been remarked, absolute isolation is harmful for man and catastrophic to reason, even when reinforced with iron courage, how much more so will it not be for the deaf person? In the centuries of brutishness just mentioned, in vain did their highly animated physiognomy, their highly expressive gestures, and the intelligence shining out of their isolation give the lie to victimizing prejudices: the ancient teachers had spoken, the old philosophers had uttered the curse. And even in our own day has not the unfortunate authority of more than one teacher sanctioned this ignominious decree? Listen, listen to the abbé Sicard himself. In the preamble to his *Course of Instruction*, he wonders: "What is a congenitally deaf person considered by himself and before any education has begun to connect him—by whatever bond—to the great family to which by his external form he belongs? In society he is a perfect nullity, a living automaton, a statue similar to the one described by Charles Bonnet and after him by Condillac—a statue whose senses must be successively opened and directed to compensate for the one unfortunately missing. Restricted to mere physical movements before the coffin in which his reason lives entombed is torn open, he lacks even that unerring instinct that controls animals destined to have only that as a guide" . . . (pp. ix-x)

. . . Up to this point the deaf person is a mere ambulatory machine whose constitution (as regards his behavior) is inferior to that of animals (xii) . . . But as the deaf person knows no speech signals and hence has no means of communication, his sensory impressions must all be transitory and his mental images fleeting. Nothing remains in his mind to which he can relate what is happening to him and which he can use as a basis for comparison. So all his ideas must be immediate and none can be the product of reflection. And because he can never combine two ideas at a time (he has no signs for retaining them) even the simplest sort of reasoning is impossible for him. Reduced to an awful solitude, he is surrounded by an endless, omnipresent, and profound silence. He cannot ask anyone a question. Does he even know what a question is? Does he know whether other people communicate with each other—whether they are not, like him, alone in the midst of their peers?

As for morality, it is the combined product of so many elements, all so remote from the deaf person, that we must doubt whether he even suspects their existence. To refer everything to himself, to act on all his natural needs with a violent impulsiveness unmoderated by any rational consideration, to satisfy all appetites no matter what, to know no limit to them other than his inability to satisfy them always, to become enraged at obstacles, to thrash at them furiously, to knock over everything standing in the way of his pleasures, with no check by the incomprehended rights of others or by incomprehended laws or by the punishments that he has not experienced—that is the sum of this unfortunate creature's morality. Moreover, as he consults only his own tastes, I suspect that no affection for anything outside himself ever enters his mind, not even the love for one's progenitors engraved by nature in animals. Do I even know whether the deaf child's heart is reached by those sweet demonstrations of maternal tenderness to which other children are so sensitive?(xiii-xv)...For him the moral world does not exist, and virtues, like vices, are without reality(xvi)...Before this new life, the happy effect of his education, he was good for nothing; he was a ferocious, maleficent animal (xxiii).

Our astonishment increases on seeing a teacher of the deaf, whose daily occupation should have convinced him of the contrary, persistently downgrade his ignorant students to a level lower than the stupidest animals, and pile paradox on paradox in the argument for this false proposition.

To combat this proposition, I shall invoke the opinion of the abbé de l'Epée and of certain men whose knowledge of mimicry and habits of observation have opened the way to these exceptional minds. But are not Abbé Sicard's contradictions sufficiently evident for me to dispense with this investigation? He himself recognizes (p. viii) that, with the exception of the sense of hearing, the deaf person is in every regard the same as other men, and, further on, he establishes that, mentally, the similarity between the deaf person and the normal child is very great, and that, sensorily, the difference between them is almost nil.[4]

We have taken these quotations at random, emphasizing statements that so thoughtlessly and pitilessly strip these poor creatures even of the squalid portion of the heaven-sent boons dispensed to all humanity.

Fortunately, we have to record here an important admission by the abbé Sicard in his subsequently published *Theory of Signs*. We only regret that, instead of recognizing his errors, he thought it unnecessary to confess frankly his complete ignorance of the natural language of the deaf. Here, moreover, are the terms in which he restores the mental faculties of which he had so unjustly deprived his pupil.

He is not so unhappy. To his lessons he brings a communicative mind, full of ideas of external objects (through the senses stimulated by these objects), which livens up his gaze, modifies his facial muscles, and controls the variety of physiognomic features and expressions that convey all his thoughts and affections . . . Finally, the uninstructed deaf child coming from his parents is no less eloquent than the hearing child who, with his teacher, has just learned the arts of analyzing thought and of speaking correctly the language his earliest teacher taught by infusing her lessons with the charm of maternal tenderness. This is the state of the deaf child at the very moment before any instruction begins; for his teacher, he is neither deaf, nor mute . . . If the deaf child already has ideas, he already has expressions; and he does have expressions, for he has signs.[5]

Then Sicard recommends that the teacher place the pupil in the right circumstances for engaging his intellectual resources.

But Sicard's remarks about the young deaf person are still a long way from the truth. If his meditations had concerned the philosophy of mimic language rather than its mechanism, if he had taken up something other than the so-called "methodical" signs (a mere physical spelling of French words), if he had not confined his horizon to the narrow use of the manual alphabet or chalk or pen, he would certainly have rendered less belated and more complete justice to our brothers in misfortune.

It was long a universally accepted opinion that the absence of speech made the acquisition of abstract ideas impossible and a knowledge of higher-order truths even less possible. To our century's shame this opinion is still so deeply rooted that the masses gave an impassive reception to the more or less successful attempts of Pedro de Ponce and the Bonets in Spain, of the Gregorys and Wallises in England, the Ammans in Holland, of the Pereires and the abbé Deschamps in France.

We think writers are wrong to credit Pedro de Ponce, Benedictine of the Spanish monastery of Oña, with the title of first teacher of

the deaf. Today it is generally recognized that Ponce's whole achievement was merely to put the principles of deaf education on a broader
foundation than did his predecessors.

Before Ponce, several isolated instances of instruction had been
attempted, more or less successfully, both in France and abroad. In
1578 Joachim Pascha had trained two of his own deaf children, but
his attempts met with no public recognition. Jérôme Cardan, one
of the most intelligent people of his time and who perhaps most
reinvigorated the philosophical school of his century, had sought to
demonstrate that the education of the deaf was not an impossibility;
he did not stop there, and had kept a written record of some important views about this quite special type of teaching:

> So we can enable a deaf person both to hear by reading and to speak by
> writing. The deaf person thinks that the written word "bread," for example,
> means the object that is being shown him; his memory retains this meaning;
> he mentally contemplates the images of things: in the same way, following
> the memory of a painting one has seen, one can paint a picture representing
> the painting, we can also paint our thoughts with the letters of the alphabet;
> and in the same way that the different human vocal sounds have received
> a specific meaning by established convention, the various written letters
> can also get the same meaning by convention [6] ... The deaf person ought
> to learn to read and write, for he can do so as well as a blind person, as we
> have shown elsewhere. The task is no doubt difficult but it is still possible.
> Signs can express a great many ideas ... The Roman pantomimes are an
> example of this. We know that a barbarian king, impresssed with the truth
> of their gestural language, entreated the emperor to take two mimes into
> his estates ... Writing is associated with speech, and through speech with
> thought; but writing can also recall thought directly without the inter-
> mediary of speech, witness the hieroglyphic writings of a wholly ideographic
> character ... The deaf know of and worship God, for they have intelligent
> souls; nothing prevents them from cultivating the arts or even from creating
> accomplished works.[7]

Eventually, Pedro de Ponce appeared, and his works attracted much
attention among his contemporaries, as they must attract that of
posterity. Single-handedly, with no outside help, he managed to
instruct the two deaf brothers and sister of the constable de Velasco,
and also the deaf son of the governor of Aragon. But what excited
universal admiration to the highest pitch was the sight of this brilliant teacher's pupils' public discussions of astronomy, physics, and
logic. According to the eyewitness reports of contemporary Spanish
writers, "they distinguished themselves so much in the sciences

that they would have passed for clever people even in the eyes of Aristotle."

After Ponce's death, the Hispanic peninsula, which has not always been the country of brutishness and slavery it is usually thought, produced another teacher, Juan Pablo Bonet, secretary to the constable of Castile, who undertook to raise the constable's brother, who had become deaf at the age of four. Bonet published a book entitled *Arte para enseñar a hablar a los mudos* [*The Art of Teaching the Deaf to Speak*]. Besides a manual alphabet, this work contains a detailed description of the movements of the vocal apparatus in the utterance of sounds. He also takes up the labial alphabet, lip-reading, but apparently attaches little importance to it and classifies it with a number of less useful methods. Nevertheless, one cannot help but be surprised to see him credit himself with this new discovery, credit that could well be claimed by his rival Ramirez de Carrion. This congenitally deaf man succeeded, in the judgment of the critics of the time, in an experiment with Emmanuel Philibert, the deaf prince of Carignan; Ramirez de Carrion proved no less skillful at teaching the reading and pronunciation of a few words. His book, published nine years after Bonet's, bore the title *Maravillas de naturaleza, en que se contienen dos mil secretos de cosas naturales,* 1629 [*The Wonders of Nature, Containing Two Thousand Secrets of Natural Things*].

At about the same time, another Spaniard, Pedro de Castro, chief physician to the duke of Mantua, established a reputation with his successful education of the deaf son of Prince Thomas of Savoy.

John Wallis, one of the famous professors at Oxford, was the first Englishman to devote himself to this humanitarian task. He surpassed his predecessors in pedagogic skill as well as in soundness of judgment. Although his work in articulation met with complete success, and his *Treatise on Speech and the Formation of Sounds* (*Grammatica Linguae Anglicanae*) received the approbation of the most enlightened scholars, he was quick to perceive that its resources for the deaf persons in his care were very feeble compared with those contained in the language of gestures. In his letter to Dr. Beverly (in the third volume of Wallis's mathematical works, *Philosophical Transactions of London,* October, 1698), he writes:

"And this [articulation training] is indeed the shorter work of the two (however looked upon as the most stupendous). But this, without the other, would be of little use. For to pronounce words only as a parrot, without knowing what they signify, would do us but little service."

So he wisely adopted signs as his point of departure.

It may be objected that by "signs" Wallis must have meant mere alphabetic letters or finger movements. I know no better way to refute this specious objection than by reporting the actual terms he uses in the same letter. "By writing first to the deaf and then explaining it to them by corresponding sentences in sign, we give them a clear understanding of simple propositions." So it is not with the manual alphabet that we explain sentences, supposedly without mimic signs otherwise known as gestures. Further on, I will have occasion to elaborate on this important question.

For the moment I shall only cite the procedures of John Bulwer, who in 1648 published his *Philosopher* or *The Friend of the Deaf*; those of William Holder, rector of Blechington; and of other Englishmen, Digby and Gregory. All these men had as their goal teaching by means of speech.

But first I must briefly draw your attention to the work of the Dutchman Van Helmont and in particular to the work of the Swiss physician Conrad Amman, who lived in Amsterdam.

Van Helmont's efforts amount to describing the mechanism of the vocal apparatus and applying Hebrew to pronunciation. He believed that only Hebrew produced the intended results. His conviction got all its force from the creation of this language directly by God Himself.

Amman's works enjoyed a good deal of acclaim; and in 1700 a French teacher, Beauvais de Préau, thought he could perform a great patriotic service by presenting his countrymen with a translation of Amman's *Dissertation on Speech*, which complements his *Surdus Loquens* published in 1692. The clarity and simplicity of Amman's procedures were so widely recognized that you soon see the abbé de l'Epée himself apply, with an alacrity that does credit to his enlightenment, Amman's principles to teaching spoken French.

Germany, which has its humanitarians as well as scholars, is pleased to count among them Kerger, who pursued this sacred mission with a zeal worthy of his talent, and who appeared to prefer pantomime to any other method of communication between the deaf; Georges Raphael, who, confining himself almost exclusively to artificial speech, raised his three deaf daughters himself, and whose soul found its greatest solace in misfortune by sharing the secret of his art with parents whom fate had treated as brutally as himself; Othon-Benjamin Lasius, clergyman at Burgdoff in the principality of Zell; and especially Pastor Arnoldi, as commendable for his high-mindedness as for his evangelical charity. Though from all appearances an advocate of the use of drawings in deaf education, Arnoldi still insisted on mimic language to facilitate the teacher's work and to ensure the pupil's success. Published in 1777, his book contains wise advice, useful instructions, and accurate observations about the natural inclinations of the deaf. Still, I think that no one will contradict me when I say that Germany would have placed in even greater esteem the Saxon Heinicke, director of the Leipzig School for the Deaf, founded in 1778 by the Elector, had Heinicke known how to do justice to an upright character while applying the stringent judgment required in such a serious issue [that is, had Heinicke been more moderate in his attack on Epée, whom he called "weak in the head"].

We come to the French teachers. There are some whose books warrant reflection on procedures and results. The more thought we devote to these works, the more impressive and productive they will appear, but they also clearly reveal what still remains to be done to complete the great train of thought delivering the deaf from the deep night in which they have been struggling for many long centuries. We see that until the advent of the abbé de l'Epée, the various teachers, Frenchmen and foreigners alike, who more or less happily succeeded each other, all strayed far from this goal, and that the honors accumulated since Epée must all be set at his feet, as rightfully belonging to him alone.

And it is here that we may criticize France, this classically progressive country, for trailing so far behind other countries in the development of this so eminently restorative art. It was only in the middle of the eighteenth century that Father Vanin, priest of the Christian Doctrine, and Madame de Sainte-Rose, sister of the Cross of the Faubourg Saint-Antoine, established this new charitable venture, one with drawings of scenes from sacred history, the other with the help of the manual alphabet and natural signs.

In Cadiz, a Portuguese Jew named Jacob Rodriguez Pereire had opened a school for the deaf which was unable to sustain itself for lack of funds. He came to Paris, that refuge for all anxious, pressured minds, and crediting himself for being the first person to demonstrate the art of teaching the deaf to speak, he presented on 7 June 1750 at the Academy of Sciences, through the mediation of the celebrated La Condamine, his first student, young d'Azy d'Etavigny. The patronage of the academy confirmed him in the usurped title of inventor of this art. Some months later, under the auspices of his protector the duke of Chaulnes, Pereire introduced d'Azy d'Etavigny to King Louis XV and the dauphin, and the next day to the royal ladies of France. The king used signs and writing to ask Azy questions about natural history. Satisfied with the deaf man's answers, the king granted Pereire an allowance of 800 francs, independent of his title of interpreter-secretary for the language of the deaf.

Another deaf person, raised by M. Lucas, architectural engineer at Ganges, and afterward by Pereire ("complete proof... a living example," said the abbé de l'Epée, "of the capacities of an intelligence denuded of the precious organs of speech and hearing"), the twenty-year-old Saboureux de Fontenay, was presented by Fréron to the king of Poland, duke of Lorraine and of Bar.

But what means did Pereire use to reach his goal? Beware of questioning him about this, for he will not reply. He obstinately refuses to make his methods public, or rather he offers to sell the government his secret for a huge sum, and also requires that it die with him. We have only one paper of Pereire's (read to the Academy of Sciences, on 11 June 1749). Now what does this paper teach us that is new, striking, or unique? Nothing that we have not already learned from his predecessors. But if it is still possible to make some inference from a letter by his putative student Saboureux de Fontenay (I say "putative" for I agree with the abbé de l'Epée who thinks that Saboureux owed the astonishing range of his knowledge just to reading), reading, writing, and dactylology (the Greek name used by Pereire to refer to fingerspelling) combine in the teacher's system which treats pantomime as an "impoverished foreigner."

The fact that Pereire enriched his manual alphabet with signs indicating the pronunciation of words and variations of intonations does not, as he wished to persuade Saboureux, constitute a method; it is an exercise, or rather a game for the fingers, which means nothing to someone with no understanding of the spoken language.

Some years after Pereire, Ernaud, who had made similar claims, received the same authorization and title from the Academy of Sciences which had admitted him to set forth the principles of his method. Nevertheless, the two rivals' subterfuge was soon uncovered. It was formally proven that they had shamelessly plagiarized from their predecessors of the previous century, Wallis, Bonet, and Amman. Even these three were not the first to unchain the tongue of the deaf. This honor dates back earlier. It is due to Pedro de Ponce. This is confirmed by his friend Francisco Vallès in chapter 3 of his *Philosophia sacra*, Ambrosio de Morales in his book *Las antigüedades de España*, and above all by the chronicler Yepès. We find further proof of it in Pedro de Ponce's notice on building a chapel (24 August 1578), and in the following extract from the monastery archives: "*Obdormivit in Domino frater Petrus de Ponce, hujus domus benefactor, qui, inter caeteras virtutes quae in illo maximè fuerunt, in hâc praecipuè floruit et celeberrimus toto orbe fuit, scilicet, mutos loqui docendi. Obiit anno 1584, in mense augusti*" [Asleep in the Lord, brother Pedro Ponce, benefactor of this house, who, amongst other virtues, which he possessed in a high degree, excelled chiefly in one that is held in the greatest estimation by the whole world, to wit, teaching the dumb to speak. He died in the month of August in 1584].

How does Ernaud differ from his rival? He rejects fingerspelling and adopts the labial and guttural alphabets.

Jacob Rodriguez Pereire and his followers, on the other hand, proposed fingerspelling as the one true way "to reach the deaf person's intelligence through his eyes as we reach other men through their ears." Fingerspelling, however, consists merely in doing with the fingers of one hand what speaking children in our schools do with two hands when they wish to talk to each other from one side of the classroom to the other without making any noise. Is this, in fact, a genuine art? Isn't it rather, as the abbé de l'Epée so clearly demonstrated, a crude mechanism, a rote procedure without life or scope. Nonetheless, Epée does recognize a real advantage in fingerspelling—it is a means of exchanging the ideas we want to express to our peers, but only when no other channel of communication is available.

Fingerspelling is helpful, for example, in dictating the proper name of a city, person, or the like, to our pupils when the good or bad quality (the attribute represented by the proper name) is still unfamiliar, and also in conveying unfamiliar technical words.

It will be recalled that we defined the labial alphabet as lipreading. Here is what M. de Gérando tells us about it in his *Education of the Deaf* (vol. 1, chap. 12, pp. 262-263): "Wallis in the *Philosophical Transactions*, number 313, relates that a brother and sister, both deafened in childhood and living in the same town as he, could from lip movements understand everything said to them, and answer appropriately." Bishop Burnet tells a similar tale about the daughter (deafened at two) of M. Goddy, a minister at Geneva (Burnet, Letter 4, p. 248).

"The world," says the celebrated Lecat, "is full of deaf people whom we can get to understand what we want. In 1700 there was a tradeswoman in Amiens who could understand anyone merely by looking at his or her lip movements; this way she entered into extended conversations. These conversations were less tiring than others, for there was no need to make speech sounds; it was sufficient to move the lips as in speaking" (Lecat, *Traité des sensations*, Vol. 1, p. 295).

The function of lipreading is, as we have observed, limited to the mechanical arrangement of the various parts and movements of the vocal organs to produce certain sounds, making each distinct. I would emphasize this last means of communication, not because I attach any great importance to it but because I am trying to make your judgment better informed. Whatever utility a guttural alphabet has for any deaf person, if it is not seconded by a more certain indicator, namely the ear, the pupil using it will always confuse intonations and articulations unless he is near some hearing person who can correct him.

Nevertheless, whatever justified criticisms we make of the two plagiarists Pereire and Ernaud, we must grant them that they made the most of their labors.

Eventually, the abbé de l'Epée appeared and, completing their defeat, produced his methodical signs. We should note, however, that at the beginning of Epée's life's work Pereire and Ernaud were quite unknown to him. Well, who could doubt the honesty of the pious ecclesiastic, who was too modest to lie to the public and too candid to lie to his conscience! Pereire had it announced in the papers that he would refute his antagonist's charges. Pereire did nothing, and the field of battle remained entirely with the victor. Later on, in Pereire's presence, Epée used methodical signs to dictate to a pupil the first five or six pages of a document that Pereire had sent him as a test: "Enough, enough, sir!" interrupted Pereire, "What I am seeing overturns all my ideas. Do you have as many signs as the Chinese have characters?"

The scope of my subject here is too narrow to treat the number of characters in the Chinese language. All I can say about the language of gestures is that, even today, few speaking people have a precise idea of what the language and its special genius consist of. Far simpler than is commonly supposed, it has a small number of constituents in an infinite number of combinations, and it is enlivened by the play of the physiognomy. It has everything required to represent all the ideas crowding into the mind and all the affections stirring the heart. In short, it alone combines the simplicity and universality of mathematics, the most perfect of all the sciences, with its ten numerals. What Quintilian and several other famous ancient writers of antiquity tell us cannot give an adequate idea of the immense resources contained in mimicry, that language of such utility for whoever has mastered it. First, we may appropriately consider it from two different viewpoints, as an instrument and as an art: as an instrument, it requires flexibility, freedom, and a grace acquired only through practice beginning in childhood. As an art, it requires life-long study. To be successful at it, one needs more than simple inspiration or the movements of the soul; one needs above all to delve into poetry, history, philosophy, and a thousand other sciences. This was recognized by Lucius and Cassiodorus, impressive authorities on this serious matter. So let us hasten to proclaim that few teachers of the deaf understand mimicry as they should: some regard it as a frivolous trifle, others—relegating it below other means of communication—mercilessly reject it as an obstacle to artistic and scientific progress.

We are far from claiming that mimicry has been exploited to its furthest limits! But to reach this extreme, it needs merely the combined efforts of all people with a direct stake in it. Yet given the different views of teachers in various schools for the deaf, and the general indifference encountered by the hard-working scholars devoted to this education (which is thought to be so limited and is not), how can we reach the goal without getting the mimic signs on paper, as has been done with arithmetical and algebraic signs? This is not impossible, but does pose some problems. Signs taken from the nature of objects, their customary uses, and their manner of being differ from one part of the globe to another. But as the principles of the language of action are unchanging and impervious to human whim, we have merely to give special characters to each arm or face movement. Surely this interesting work will, sooner or later, stimulate a general competition of essays and investigations, throwing a powerful light on the study of human understanding as well as on a host of questions hitherto regarded as insuperably difficult.

The *Mimography*, written by my poor friend the former *censeur* of the Royal Institute of Paris, M. Bébian, whose recent loss is mourned by the deaf, seems to portend the goal toward which all we teachers of the deaf are heading. For many years I myself have been mining this land which covers a rich lode, and perhaps I am on the verge of the discovery of a precious vein that will reward me for all my labors.

But, gentlemen, before turning exclusively to the abbé de l'Epée, that immortal genius for whom heavenly glory is reserved because of his overthrow of all the ancient system, allow me to say a word about another French teacher, the abbé Deschamps, chaplain of the church of Orléans, although his *Elementary Course of Education for the Deaf* was published some five years after Epée's *Instruction of the Deaf by Means of Methodical Signs*. This discussion will lead me directly to Epée's book with which, faithful to the program you have stipulated, I shall conclude this paper which, to my great regret, may be unworthy of your attention.

First, let us speak freely, the abbé Deschamps's book is merely the more or less felicitous application of the methods of his predecessors, and I find it hard to understand how someone so perspicacious can display such puzzling obstinacy in denying the value of Epée's discovery. Deschamps's fixed and unshakeable idea is that, as pupils are learning to pronounce words, they must "be adding to the sum of their ideas, correcting them, and combining them as do developing normal children." This idea soon met with a judicious critic and formidable opponent in the person of the deaf Desloges, a poor bookbinder-paperhanger and self-styled student of pantomime, which he learned from a congenitally deaf, illiterate Italian manservant to a writer for the Italian Comedy. As soon as it appeared, Desloges's *Observations of a Deaf Person* was in vogue. Here is how he himself tells his story (Preface, p. 7 and following): "For a long time I was unaware of sign language, and my few signs were scattered, isolated, unconnected. I did not know the art of combining them to form distinct pictures with which to represent ideas, communicate to others, and converse in sustained, connected discourse." I also cannot resist the urge to cite a passage from a letter from this deaf laborer to the editor of Bouillon's *Journal encyclopédique*:

Several people seem surprised that I have called myself a strange writer of a unique kind. They are unaware that no writer has ever been in the same situation as I. Let you, gentlemen, be the judges. Deaf from the age of seven, left to myself and without education from the time that I could read and write a little, I came to Paris at the age of twenty-one, and entered into an apprenticeship against the advice and wishes of my parents who judged me incapable of learning anything. Obliged to look for work in order to subsist, without support or protection or resources, twice reduced to the poorhouse for lack of work, I was forced into constant struggle against poverty, prejudice, insult, the cruelest teasing from parents, friends, neighbors, and coworkers who called me an animal, an idiot, a madman who claims to be rational and more intelligent than they but who will someday be committed to the Petites-Maisons—this, gentlemen, is the situation of the strange deaf author; these are the encouragements, the counsels he received. It is in these circumstances—tools in one hand, a pen in the other—with which he composed these observations, etc., etc., etc.

But let us return to the abbé Deschamps, and note his error in limiting the first phase of teaching to pronunciation and relegating mimicry to the final one. In my opinion, the reverse procedure would be more reasonable, for will not the deaf person's a priori instruction through articulation resemble that of a parrot so long as mimicry is not brought into play? But this last method can be conveniently foregone only if we are certain that the pupil's education is far enough advanced that he can understand the meaning of unfamiliar words.

The most noteworthy feature of the abbé Deschamps's paper is the attempted extension of his treatment to include the congenitally blind and the blind and deaf—the first study, we are assured, to have laid out the principle of books printed in relief for use with both these groups in teaching reading.

But, gentlemen, I can imagine your justified impatience, and I would be guilty if I delayed your satisfaction any further. You are eager to follow your illustrious compatriot, the abbé de l'Epée, throughout his arduous career, from the day that his genius, lit by the torch of charity, came to give a new life to outcasts regarded by the world with fear to the day when, reaching his journey's end, his unsteady hands let go of the task that in the future was not always entrusted to hands as skilled and well-intentioned.

The great Epée was condemned for life to carry out the humble duties of the deaconship with no hope of reaching the priesthood, which made him vulnerable to persecution by the envious, and that was because his conscience forbade him to approve the *formulaire* a profession of a certain faith decreed by the clergy's General Assembly in 1655 following quarrels between the Molinists and the Jansenists—a *formulaire* he was required to sign according to the prevailing custom in the diocese of Paris when at seventeen he presented himself to receive holy orders.

But the impenetrable design of heaven reserves a sweet consolation for the virtuous soul: it silently prepares suitable fuel for the flame of charity that sets the soul aglow. One day chance, or rather an invisible hand, leads the abbé de l'Epée to the home of two twin sisters whom he finds at their needlework. Their mother is out. He speaks to them, but their eyes remain fixed on their work. He questions them softly—both remain silent. Eventually, the mother arrives and explains all: the two young women have been deaf from birth and Father Vanin, who had begun their education, has just died. Touched by the spectacle of this distressing fate, Epée conceives the idea of completing this beneficent task. He longs to fling himself into an unknown career, one bristling perhaps with insuperable problems, for the good priest, hitherto devoted to other works, has no idea that anyone except Father Vanin had ever undertaken to educate the deaf. He is unacquainted with the investigations of Pedro de Ponce or with the theories of Wallis or of Conrad Amman. But some supernatural instinct revealed to him the secret that helped him repair nature's injustice, restoring its victims to civic rights and human prerogatives. He creates a new method which invalidates all the previous so-called methods and refutes the persistent attacks of envy and incredulity. The alacrity with which his method was adopted in the vast majority of schools for the deaf attests to the superiority of Epée's work.

Until then, as I have just explained, all educators of the deaf interpreted the principle that "our mind contains nothing that did not get there by way of the senses" as meaning that their only job was to give these unfortunates the mechanical use of speech. To the contrary, Epée was the first to espy in their still-imperfect mimic language a surer, quicker, simpler means of communication and a more direct and therefore clearer translation of thought. And he made hidden treasures spring forth—truth, flexibility, the richness of an idiom that belongs to all nations, indeed to all mankind, an idiom that admirably resolves the problem of a universal language which scholars everywhere have sought for centuries in vain.

From the simple argument that the deaf can be educated with the help of gestures the way we educate other people with the sounds of the voice, and that both groups can master written language, the indefatigable Epée brought forth a new world, a whole generation. One man's wisdom brought the art of speaking with fingers and arms, of hearing with the eyes, so far that, unaided, he brought to fruition the most perfect and well-ordered system of intellectual and moral emancipation. O, it is here or never that we can join with Horace in exclaiming: "Our heart by a tale is much less affected / Than our eyes by a true picture presented."

And would it be believed that there were in France persons with enough animosity against their homeland to contest the credit to a fellow Frenchman for constructing the most beautiful human language, and also to maintain that the credit for this revival rightfully belongs to Pedro de Ponce? But all will be explained. We hasten to announce that after an extensive search the precious manuscript of Ponce's work was found, thanks to the initiatives of the learned Ramon de Sagra, who was consulted on this matter by the baron De Gérando, an administrator at the Royal Institute for the Deaf of Paris.

Before the abbé de l'Epée, everything possible for the deaf was thought to be done by teaching them the mechanical movements of the tongue and putting the vocal organs into play. But the deaf person wished, in addition, to combine his ideas with art and to express himself with order. In his eyes, nothing proved better the importance of method at the beginning of the deaf person's education than the innumerable errors constantly made by hearing people in speaking or in writing, as a consequence of the lifelong lack of reflection about their native language. So Epée endeavored to teach his pupils to distinguish the persons, numbers, tenses, and modes of French verbs, and to understand their objects as well as the cases, numbers, and genders of nouns, adjectives, and pronouns; and finally, the differences between adverbs, prepositions, and conjunctions. It was not enough to give the pupil a method; he also needed a dictionary with an exact definition for every term and the correct expression for every particular idea. In publishing his *Instruction of the Deaf by Methodical Signs* and eight years later his *True Manner of Instructing the Deaf, Confirmed by Long Experience*, Epée had anticipated a universal wish. As for the eagerly awaited dictionary, the idea had at first intimidated him as unfeasible. Nevertheless, once judicious examination suggested that the project would merely require one voluminous book, Epée soon realized that he had to expunge a host of words that would be of no value in the education of the deaf. (In this regard Epée confesses with his habitual simplicity that if many a scholar is ignorant of some three thousand words, he himself is ignorant of an even greater number.) So he set energetically to work, less for the sake of the deaf than for the sake of the teachers to be trained; for in all his lessons, he says, he was himself the living dictionary that explained the meaning of the words.

What powerful, original, active, tenacious genius this humble priest must have been gifted with to reach so high after starting so low! From the beginning of the world's existence many sublime truths have been sleeping unknown, buried deep in the womb of nature; there are, moreover, truths that man roots out but abandons as soon as they are proclaimed, for they resemble those will-o'-the wisps that lead the traveler astray. Thus Descartes and after him Leibniz encouraged the world of learning to hope for a universal language, but both philosophers died before realizing this magnificent promise. There eventually appeared the modest teacher of the deaf who told a startled France: "The universal language that your scholars have sought for in vain and of which they have despaired, is here: it is right before your eyes, it is the mimicry of the impoverished deaf. Because you do not know it, you hold it in contempt, yet it alone will provide you with the key to all languages; it is still indigent, forsaken, dressed in rags; well, we can purify it, embellish it, enrich it. Our methodical signs will reveal what they can do in practiced hands." And we saw Epée first revive the ancient pantomime whose wonders had been consigned to the domain of myths. Certainly, this great work of reconstruction was not accomplished without forceful attacks by theologians, philosophers, academicians from all countries who maintained that representational signs would not help to get metaphysical ideas into the mind of the deaf person. Epée could prove to his opponents that an idea is no more intimately bound up with the sounds of speech than with the written word, and that the only thing required to activate the idea in the brain is an intermediary stimulating the eyes or indicating the meaning of the word.

Wishing to convince as many people as possible, Epée often opened his classes to the public. Among his outstanding pupils was one Clément de la Pujade whom he had trained to render in a clear and intelligible voice a five-and-a-half page discourse in Latin, and to participate in a discussion about the definition of philosophy. There was also a deaf girl present who recited the whole of the twenty-third chapter of the *Gospel According to Saint Matthew*, and who used to say with her teacher the office of Prime every Sunday.

On leaving these exercises, the academicians unanimously exclaimed: "I would not have believed the detail gone into; I had to see for myself to be persuaded." But how regrettable it is for the glory of this sublime teacher, and especially for the good of humanity, that he did not also know how to implement his clear and carefully elaborated principles of rational education. How much more rapid and complete the progress of the deaf would have been if his demonstration had kept abreast of the theorem! The human mind has unfortunately its limits and its first guides are destined not to accompany it into the Promised Land.

To translate French words, Epée looked up derivations from Latin and Greek; he tried to contort the language of gestures, bending it to the habits and genius of conventional language without realizing that one language grafted onto another necessarily becomes a mistranslation. Mimicry recognizes no master other than nature and reason; its syntax is fixed, as opposed to the changeable syntaxes of spoken languages, particularly the syntax of French. The mimic performance is quite independent of grammatical rules; it soars as quickly as thought. Epée had no idea of the range of the instrument he had created. To cite only a few examples from a thousand possible ones, here is his analysis of the words *satisfaire, introduire,* and *intelligence.*The sign *satisfaire,* he said, is made up of two Latin words, *facere* and *satis* (to do enough); *introduire* is made up of *ducere* and *intro* (to lead into); *intelligence* is taken from the Latin adverbs *intus* and the verb *legere* (to read into).

Hence the unfortunate deaf person had to be removed from his village and made to learn Latin before he could be taught French. But was it not whimsical, and profitless to the child, to choose the longest route to the urgent goal? That, unfortunately, is not the only error the abbé committed when it came to nomenclature. He was no luckier with grammar.

In teaching the use of articles, for example, he says:

We have the deaf person observe the joints of our fingers, hand, wrists, elbows, and so on, and we call them "articles" or joints. Then we write on the blackboard that *le, la, les, de, du* and *des* connect words the way that our joints connect our bones (grammarians will forgive the divergence of this definition from theirs), whereas the movement of the right index finger extending and bending several times in the shape of a hook becomes the methodical sign that we give to every article. We express gender by putting the hand on the hat for the masculine article *le,* and on the ear, where a woman's coiffure terminates, for the feminine article *la* (*The True Manner of Instructing the Deaf,* p. 18).

To give the general sign for grammatical case, Epée had the pupil roll one index finger over the other with a downward motion, that is, by lowering the hand from the first to the sixth position. Epée accompanied this rolling with the sign appropriate to the position of each case on the blackboard. The nominative case came first, the genitive second, the dative third, and so forth.

In addition, here is his explanation of the difference between the indefinite past, the definite past, the anterior past indefinite, past anterior definite. He made the sign of the first, the second, the third, and the fourth pasts, the past being expressed by bringing the hand to the shoulder.

First, don't these examples show that these signs are perfectly inconsistent with logic? Need it be pointed out that to distinguish between the different past tenses, the teacher should make the student appreciate the relations between the various temporal states expressed by modifications of the verb?

To pursue this grammatical controversy any further would take me too far away from my topic. But it reminds me of Diderot's observation about the congenitally deaf in his remarkable letter to the abbé Batteux concerning the latter's *Treatise on Imitation in the Fine Arts*: "We are never certain of making the congenitally deaf person understand the difference between the tenses of *je fis, j'ai fait, je faisais,* and so forth."

I prefer to leave the refutation of Diderot to people who have witnessed the lightning speed with which our children grasp these supposedly difficult distinctions, and apply them both appropriately and promptly.

In any case, the slight mistakes just noted in Epée's method are barely detectible stains, leaving untarnished the glory of his creative spirit. Do not his writings, apart from their firmly held beliefs, breathe that passion for the truth characteristic of the highest intellects? Furthermore, is there a single chapter where Epée does not invoke the reader's help, where he does not entreat the reader to indicate whether he knows any better signs than the author's? How much more glory still blazes therein! We are no less impressed by the depth of his analyses than by the extreme clarity and attractive simplicity of his diction. His style has an ineffable earnestness akin to virtue, and his is the eloquence of charity. He does not dazzle with the false brilliance assumed by ignorance and charlatanism in order to deceive. The finishing touches to his genius are his naturalness, candor, and lack of guile. So why should we be surprised to see the humble priest use such great and powerful arguments to silence his detractors, and to convert the merely curious into believers in his method? Why such amazement at the sight of the modest conqueror dragging in his wake myriad imitators from all nations, including powerful sovereigns desiring to make their deaf subjects enjoy the treasures of education that the burgeoning school of Paris will soon distribute liberally to all the deaf of France?

We have seen that Epée's system (the only one employed in the classroom) consists in getting the sign framed by the word rather than by the idea. This was also the abbé Sicard's system, as well as that of all his disciples with the exception of M. Bébian. After publishing two papers on the art of educating the deaf, abbé Sicard presented the public with his *Course of Instruction for a Deaf Person*, which became immensely popular. Let us attempt to judge it without prejudice or partiality.

The imagination, we must confess, becomes apprehensive on seeing only a wearisome amplification, to say the least, of the teacher's points, apart from a host of procedures that are no doubt ingenious, but that reveal the facility of a systematic mind maneuvering at the expense of cold reason. It is pointless to ask why Sicard divided his book into twenty-five "methods of communication"; in vain do we wonder why he put the fifteenth method, "On tense: Divisions made, Notions of the world system," before the sixteenth, a discussion of adverbs. Sicard says that the celebrated Massieu had to know the twelve signs of the zodiac before he could use the word "today," which Sicard calls an adverb (or an ellipsis for the prepositional phrase beginning with *dans*). Here is an example of Sicard's explanation of the adverb *aujourd'hui* [as used in the sentence]: "In the daylight of the current day, the sun is in the sign of the ram."

> *Dans le jour de le jour présent.*
> *À le jour de jour présent.*
> *Au jour de jour hui.*
> *Au jour de hui.*
> *Aujour d'hui.*

Do you want to know how he goes about explaining the word *comment*? He transforms it, he says, into *de quelle main* or *de quelle action de la main* or *de quelle manière*.

> *de* or *avec quel esprit*
> *de* or *avec quelle main* } *de quâ mente*
> *de* or *avec quelle manière*

> *de quâ mente*
> *de quo mente*
> *de co mente* } *comment*
> *de com mente*
> *com mente*

Doesn't this appear to be a long series of paraphrases designed to repel even the most intrepid mind?

And while we are on the topic, I shall report the comment of a superb teacher, M. Bébian, who gives the following characterization of Sicard's book: "It is a kind of philosophical novel written more for the entertainment of amateurs than for the instruction of teachers."

Sicard's *Theory of Signs as an Introduction to the Study of Languages* in two volumes (Volume I, 580 pages; Volume II, 650 pages), is no better. The author got the idea for it from Epée's dictionary. Except for a few minor changes, this dictionary is copied from Richelet's abridgment as corrected by Wailly. Sicard's untimely death prevented him from putting the final touches to it. The book is divided into several sections: physical objects, adjectives, abstract nouns, and so on. Dictation of the word *arbre* [tree] requires three signs: the first sign represents something set in the earth, the second one progressive growth and rising, the third one the branches coming out from a trunk and being stirred by the wind. For the word *professeur* [teacher] he makes: (1) the signs for a public or private room in a high school or institution; (2) the signs for grammar, logic, metaphysics, languages, arithmetic, geography, geometry, and the like; (3) the signs for the action of gathering young people together and speaking to them and teaching them publicly. What needless paraphrases these are when all that is needed to give full expression to the ideas is a single sign!

Be that as it may, the abbé Sicard's service has earned him a distinguished place among the most commendable teachers and true benefactors of humanity.

No one was capable of grasping the whole of Epée's thought and of making it fruitful. Eventually, the man appears. After silently devoting his whole youth to the study of the language of the deaf, M. Bébian rid the curriculum of all the excess intellectual baggage that merely slowed down the students' progress, and he brought teaching back to the simplicity and truth that Epée had never diverged from for an instant. Through much devoted effort, Bébian managed to dethrone the old method and restore more ingenious and truer methods to their rightful, primary role. Before Bébian's time, for instance, the signer resorted to finger shapes to indicate the initial letters of *temps* [time], *pendant* [while] and *durant* [during], and it was thought that this initialization enabled the deaf person to grasp the respective meanings of these expressions and the difference between them. But this was impossible; continuing such a puerile game from generation to generation was merely to perpetuate a deadly tradition. Replace it, as Bébian did, with a clear and precise demonstration with natural language, and corroborating this demonstration with practice—the greatest teacher of all—and you will be spared recurrent mistakes by your pupils, endless groping, and a great deal of lost time.

To prove that mimicry is no more similar to any instructional language than poetry is to geometry, I need only consider one point of comparison. My explanation proceeds by analogy, and I choose randomly two among many possible examples. The Latin *morem gerere alteri*, is translated literally as "carry the custom to another" instead of "defer to this person's wishes"; *Lacrymas dilectae pelle Creusoe,*—literally, "hunt the tears of the beloved Creuse"—really means "Hold back the tears you are shedding for your dear Creuse." Now, if we stuck to the literal translation, would we be shedding any new light on the matter? No, obviously not. So, with mimic syntax or expression, why not stick to the underlying meaning rather than the external form in the translation of, say, some figurative Latin expressions into another language, French for example? The need for clarity in translation requires the choice of an equivalent French expression, not a slavish copy of the original.

On the other hand, sign—which is more felicitous than any conventional language and more scrupulously faithful in reproducing the fleeting facial expressions of conventional language—lends itself with marvelous agility to the great variety of forms of discourse. It reflects thought whole, as in a mirror, with contours of the greatest delicacy; thought materializes itself there, so to speak; understandable from the start—visible, palpable, concrete—while even the richest languages constantly resort to borrowing to express particular ideas. Also, languages all leave it to the imagination to supply what they themselves lack and to embellish what they represent; like Aristotle's scale which explains each virtue by placing it between the two corresponding vices at each extreme—a scale whose lacunae were notable because, said Aristotle, "I should not be blamed if my tongue has fewer words for virtues than for vices." But if, like Chateaubriand,[8] we admit that "Christianity has solved the problem by revealing that virtues are virtues because they flow back toward their source, namely, God," the outcome will be just as decisive in favor of the language of gestures.

Despite my optimism, it may be objected that the present system of signs is still imperfect and that, both in the schools and outside them, a considerable number of false and inexact expressions still seem mysteriously to evade the fortunate prohibition of the old system of signs and continue to be preserved through ignorance. I agree. So we must condemn the casualness of certain teachers who tolerate these expressions, for it is now widely recognized that the rightness of signs creates the rightness of ideas, and that the rightness of ideas has the same influence on the rightness of signs. Nevertheless, it will take the authority of some enlightened teacher to efface the remaining vestiges of barbarism. Who knows whether this beneficial innovation will not sooner or later be adopted by other schools, in France or abroad? The triumph of logic is inevitable in the near future.

It will be the teacher's role to make an accurate collection of the various signs, with the false ones corrected. It is also up to the teacher gradually to lead the pupil to take the new ideas suggested by usage, and to recast them in new signs. The deaf person's spontaneous association of ideas and signs will unfailingly produce a situation similar to that of the hearing child who always gets pleasure and instruction from the happy and frequent convergence of circumstances, in lively scenes from human life, and in the moving spectacle of nature. However—and this is a generally recognized truth—the abbé de l'Epée's method is superior to all others because it teaches one to think correctly, to express ideas as they occur in the mind, and to consider all possible aspects of thought. This is the method of reason—the method of the most celebrated philosophers who constantly expostulated against the bad practices that keep children going from words to ideas instead of going from ideas to words, and contenting themselves with the "approximately" which, leaving minds in suspense, often barely allows them to reach agreement, still less to understand each other.

The deaf child differs from normal children only in his lack of a sensory modality. His inferiority in this respect is also more apparent than real. His infirmity is less to blame than his isolation. His intelligence is dormant for want of exercise and communication. His impatient curiosity searches about for nourishment but, a veritable Tantalus, his hunger frequently goes unsatisfied. All the powers of his mind rebel against this imprisonment within the narrow sphere of sensations. As soon as the mind receives impressions, they depart like a dream. How, in fact, could impressions continue to exist if his mind has nothing to preserve or recall them? So the deaf person is flighty, inconsistent in his tastes (a widely held criticism and perhaps a shade excessive). But does he know that inconsistency does not bring happiness?

Provide then the deaf person with materials for his natural mental activity! You will soon see him in possession of that great intercourse of ideas brought about through the mediation of speech and its most beautiful product, the precious storehouse of knowledge. Analogy and reflection will do the rest for him. The more he develops his relations with other men, the more he will discover the hidden reasons for their actions and will also learn to appreciate and understand them. Thus he will naturally be drawn to study by himself, to reflect on the consequences of his behavior.

Does not the influence of sign language on the deaf person's intellectual development—as great an influence as speech sounds have on the hearing child's mind—reveal that he can be given a great deal of knowledge without the help of written language and that this knowledge can later serve to interpret spoken language? Later on, the written language records acquired ideas, puts them into methodical categories, and makes them more precise, thus lightening the burden they put on memory and giving the understanding new energy or at least giving it freer use of all the energy at its disposal.

On the other hand, one additional consideration will doubtless not have escaped you. The longer the pupil's faculties remain profoundly comatose, the more arduous the teacher's job becomes, and the greater care and perseverance are required to achieve this kind of metamorphosis. This is the price of success. But all the time will be devoted in vain and your sacrifices will increase if you have not previously acquired the habit of reading deeply into your pupil's soul and mind and of penetrating the recesses of his innermost feelings. This close examination must invariably lead you to the discovery of a germ of independence in him which, cultivated, will produce ample fruit, for he will always ally himself with the controlling authority, provided that it is neither illegitimate nor tyrannical and, most important, provided that he sees it only as superior knowledge and a legitimate resource exercised with moderation and firmness. Act so that the yoke of obedience never seems heavy. Lighten it with good temper and you will gain his affection and confidence. He will soon seek out his teacher and benefactor all the more eagerly, as the deaf person is more sensitive than the normal child to scorn and inhumanity. When he espies a threatening countenance, he runs trembling for refuge in the arms of a dear one. And do you still refuse to credit him with even rudimentary reasoning ability? You agree that the hearing child frequently thinks, judges, and acts without reflecting, but you create a separate category for the deaf child! Oh, to realize your error, merely contemplate the deaf child when the teacher cannot yield to one of his desires, when the teacher is obliged to frustrate him, and you will see how cunning the child can be, inventing a thousand schemes to get what he wants!

And if we now consider him left to himself, unrestrainedly grabbing whatever pleases his disordered appetites, without a shield against bad examples and brute passions, oh, what a sorry and fearful spectacle he presents! Who will teach him to shun the chance to do evil? Who will teach him to resist the temptation to break the law he does not know about? In vain will justice spread before him the staggering profusion of repressive forces with which society arms him for his own defense; jealousy, hate, and fury will wrangle in his tender soul and be reflected with a savage energy in his features. Will society be endangered because the passions of this brutal son of nature have been unleashed? Who will check his terrible inclinations, who will arrest and prevent the deplorable consequences? Only education has the right and the power to work this miracle. Education will refine his manners and enhance his soul's dispositions; it will extend his intellectual horizons. Enriched with the same blessings, his relations with his peers and with hearing people will complete what education began. He will have a fuller appreciation of the meaning of virtue, and of the vileness of an action against nature, against wisdom; he will gain a greater conviction that life in society must be the constant application of universal morality, and that any infraction of its laws is a crime before God and man. These are the benefits that the deaf person will gain in our yearly banquets perpetuating the memory of our intellectual father's birth and in the monthly meetings of the Central Society of the Deaf of Paris.

Let us pause here. It would not become us, the founders of this society and of its sacred olympiads, to describe the extraordinary revolution that they have brought about in the habits of our poor brothers and to point out the progress of the civilization to which they are admittedly indebted. Has not all of France seen the deaf suddenly break, scarcely a few years ago, the chains in which the most squalid quackery had pitilessly sworn to bind them? They are no longer beasts of burden, these pariahs condemned to serve as a plaything or doormat to charlatanism: they are citizens and human beings worthy of the foremost nation in the world and the great family of Christ. There they are, understanding the close ties of community, wholeheartedly dedicating themselves to its duties, ardently plunging into literary, scientific, artistic, and industrial professions with no other goal than the general good and the glory of France. Is this not the best rebuttal to the constant accusations of people too lazy and superficial to get to the bottom of things or so intent on prolonging old abuses that they tremble at the breaking of each link in the huge chain of the old slavery?

The preceding suggests that we must take the greatest possible care in the selection of a teacher for the deaf. As I have suggested, the most important qualifications are a perfect knowledge of, and extensive practice with, the language of action. Unfortunately, it must be confessed, the people long entrusted with the fate of the Royal Institution of Paris have not always understood this. The position of the deaf instructors has sometimes been inequitable, and too often it has been forgotten that with equal justice they perhaps had the right to equal consideration.

Forgive me, gentlemen, for this digression. I wanted to give, as best I could, an idea of the deaf person's natural language. There still remains another topic to discuss, speech. I must determine its importance in instruction and its potentiality for fostering intellectual development.

First, we should note that speech, like lipreading, is merely an adjunct, say the first-rate teachers, suitably used only with great caution and appropriate only for training pupils judged to have an aptitude for it, taking care not to impose it on every one or, above all, not to force it on pupils with an unconquerable aversion to the task.

If, however, as certain instructors have claimed, the education of the deaf reduces to articulation, lipreading, or even fingerspelling, we could only begin to teach them a subject, arithmetic for example, when they had made sufficient progress in the study of spoken language to understand explanations given orally. Tell me now, how many final-year students can grasp an arithmetical proof with only the aid of writing! Possibly not a single one. So what would happen if we had to resort to artificial speech? Lipreading is merely a kind of guessing in which the meaning of the visible syllables helps one decipher, to supply, or to guess, what remains out of sight. Far from leading directly to the interpretation of thought, lipreading constantly needs to be interpreted by thought. It can serve as a memory device for predictable phrases in everyday conversation; but it will never be a medium of regular instruction or of the cumulative elaboration of ideas. In vain do we fight the force of truth; we end up yielding to evident certainty and dropping a once-promising instructional system that threatens regression to the cradle.

What is the source of this tenacity that resists both the voice of reason and the lessons of experience? I cannot and must not accuse only the ancient predilection to give speech the leading role in mental development. This has been and will long be the major obstacle to progress in the education of the deaf. People readily grant that our students have no trouble discriminating a tree, a house, a cow, a horse, food pleasing to their palates from substances repugnant to their senses of smell and taste, the person affectionately making them welcome from the person harshly spurning them with disdain; they now dispute the abbé Sicard's assertion ranking the deaf person beneath the lower animals, which even denies him any filial affection. They may grant that deafness does not extinguish every spark of intelligence or nuance of tenderness. Some people would even ascribe to the deaf person a feeble notion of private property. But do not talk to them about abstract ideas acquired without speech or writing. If they deign to respond to this philosophical heresy, it will be to demolish you with some long words from metaphysics. Then they majestically cloak themselves in clouds of aphorisms, and that's that.

Indeed, open any book concerned with the education of the deaf (either directly or indirectly) and you will find much the same prejudices concerning the impossibility of acquiring abstract ideas without the help of speech. I have yet to come across a single hearing person who in a discussion of this topic (and what hearing person can resist the itch to get in a word on it?) did not from the beginning throw these big words in my face. So I have often gone looking for this fearful monster who troubles all minds and, to my shame, I confess that I have discovered nothing. The words "abstract ideas" conceal some mystery that my feeble understanding cannot discern; foiled in my search, I must conclude that it is merely an unreal ghost that the imagination creates and then becomes alarmed about. But this is no place to undertake a discussion of metaphysics.

Nevertheless, let us observe that in dealing with the deaf from rural areas, we can and must treat the matter of articulation from a different point of view. Education has not yet made its way into the country cottage. For the most part, the poverty-stricken deaf are born of parents who cannot read or write. So to a degree these deaf people will find it useful to know how to make themselves understood with their voices. Let them not fear to speak in laborious and disagreeable sounds; let them not even fear the hoarse grunts coming from their chests! The field worker's ear is less delicate than the city dweller's.

But it will be objected that some deaf people manage to articulate intelligibly. Doesn't that simple fact invalidate my argument? Yes, I would even grant that some deaf speakers can make themselves understood, even in extended discourse. All the same, I beg you to place these children next to someone unaccustomed to their sham speech: will you then dare to maintain that the sounds they make are as distinct to this stranger as to the persons used to hearing them?

No one believes that the deaf person finds it far harder to articulate than to read lips, for human curiosity is such a powerful incentive! To guess a word or phrase it is often enough to perceive the first or second syllable of the word or even just the beginning of the phrase. Thus the abbé de l'Epée took care to suggest that observers stand to one side if they wanted their speech not to be understood by the deaf person.

Epée owed the use of this new method to a strange circumstance. In his classes one day, a stranger presented him with a book in Spanish, assuring him that if he decided to buy it, he would be rendering the bearer a great service. The abbé, who understood no Spanish, at first refused; but on opening the book at random and casting his eye on the Spanish manual alphabet in copper-plate engraving, consented to purchase it. Imagine his surprise at seeing on the first page: *Arte para enseñar a hablar a los mudos*. He said, "I had little difficulty guessing that the title meant *the art of teaching the deaf to speak*, and immediately resolved to learn Spanish so that I could render this service to my pupils."

As Epée gladly and publicly gave credit for this treatise to Juan Pablo Bonet, one of his assistants told him of a very good book in Latin on the same subject written by Conrad Amman, entitled *Dissertatio de loquelâ surdorum et mutorum*. Epée made sure to profit from this tip, and he knew how to make such good use of the treasures collected through the experience of his two predecessors ("mentors" he liked to call them) that his own treatise became in turn the cicerone of teachers in France. By universal admission, Epée's precision and clarity leaves nothing to be desired.

It remains for me, gentlemen, in fulfilling the last condition of your proposal, to indicate impartially the share of glory and gratitude that redounds to France and to the abbé de l'Epée, by judging, the documents in hand, the debate arising from the well- or ill-founded claims of other men or nations.

At about the same time as the debate, Epée's reputation rose to even greater heights because of challenges against him by some formidable adversaries. Heinicke, director of the Leipzig School for the Deaf, founded in 1778, dared to protest the unanimous public support given the French teacher. Like Pereire, Heinicke jealously concealed his teaching method from public knowledge. He was even more jealous of the many stunning successes obtained by the abbé' Storck's pupils who had learned with Epée's basic method. Heinicke tried, at the court in Vienna, to disparage Epée's basic principles and to get Epée's disciple to throw his lot in with Heinicke's school, claiming that none of the methods followed up to then compared to his. Informed about Heinicke's unjust acts, Epée addresses him directly, calls him to a gloves-off confrontation, and begins to elaborate his own theory. Rather than accepting the challenge, Heinicke shrouds himself in mystery. From this debate only a single response of his remains, while we do have the very lengthy ones of Epée. Further, Heinicke did not take on the question openly; he avoided controversy instead, taking refuge in his vanity as in an impregnable rampart. After writing grandiloquently to the abbé Storck that (1) vision cannot stand in for hearing, (2) abstract ideas cannot reach the minds of the deaf, even by means of written words supplemented by methodical signs (an opinion triumphantly refuted by Epée on the authority of his pupils' successes and his spectators' unanimous reports), Heinicke dares condemn his rival's method by pleading the need to teach speech before anything else.

Here is how he reasons: "Written or printed letters are like the footprints of flies or spiders; they lack a sufficiently simple or distinctive shape for our imagination to recall them in their absence; and when our mind has a distinct recollection of one letter separatd from the others, how is it possible that the mind clearly represents a whole word which often includes many letters? The deaf cannot think with these signs; and it is not in signs that objects materialize in their dreams."[9]

Against these objections, Epée sets the authority of experience; even better, he sets up Heinicke against himself. Finally, as truth-loving as he was eager to defend the theory that his conscience suggested was the best, Epée takes as arbiters the most respected learned societies of Europe; but all of them, frightened beforehand of the possible results of the debate, judge it fitting to withdraw into total silence; an exception was the Academy of Zurich which, devoting considerable time to this interesting question, decides in favor of Epée. The academy founds its judgment on the apparently equal suitability of methodical signs and speech as intermediaries between written words and ideas, because "signs represent objects as they are by imprinting the accurate image of them in the mind." The academy also solemnly recognizes with Epée, "that every word means something, and there is nothing that cannot be meant by one or more words, whether the thing is dependent on the senses or totally independent from them, and in every language scholars can analyze the meaning of any word by using just the number of other words needed to make clear what is not initially understood" (*True Manner of Instructing the Deaf*, chap. 14).

At about the same time, M. Nicolai, a member of the Academy of Berlin, who had observed a demonstration by the pupils of the Imperial Institution of Vienna, launched a violent attack on Epée's method. He had proposed to the abbé Storck to perform some act in front of a group of deaf persons, then to have them write a description of the act without his dictating the words for it. The challenge is accepted. Nicolai strikes his breast. The appointed pupil writes: "hand," "breast." Nicolai rises and leaves, convinced that the pivot on which all of Epée's method must revolve is the vocabulary of concrete objects, and in a Berlin newspaper Nicolai publishes a letter to this effect, reprinted by the *Journal de Paris*. Ever moderate, Epée addresses Nicolai a carefully written letter justifying his pupil's reaction, and sends another letter to the Academy of Berlin asking it to serve as judge between one of its members and himself. To improve his chances of getting a decision from this body of scholars, he solicits the mediation of Prince Henry who had observed his demonstrations in Paris.

The results? Inconclusive. Dispensing with a confrontation between the two opposing systems, the recorder Formey declared that it was up to experience to split the difference. To evade the question this way was to resolve it.

Furthermore, Epée's two letters were published in the *Journal de Paris* for 27 May 1785.

Let us frankly confess, however, that Nicolai's objection, based on the pupil's confusion in this decisive situation, still kept all its force, for Epée seemed to undertake more the training of the deaf people's memory than their judgment, witness his public demonstrations. Epée answered his critics by saying: "I understand Italian but I cannot write in it; the deaf understand French, for they translate it with signs, and that is enough for me."

Be that as it may, let us contrast those jealous and self-seeking criticisms with an impartial panegyric by another of Epée's antagonists. The abbé Deschamps says:

However little we reflect on the foundation of Epée's art, we will be amazed to see how much time, trouble, and labor he required to create this beautiful, methodical system; how extraordinarily diligent the search for signs to serve as roots or derivations or endings. Abstract ideas, like the ideas we form with sounds—everything is grist for the mill of sign language. The creation of a language that has reached such a high degree of perfection required the deepest meditation, the soundest judgment, and the sharpest imagination combined with a thorough grounding in grammar. Only a genius like Epée's could invent a sign language substitutable for speech, quickly and easily performed, and clear in its principles. This is the abbé de l'Epée's accomplishment, and it merits universal acclaim.

At about the same time, the philosopher Condillac set his weighty authority onto the scales.

From the language of action Epée has created a methodical, simple, and easy art with which he gives his pupils ideas of every kind, and I dare say ideas more precise than the ones usually acquired with the help of hearing. When as children we are reduced to judging the meaning of words from the circumstances in which we hear them, it often happens that we grasp the meaning only approximately, and we are satisfied with this approximation all our lives. It is different with the deaf taught by Epée. He has only one means for giving them sensory ideas; it is to analyze and to get the pupil to analyze with him. So with simple, methodical analyses, he leads them from sensory ideas to abstract ideas; we can judge how advantageous Epée's action language is over the speech sounds of our governesses and tutors. I thought it proper to seize this opportunity to do justice to the talents of this teacher who I think does not know me, although I have been to his institution and seen his pupils, and he has acquainted me with his method.

Here is what Condillac also says in his *Grammar*, published four years after *Instruction of the Deaf with Methodical Signs*:

Because the language of action is determined by the structure of spoken languages, we did not choose its first signs. It was nature that gave them to us, but in doing so, it put us on the road to inventing some ourselves. Consequently, we became able to express our thoughts with words, and this language could be composed of both natural and artificial signs. Note that I say artificial signs, not arbitrary signs, for we must not confound the two. What, in fact, are arbitrary signs? Signs chosen without reason and by whim. Arbitrary signs are incomprehensible . . . On the contrary, artificial signs are ones whose choice is based on reason. They must be invented so artfully that the understanding is prepared for them by signs already understood.

And yet, Condillac had previously formed a quite different opinion of the intellectual and moral state of the deaf, an opinion reported in the first volume of his *Essay on the Origin of Human Knowledge,* and shared by M. Destutt de Tracy and other contemporary philosophers, among them M. de Bonald. Condillac declared the deaf incapable of conceiving metaphysical ideas. In a paper read in Year IV at the French Institute, and published in the first volume of the collection of the class of moral and political science, Destutt de Tracy proclaimed that "symbols alone give body to archetypal ideas and ideas of generalized substances, and without artificial symbols and perhaps just symbols, there are no abstract ideas, and without abstract ideas no deductions." He retracted this claim some years later. He recognizes that a gesture or cry, no less than a word, can express an abstract idea; that "artificial symbols, of whatever nature, can present themselves and note ideas of every kind, and the degree of complication they make possible as well as the combinations that can be created, do not depend on the intrinsic nature of symbols but on their degree of perfection that makes them capable of expressing nuances."

Let us add the testimony of a critic whose voice has long enjoyed Europe's respectful ear and whose judgments were oracular. Let Epée speak for himself:

Another kind of scholar, known throughout Europe, had announced in an occasional paper of his that my deaf pupils could only be semi-automatons. On being informed of this, I took the liberty of writing to him in the following terms:

"No, sir, I can no longer suffer that a man with such estimable talents as your own is so attached to the way he received the first fruits of his knowledge, that he imagines that we can acquire them in no other way. Are we metaphysicians or are we not? If we are, can we say that ideas are more closely connected with the speech sounds we hear than with the written characters we see?"

Fifteen days ago M. Linguet did me the honor of attending one of my classes, stating his name upon entering. Immediately I begged him to formulate some metaphysical idea of his choice, assuring him that one of my students would express it in writing.

As he preferred not to make the choice himself and deferred to me, I pointed out that he was the one in doubt, not I; so it was up to him to indicate what he judged appropriate; but unable to overcome his resistance, I tell him: "Here, sir, are some metaphysical ideas: 'intellect,' 'intellectual,' 'intelligent,' 'intelligible,' 'intelligibly,' 'unintelligibly,' 'unintelligibility.' Here are eight words related to the intellectual faculty, but whose methodical signs are different from each other: 'comprehensible,' 'incomprehensible,' 'conceivable,' 'inconceivable,' 'conceivably,' 'inconceivably,' 'idea,' 'imagination,' 'imaginable,' 'imaginably,' 'faith,' 'belief,' 'believable,' 'believably,' 'unbelievably,' 'incredulous,' 'incredulity.' I then asked him to pick one of these ideas for me to dictate by signs. He wanted me to choose, but at my insistence he settled on the word 'unintelligibility,' which he probably thought was the hardest. Seeing his surprise at the student's promptness in expressing the word, I tell him: "It is not enough, sir, that you saw the word you asked for; I must explain how I dictated it so quickly. I need only five signs performed in an instant, as you have just seen. The first one expresses internal action, the second the action of a mind reading internally, that is, one that understands what is being proposed, the third asserts that this state of mind is possible. Does this not yield the word "intelligible"? And doesn't a fourth sign transforming this adjective into an abstract quality produce the word "intelligibility"? Finally, a fifth sign adding negation gives us the whole word "unintelligibility."

After proposing five or six other words and then stopping, as I begged him to continue, M. Linguet replied that that would be going to needless lengths and that he no longer doubted my ability to give an exact account of all my signs. However, he added, he still wanted to know whether the deaf, though able to give accurate expression to metaphysical ideas with signs, knew in general what a metaphysical idea was. I wrote on the blackboard: "What do you understand by *metaphysical ideas*?" Immediately, while I chatted with Linguet, a deaf girl wrote out the following answer: "I understand ideas of things independent of the senses, which are beyond our senses, which make no impression on our senses, which cannot be perceived by our senses."

Linguet then asked me to effect a reconciliation between him and the deaf who would be dismayed by his claim that they were semiautomatons. So I dictated the following words with signs: "Monsieur is a scholar who agrees that this was indeed the idea he had about you, but who is now persuaded of the contrary."

If Epée congratulated himself on the eagerness of scholars and great notables, if he took pride in the expressions of interest elicited by his pupils, it was not for his own sake but for theirs. All his thoughts and wishes had no other purpose than the future of these unfortunates; and when the waves of a numerous and brilliant audience receded, Epée, surrounded by his pupils, would offer to God, the source of all knowledge, the glory they had just earned. That is how, early on, he instructed them to guard against vanity, that great enemy of innocence; that is how he chose to sanctify their lessons.

During one of his stays in Paris, Emperor Joseph II paid several visits to the modest teacher's classes. The emperor had previously been to the school of Epée's rival, the Portuguese Jew Pereire, and had come away dissatisfied. The good monarch had readily perceived that Pereire's method was mere self-serving calculation, while for Epée everything was sacrifice and altruism. Joseph told his sister, Queen Marie-Antoinette, about Epée and his pupils; she wished to see them, and like her brother, she came away delighted with these marvels.

When the emperor consulted Epée about how to bring up a young deaf Viennese girl from a powerful family, Epée replied: "Your Majesty would merely have to send her to me in Paris, or failing that, send me an intelligent person some thirty years old whom I would teach to achieve complete success in this undertaking." On his return to Vienna, the emperor sent Epée the following letter:

> . . . the establishment that you have devoted to public service and whose astonishing progress I have had occasion to admire prompts me to recommend to you the abbé Storck, bearer of this letter. I believe that he has the requisite qualities for learning to direct a similar establishment in Vienna.
>
> I am acquainted with him only through his bishop who made the selection for me and who believes he can answer for him. I trust you will be willing to take him under your direction and communicate to him the method that you have so painstakingly established. Your love for the good of humanity and the glory of restoring new subjects to society leads me to hope that you will extend your wholehearted charity to the German deaf by training a teacher who, through their eyes, will provide them with an adequate means for thinking and combining their ideas. Adieu.

The pupils coming to Paris from the Vienna school have praised the well-known graciousness of Joseph II, who communicated with them himself by fingerspelling.

Epée devoted to the deaf not only all the resources of his exceptional genius, but also all those of his modest fortune. Only as a kind of favor were rich pupils admitted to his classes, which were not for the well-to-do, but for the poor: "Without the poor I would not have undertaken the education of the deaf: the rich have the means for finding and paying a teacher."

For the sake of his pupils Epée went so far as to deprive himself of basic necessities; he wore cast-off clothing so that they did not go naked; he was satisfied with the plainest food so that they would not go hungry. He was the Las Casas [known as the apostle of the Indies] of the deaf. He sacrificed everything for them. He paid for the board and room of some; others he supported completely. He borrowed on the strength of his future income, and he borrowed from all his friends. The government gave him nothing; he supported up to fifty or sixty poor deaf children. His brother, executor of their joint inheritance, criticized his liberality. Not only did the abbé spend what he himself owned, but also everything that his dear brother, the hard-working architect, could amass through his daily labor. His mother made the same complaints of him—unusual but constant topics, for the good ecclesiastic was incorrigible. And when the infirmities of old age afflicted him during the hard winter of 1788, he even did without wood and ended this privation only at the constant entreaties of his pupils, who were alarmed about the life remaining to their worthy teacher and good father. Even long afterward, he was heard to reproach himself for this minor expense as a sinful waste: "My poor children," he said to his pupils, "I have wronged you by at least three hundred *livres*."

Among the multitudinous virtues adorning Epée's career, some are a pleasure to relate. Joseph II, marveling at the modest teacher's miracles, wanted to ask Louis XVI for an abbey for Epée, and in case he encountered obstacles in this regard, he decided to give him one from his own land. "I am overwhelmed, Sire," responded the abbé de l'Epée. "If when my undertaking still had no chance of success, some powerful mediator had requested and obtained a lavish grant for me, I would have accepted it so as to employ the resources for the benefit of the institution. But I am now old; if Your Majesty wishes the deaf well, the benefice should be placed not on my head, which is already bent toward the grave, but on the work itself. It is worthy of a great prince to perpetuate this work for the good of humanity."

Another example of disinterest! In 1780 the ambassador of Catherine II of Russia, a just appraiser of Epée's worth, came to offer him rich presents on the empress's behalf. "My lord," replied the abbé, "I never accept gold, but tell Her Majesty that if my work appears of some value, the only favor I ask is to send me a deaf person to instruct."

His unfailing charity held the deaf all over the world in its embrace. Moved to universalize his kindness, he was seen at an advanced age spiritedly pursuing the study of several foreign languages with no other teacher than dictionaries and grammars. He even allowed that he was ready to learn any language in order to teach a deaf person from some country where that language was spoken. Unpaid teacher of this outcast class, Epée would have thought he was doing only a small part of his duty if he offered his services just to his own country; he said to all governments: "You have subjects whom some infirmity has cut off from the society of their peers; I can make them men, citizens, Christians. Here I am, use me!" His evangelical fervor extended even further; he wanted brought to him for instruction deaf persons struck down by smallpox or any other disease at the age of two or three.

What eyes are not awash with tears every time the French stage has presented M. Bouilly's play—a dramatic classic written more with the heart than with the mind—the history of a deaf man, known as the count of Solar, whose protectors were Epée and the duke of Penthièvre, ancestor of our King, Louis-Philippe?

It must be added that some persons we have met maintain that in the trial of the deaf adventurer, as they term him, Epée's good faith was conspiratorially exploited, and as proof they cite the second ruling of the high judicial court of Paris. But why would we decide in favor of one decree rather than another? Why would we think the second judges were any more infallible than the first ones? Two extracts from this trial, which we have in hand, are enough to convince us. One is Epée's *Mémoire à consulter* for M. Bonvalet, attorney to the court and tutor to the young deaf count of Solar; and the other is the well-argued letter that he addressed to M. Élie de Beaumont, defender of a certain M. Cazeaux, to reveal his errors and to defend his client against the accusations. Le Chatelet hurriedly convenes, listens only to the truth, and pronounces in favor of the deaf person. The court, which had the time to be more circumspect, honors the rights of a powerful family. To absolve Epée's heart, the court is forced to incriminate him, that superior person to whom we owe what is perhaps the most magnificent, beautiful creation of our era. Now that time has passed over both trials, I think we need not belabor the facts overmuch in order to decide the question.

Despite this notable setback, Epée's reputation had reached its zenith; foreign learned societies declared in his favor against the barbarians who denied his miracles; men distinguished by their enlightenment, fortune, or social position, and the greatest personages from all countries flocked to pay him their admiring tribute. People came from all over the world to obtain from his method the material for regenerating that teeming class of unfortunates; but Epée—increasingly self-abnegating, concealing his glory, happy with the title of teacher of the deaf—refused with modest dignity to accept either the rich benefice proposed by Joseph II or the magnificent gifts of Catherine of Russia. Even as a youth of twenty he had given stunning proof of this self-abnegation by declining a bishopric offered by the cardinal de Fleury in recompense for a personal service rendered by Epée's father. Who could have predicted that after thirty years of unremitting labor Epée would be reduced to vainly holding out his hand to the powers that be for the sake of his deaf children, that he would vainly beseech those powers to ensure the posthumous existence of his famous school, which he had founded at his own expense, which he maintained at the cost of repeated personal sacrifices, and which was destined to serve as a model for all schools in both the Old and New Worlds?

Only Louis XVI came to Epée's aid. In 1785 the king granted the institution a home next to the former Celestine convent, and from the royal privy purse he accorded Epée an annual subsidy of 6000 *livres*. But it was only two years later that the reform-minded Constituent Assembly, the first to dare to put the axe to the tree of abuses, decreed (in the sessions of 21 and 29 July 1791) that Epée's institution would be maintained at state expense as a monument worthy of the French nation. Article 1 of the decree, rendered the same day, states: "The name of the abbé de l'Epée, founder of this institution, will be placed among the ranks of those citizens who have merited most of humanity and the nation."

By the decrees of 12–14 May 1793 the National Convention, Herculean heir of the solicitude of its predecessor, wishing to continue its patronage of the institution founded in 1786, placed it under the auspices of the reverend prelate M. Champion de Cicé, the archbishop of Bordeaux, to be headed by the abbé Sicard.

In 1794 the Paris institution was transferred to its present site in the former seminary of the archbishop of Paris, Saint-Magloire, 254 and 256 Rue du Faubourg Saint-Jacques.

Although Epée missed the consolation of dying in the certainty that his method would live after him, at least he must from the abode of the happy contemplate with joy the abundant harvests produced by his school. The teachers who have contributed the most to its flourishing are the already mentioned abbé Storck, the abbé Sylvestre whom the papal nuncio Doria Pamphili brought from Rome, Ulrich of Zurich, Dangulo and d'Alea in Spain, Muller of Mainz, Michel of the Tarentaise, Delo and Guyot in Holland, the abbé Huby of Rouen, the abbé Masse, first designated by the Commune to succeed Epée; the abbé Sicard, Epée's permanent successor, the venerable abbé Salvan, second teacher, charged with the education of the deaf girls (who died a year ago in the heart of his birthplace, the Auvergne), and above all, M. Bébian, our former director of studies (whose books have become classics and are worthy of study by all French and foreign teachers), to whom in 1817 the Royal Academic Society of Sciences in Paris awarded the prize for a eulogy of our illustrious founder.

Would not the eagerness of all these missionaries of civilization to adopt Epée's method (except for some modifications necessitated by time and experience) be enough, apart from their enthusiasm and gratitude, to proclaim to the civilized world that he is the unique creator of the true art of compensating for hearing with sight, and for speech with writing—a title already unanimously granted him by his far-sighted contemporaries? Yes, his method is the torch we must uphold if we are to proceed with a firm stride along the bramble-bristling path. If we pay no heed to this beacon, we will soon go astray. Therefore, teachers of the deaf, let Epée's books be your lifelong texts and daily rule-books, while acknowledging the vagaries of his genius that show us that he is human! Above all, beware the presumption, the vanity that leads you away from that salutary beacon! Trust his experience to alert you to the reefs!

Though we must admit that France had predecessors in the difficult birth of an art that raises so many unfortunates to human dignity, our dear homeland can at least pride itself on producing in one of its children the immortal union of the most sublime genius with the most zealous charity—a union that eclipses so many glories and before which so many scepters are lowered! Let France glory in having endowed religion with such a commendable minister, humanity with such a fervent benefactor, and a vast unhappy world-scattered family with an admirable legislator and an untiring exponent of a hitherto scarcely imaginable science.

In conclusion, gentlemen, please allow me to record the public expression of a wish consistent with the spirit of charity animating the whole life of the man we are pleased to call our intellectual father. May the education of his children no longer be the privilege of an elite, but may its blessing extend to all, in whatever class they belong, in whatever religion they are reared! May our legislative assemblies, may our departmental and municipal assemblies have constantly in mind the sacred debt that society contracts with each of its members, to which the unfortunate deaf must, by reason of their disability, lay an even greater claim! I have no doubt that this appeal by one of their brothers will be heard. These assemblies will not trail behind the philanthropic movement that marks our century's progressiveness. My guarantee is the solicitude of the government itself, which has ordered its prefects to collect the necessary statistical information about these unfortunates, the data from two generations ago being now insufficient and inexact. May the government use this information to increase the number of the deaf called to profit from a liberal education! May this information serve the government to multiply the number of institutions dispensing this education! May every department have at least one such institution! And as corollaries of these establishments, let the regions of France with deaf people be implanted with small intellectual centers where they will be prepared for public education and where they will later return to distribute some of the bounty they will have harvested! May enlightened philanthropists become protectors of the children leaving our schools with an education, a trade, good will, and courage! May they send these graduates among speaking people, from whom they will ask only work and equity!

It would be worthy, gentlemen, of a society of equals that had its heart set on honoring the greatest man of Versailles, to make this society the organ of the wishes of his adoptive children and in their name to appeal to the generosity of the world's most enlightened nation, and so to evoke the interest of a power eager to extend to the sons of all the citizens a common patrimony of benevolence.

NOTES

The notes to the Introduction are by Lane and Philip. Notes to Chapter 2 were appended by the original publisher; notes to the other chapters were appended to the original documents by their authors. Comments by Lane and Philip are in brackets.

INTRODUCTION

1. Linstok Press, 9306 Mintwood Street, Silver Spring, Md.

2. E. Klima and U. Bellugi, *The Signs of Language* (Cambridge, Mass.: Harvard University Press, 1979).

3. H. Lane and F. Grosjean, *Recent Perspectives on American Sign Language* (Hillsdale, N.J.: Lawrence Erlbaum Associates, 1980).

4. A. Gentile, "Further studies in achievement testing, hearing-impaired students, Spring 1971," in Gallaudet Office of Demographic Studies, *Annual Survey of Hearing-Impaired Children and Youth* (Washington, D.C.: Gallaudet College, 1973. These results were also reported in D. Moores, *Educating the Deaf* (Boston, Mass.: Houghton Mifflin, 1982). Also see E. Mindel and M. Vernon, *They Grow in Silence* (Silver Spring, Md.: National Association of the Deaf, 1971).

5. Mindel and Vernon, *They Grow*, p. 102. See also J. Schein and M. Delk, *The Deaf Population of the United States* (Silver Spring, Md.: National Association of the Deaf, 1974).

6. See H. Lane, *When the Mind Hears* (New York, N.Y.: Random House, 1984).

7. T. Arnold, *Education of Deaf-Mutes: A Manual for Teachers* (London: Wertheimer, 1888).

8. K. Hodgson, *The Deaf and Their Problems* (London: Watts, 1953).

9. R. Bender, *The Conquest of Deafness* (Cleveland, Ohio: Case Western Reserve University Press, 1970).

2. PIERRE DESLOGES

1. The author, Pierre Desloges, was born in 1747 at Le Grand-Pressigny, near La Haye in the diocese of Tours. He is a bookbinder and paperhanger by trade. He resides in the Petit-Hôtel de Chartres, rue des Mauvais Garçons, Faubourg Saint-Germain in Paris.

2. To the author's description of what remains of his speech (a description that is surprising in its precision), I would add some facts that his deafness makes it impossible for him to know: his voice is extremely weak, merely a low indistinct murmur in which dental articulations are noticeably predominant and take the place of the ones required by correct pronunciation. I have vainly implored him to give his voice greater volume and life, but he has always given me to understand that this was impossible. If that is so, it must be that his cruel childhood malady affected his vocal and auditory organs both.

   I understand that with a great deal of effort and practice I would manage, as he says, to identify the inchoate sounds of his speech; I have seen too little of him to try this. The most convenient way to converse with him is with pen in hand—that is what I have always done. Fortunately he knew how to combine the principles of reading and writing with the knowledge remaining of his early childhood language. Practice in reading has maintained and strengthened his knowledge of written language; his reflectiveness and natural talent have done the rest.

3. These experiments show what the nature of hearing is for our author and for all similar unfortunates: it is to have the perception, through touch or through a disturbance in the surrounding air, of certain perturbations occurring in nearby objects. For such people audition is merely the exercise and effect of touch in the strict sense. I am persuaded that our author, as intelligent as he is, no longer has the least trace of the precise idea we attach to the word "hear." His explanation, which will

be of inestimable value to readers of a philosophic turn of mind, gives more than ample proof of this.

4. According to estimates by M. Pereire and the abbé de l'Epée, more than half the deaf who have studied with them were not completely deaf—their ears, like ours, could experience true hearing of very loud and piercing noises. But these partially deaf people are no more advanced for all that. For a child to suffer all the misfortunes of profound deafness, the only thing required is that his or her ear be obstructed to the point of an indistinct perception of speech sounds. Ignorant of the conventional sounds of spoken languages and of the ideas we attach to them, he necessarily becomes mute. As for our author, he appears totally deaf; the sharpest whistling noise makes no impression on his ears.

5. Indisputably, the primary advantage of sign or mimic language is its clarity and precision; in these respects it surpasses spoken languages. Spoken languages can depict ideas only through the mediation of sounds; sign language depicts ideas directly. So spoken language, if I may be allowed to speak this way, is further from objects than sign language—spoken languages represent things only through a veil that must always be penetrated to reach an understanding of the thing expressed by the word.

    When I am addressed in any European language, I must necessarily have two consecutive and independent perceptions: the perception of the sounds or words of this language; the perception of the ideas to be attached to these words. And because these two perceptions are, as I have just said, independent of each other (by virtue of the purely arbitrary relation between words and ideas), then from what a speaker in any language says to me, I see that he, like me, understands the words of this language, but I am not actually certain that he attaches the same ideas to them as I. This is particularly true of children, for they use language for quite some time without attaching any clear idea to the individual words. Well, how few adults are not children in this regard.

    On the other hand, in sign or mimic language I necessarily go directly from the perception of the sign to the perception of the idea in just the way that when I see the outline of a tree, a house, or the like, I cannot help having the idea of this tree, of this house, and so on. So when a person depicts some objects with a gesture, the results are two great advantages that point up the excellence of sign language: my certainty that the gesturer has a clear conception of the object he is representing, because of the impossibility of depicting, with either pencil or gesture, what is not conceived in this way; my certainty that this manner of depicting my ideas will communicate them just as I conceive them, for he can see them only the way I represent them and I can represent them only as I conceive them.

    I am so persuaded of the great benefits of sign language that, were I to educate a normal hearing child, I would make frequent use of sign. I would get him used to translating his phrases into sign so that I would be sure that he attaches a clear and precise meaning to them. This exercise, which children take as fun, would be extremely valuable for my pupil and would furnish me with proof that I was not training a parrot.

6. Certainly, we can only applaud the wishes of the abbé Deschamps and of our deaf author on the publication of a dictionary of sign. I have even encouraged the abbé de l'Epée to take it up, but he has always seemed convinced that reading these signs would be less impressive than seeing them.

   Epée and I are in complete agreement. Learning signs from a dictionary would be boring and tiring, whereas learning them by seeing them demonstrated is a game. Besides, just seeing signs in a book would result in misunderstanding. Further training and practice would be indispensable. Would one ever become a painter by making do with books on the theory of drawing and painting? Does one not need the constant manipulation of pencil and brushes? As sign language is just a natural depiction of ideas, any progress we make in it requires the same behavior as that required to develop a talent for drawing and painting, with the difference that to excel in the latter arts requires several years of assiduous study, whereas only a few weeks are needed to achieve passable fluency in sign language.

   The abbé de l'Epée is currently overseeing the compilation of a dictionary of signs.

7. Let us speak frankly. Lipreading or lip-guessing is more plausible-seeming and awe-inspiring (owing to its unexpectedness) than it is genuinely useful to the deaf. We know that M. Pereire works on getting his pupils to speak. He certainly has all the patience and talent required for success, but I must admit that even the best among his pupils still speak very poorly. Their pronunciation is loud, slow, disjointed, and grating on the ears because of the effort it evidently costs them.

   The abbé de l'Epée gets no better results. Not that the able teachers are to blame. They do everything humanly possible. But the voice can be guided correctly only by hearing, and no other guide can adequately replace hearing. So the better-educated deaf make little use of speech. I know and have several times seen the pupil who has earned the most honor for M. Pereire [Saboureux de Fontenay]. This young man is very learned, with a great deal of knowledge in a variety of subjects, being especially well-versed in languages. He himself agrees with me about everything I have just claimed, and will converse only in writing. Generally, all other deaf people express the same repugnance for speaking; the more enlightened they are, the better they appreciate the inadequacy of their speech.

As for the art of lipreading, it may doubtless have some utility; we should not ignore it in the education of the deaf, but we would be unwise to put too much reliance on its help. In talking to a deaf person, one must have the habit of speaking in a certain way to be understood by him; even so, this is practicable only for short and common phrases; for fairly long and quickly articulated phrases, I have yet to come across a deaf person who could follow and understand them.

In the pulpit and at the bar we have orators whose pronunciation is extremely careful and distinct, but I strongly doubt whether any deaf person can ever be enabled to understand them by looking at their lips. Unless I am mistaken, this art will never reach that point. Half of all speech articulations are made inside the mouth so that, normally, they are hidden from view. And even when articulation is slow and forceful—making the speech mechanism maximally visible—lipreading is still not easy and, for even the most intelligent deaf person, requires long association with the speaker. This was made quite evident to me in conversation with the author of this book. Whatever pains I took to articulate clearly, he could understand only a few of my words and we were obliged to resort to pen or pencil.

So the soundest part of the education of the deaf is reading and writing combined with an understanding of the language in which they are taught. With this knowledge and the right talent, they can go as far as other people in the pursuit of knowledge.

Indisputably, the surest way to communicate with the deaf is in writing and sign language. One can scarcely live with a deaf person and take an interest in him without promptly getting into the habit of speaking and listening to him in sign language. Every person carries the seed of it, so to speak, within himself; circumstances effortlessly promote the seed's germination and the language flowers without teacher or method.

8. In practicing an art as useful and interesting as the education of the deaf, it is especially dangerous to make a mistake and lay down principles that deflect the effort from the proper path: the wise observations of our deaf author seem to me highly appropriate for correcting the abbé Deschamps and for focusing the public's ideas on the true elements of a new-fledged art, which is excusably still not fully explored.

The main point of contention between the abbé Deschamps and his opponent may be reduced to this: what should the primary medium for the education of the deaf be, lipreading or the use of natural and methodical signs?

First, we should see what the two opponents agree on: this preliminary discussion will shed a great deal of light on the question and enable everyone to judge the issue.

The abbé Deschamps acknowledges the utility of signs or mimic language. He himself makes frequent use of it in his own lessons.

On the other hand, his opponent agrees that lipreading is a useful exercise and should form a part of the education of the deaf.

So the opinions of the two writers are not nearly as far apart as they appear to be; they are closer than they themselves realize. For their whole dispute comes down to determining which of two mediums, which they both regard as good, will be the basis of the education of the deaf. So the only decision concerns the primacy of one of these two methods.

Here is a thought that will, I believe, prove helpful in achieving a permanent solution to the whole difficulty. So certain is it that signs are the one means of communicating with the deaf that it is impossible to imagine any other. In the act of reading, whether of books or of the mouth or by the sense of touch, the deaf see in the written material only signs, nothing but signs; we will never get them to understand anything except through signs. "For hearing people," as the abbé Deschamps very well puts it, "speech is spoken sounds, words; for the deaf, it is silent signs made with the speech apparatus to which they attach their ideas."

Therefore, it is one of the uncontestable principles of the abbé Deschamps that the deaf person, when we are speaking to him or he to us, actually sees or makes only signs, signs or signals in the most literal sense.

But what a difference there is between these sort of signs and those of mimic language or signs in the strict sense. By the writer's own confession, the deaf person finds the former extremely difficult to comprehend and to perform. In addition, they are all absolutely arbitrary.

On the other hand, the signs of mimic language are always readily comprehensible, for they are just an image or gestural depiction of the thing meant. The deaf person performs these signs with great ease, and makes constant use of them—they are his true language. Moreover, these signs are not the least bit arbitrary; they necessarily give the idea of the thing of which they are the image and representation.

To make all this clearer, let us consider an example.

Suppose we want to evoke in the deaf person the idea expressed in French with the word *chapeau* [hat]. Can the abbé Deschamps doubt that I could accomplish this more quickly and easily by making the natural sign expressing the idea of hat than by getting the deaf person to note the play of the speech apparatus when I utter the word *chapeau*?

With a gestural demonstration, I give him, at once and without needing any explanation, the idea of *hat*.

With the demonstration by lipreading, I give him no idea at all in the strict sense. He sees that I am making certain movements with my mouth, and that is all. So it must be the case that: (a) I am teaching him to distinguish these movements from all the others I can make with my mouth, (b) I am giving him a clear and vivid idea of this by frequent repetition, (c) up to this point the deaf person knows nothing if I do not further teach him by repeated practice that this series of mouth movements is connected with the idea of *hat*—a connection he would surely never have suspected, (d) there remains another, even more difficult task of getting him to make the same movements and of getting him to pronounce the word *chapeau* himself. What a bore! What repellent difficulties both for teacher and student! Sign for sign, is it not better to prefer the simplest and easiest signs, especially at the start?

In all the arts and in all kinds of education it is an accepted principle that we must go from the known to the unknown, and that the first elements cannot be oversimplified. So I think that a reflective person will judge that a deaf person must begin the study of reading and writing of any language with the help of his natural signs. Truly, for him these signs are the chief instrument of all the knowledge that he can acquire. Only when he has advanced beyond these first exercises should we be seriously concerned with the role of pronunciation on which, again, we should not rely more than is convenient (as was remarked in Note 7).

But in this system, objects the abbé Deschamps (p. 32), you impose an additional burden on the teacher—the burden of learning sign language.

Were this problem as real as the writer supposes, I doubt that people with enough spirit to take up such a hard task as the education of the deaf would be much deterred. The abbé de l'Epée's door is always open, and he has already taught sign language to a great many people, so it is not terribly difficult to improve one's knowledge of it, either with his help or that of his students.

Furthermore, sign language, as our deaf author wisely observes, is not a bed of thorns. A fairly intelligent teacher will always know enough naturally to begin his lessons. Continual practice will soon make him a skilled signer.

Finally, I am deeply persuaded that the abbé Deschamps actually does base his instruction on sign language, though without realizing it. His apparent coolness toward sign is in reality just a misunderstanding. I assume he has enough integrity and candor to agree and to yield to the force of the reasons he finds in his opponent's observations.

9. This example plainly shows us that sign language is a running definition of the ideas expressed in it, but a necessarily clear and unambiguous definition, for it consists entirely of images. The person using sign language can doubtless be mistaken, but we see in each expression—as through a transparent mirror—the precise idea he has of objects. If sign language were to gain universal currency, it would be an invaluable aid in the pursuit of truth. We would at least understand each other, and there would be no issues that we could call *arguments about words*. It would be practically impossible ever to have *arguments about signs*.

10. It is indeed surprising that all the abbé de l'Epée's demonstrations of the utility of sign language—designed by nature itself to become a universal language, a bond of communication between all men—have not yet inspired anyone to learn it. We grow pale poring over books in pursuit of an inadequate knowledge of dead and foreign languages, but

refuse to devote a few weeks to the learning of this simple, easy language which could become a supplement for all other languages.

5. R. A. SICARD

1. Massieu's plea to a judge. The event was reported in all the newspapers of the day. Here is how it appeared in an English paper, along with the journalist's comments.

> Among the interesting events that characterize this century, the denunciation of Jean Massieu, age eighteen and a congenital deaf-mute, is among the most extraordinary.
>
> This young man, a pupil of the abbé Sicard, successor to the abbé de l'Epée in the humane and unusual calling of teaching deaf-mutes, pleaded his own case against a common thief before a tribunal, without needing to be represented by a lawyer; he himself wrote out what happened, with the noble sincerity of innocence and the ingenuity of a primitive man deeply imbued with the idea of the sacred rights of nature; as if nature had itself been charged to recall the events, and to demand redress and vengeance against violence! Here is a transcription of the truly curious and unique monument to the efforts of a human mind deprived of normal education.
>
> Jean Massieu to the judge: "I am a deaf-mute. I was watching a procession of the monstrance for Corpus Christi on a main street, in the company of other deaf-mutes. This man noticed me. He saw a small billfold in the right pocket of my coat; he slyly approached me and took the billfold. Alerted by a touch on my hip, I quickly turned toward the nervous thief. He threw the billfold onto the leg of another man, who picked it up and gave it to me. I grabbed the thief by his jacket, and held him tight. He became pale, then livid and tremulous. I summoned a soldier and showed him the billfold, signing to him that this man had stolen it. The soldier took the thief and brought him here. I followed. I ask you to judge us.
>
> "I swear before God that this man stole my billfold. He will not dare to swear before God.
>
> "I beg you not to sentence him to be beheaded, for he is not guilty of murder, but only to serve as a galley slave."
>
> The thief did not contest the accusation. He was sentenced to three months in the Bicêtre prison.

2. In May 1785 the abbé de l'Epée wrote to the Academy of Berlin to ask them to invite M. Nicolai, one of its members, to meet Epée's challenge concerning his method, which Nicolai had taken the liberty of disparaging in one of his writings. Epée submitted the judgment of this dispute to the Academy's tribunal. The *Journal de Paris* of 27 May 1785 published the letter of the abbé de l'Epée, which is too lengthy for inclusion in this note. He sent to the Academy the letter he himself wrote to M. Nicolai. It appears in the same edition. Here is an extract from M. Nicolai's intemperate reply.

I was not talking about your school, monsieur, but about that of Monsieur Storck. If his method, which gives deaf children only vague words and few clear ideas, is also yours, that is surely not my fault. If your method were better than his, I would be glad for you; but let us not argue the point. I have stated that M. Storck's method is inadequate and inappropriate. I still maintain this, and give the reasons for this in my book . . .

If M. Storck has not seen fit to make any response to my arguments and the facts I cited in my book, I do not see why you are so agitated about a German book that must be unknown in Paris, like so many other and more worthy ones.

It is truly astonishing that M. Storck did not reply himself, at the time, to M. Nicolai, and that he referred the troublesome matter to his teacher whose doctrine he should have defended.

3. Extract from a letter from the abbé de l'Epée to M. Sicard, 25 November 1785: "I sincerely applaud your successes, my dear *confrère* (I am setting the example for you, I now refuse the appellation *maître*), but I fear that you will be led astray by the desire to make your pupils into metaphysicians. Do not hope that they will ever be able to express their ideas in writing. Our language is not theirs: their language is sign language. Let it suffice that they know how to translate our language into theirs, as we ourselves translate foreign languages without being able to think or express ourselves in those languages. Is there not enough glory for you in sharing mine? And what must you do to obtain it? Let your pupils, like mine, learn to write from dictation in signs . . ."

4. The Institution for Blind Youth finally found its true function. Established as an integral part of the *Quinze-Vingts* (Hospital for the Blind), it was confided to the enlightened, moral, and religious Citizen Bertrand, who thought that in the restoration of these unfortunates to the principles of Catholic morality (so necessary in misfortune) there was no reason for consulting them, and it is the commendable Citizen Saignetter, general agent for the hospice, who is training them to earn a living upon their return to their families. Now the name formerly given to these unfortunates is no longer a mockery or piece of irony, and they are truly blind workers.

5. Champion de Cicé was the first person in France to conceive and execute the plan to provide the abbé de l'Epée with a successor. "It was he who sent me to the celebrated priest to learn the art of educating the deaf . . ."

6. R. A. Sicard, *De La Théorie des signes pour l'instruction des sourds-muets . . . Suivie d'une notice sur l'enfance de Massieu* (Paris: Imprimerie de l'Institution des Sourds-Muets, 1808).

7. Letter from M. de l'Epée, 18 December 1785:

What, my dear confrère, your pupils still do not know how to write short sentences from dictation by signs! What on earth are you doing? What game are you playing? You wish absolutely to make writers of them when our method can only produce copyists. You have attended all my public lessons; have you ever seen the observers require of my pupils what you seek from yours? If sometimes they were given questions to answer, they were always familiar little everyday requests always asked the same way. You have seen the most distinguished figures of the court and of the city, and even foreign princes, require nothing more than that. Believe me, my dear confrere, give up these pretensions (which have a little of the Garonne about them) and be content with the modest portion of glory that you see me enjoy. Teach your children promptly declensions and conjugations; teach them the signs from my dictionary of verbs; teach them the parts of the sentences according to the table whose model you have, without flattering yourself that your pupils can ever express themselves in French any more than I can express myself in Italian even though I can translate from it very well . . ."

8. For a more extended treatment, see volume 1 of my *Eléments de grammaire générale* (Paris: Bourlotton, 1799), or the third edition enlarged (Paris: Déterville, 1808), pp. 25–29. This book, as well as my *Manuel de l'enfance* (Paris: Le Clère, 1797) and *Catechisme à l'usage des sourds-muets* (Paris: Institution des Sourds-Muets, 1796), can be purchased at Le Clère, printer-bookseller, and at Déterville, bookseller, 16 rue du Battoir, Paris.

9. For a more extensive treatment of this subject, see Volume 1 of my *Eléments de grammaire générale*, second edition.

6. R. A. BÉBIAN

1. It would be the same with the privation of taste and smell. Clerc, of whom I have just spoken, is also deprived of the olfactory sense.

2. Francisco Vallès, *De Philosophia Sacra* (Turin: Nicolai Beuilaqual, 1587), chap. 3, p. 53.

3. Personal communication to Gall from Emmanuel Nugnez de Taboada.

4. He died in August 1584, at the convent of San Salvador de Oña.

5. Juan Pablo Bonet, *Reducción de las letras y arte para enseñar a hablar a los mudos* (Madrid: Abarca de Angulo, 1620). [*Simplification of the Letters of the Alphabet and Method of Teaching Deaf-Mutes to Speak.* Translated by H. N. Dixon (Harrogate: A. Farrar, 1890)—Trans.]

6. John Wallis, *Grammatica linguae anglicanae, cui praefigitur de loquela*

sive de sonorum omnium loquelarium formatione tractatus gramma-tico-physicus. Translated by J. Greenwood (London: Beltes-Worter, 1729).

7. Letter from John Wallis to Thomas Beverly, 30 September (1698), *Phil-osophical Transactions of the Royal Society* (1698) 20: 353–360.

8. Pierre Desloges, *Observations d'un sourd et muet sur "Un Cours élé-mentaire d'éducation des sourds et muets," publié en 1779 par M. l'abbé Deschamps* (Amsterdam and Paris: B. Morin, 1779). There is a review in the *Mercure* of December 1779 in which we find, in addition, a letter by M. Desloges. I have just obtained this booklet, which I had long been looking for and of which I had read only a few passages. I think that people will be grateful to me for publishing something by this unusual author . . .
   [Here Bébian quotes Pierre Desloges, above, pp. 31–32. "I became deaf," etc. Quote up to "settled in Paris."]
   Before his illness, Desloges had learned some basic reading and writing of which he kept some memory and from which he later drew exten-sively. He was a poor working man, a paperhanger and bookbinder, deprived of any outside help in his education.

9. Charles-Michel de l'Epée, *Institution des sourds-muets par la voie des signes méthodiques* (Paris: Nyon, 1776), p. 155.

10. At a public demonstration by the abbé Sicard, some spectators gushed at hearing a deaf person speak. "Messieurs," said the celebrated teacher, "if I could pay a laborer for this work, no pupil would leave this school without knowing how to speak."

11. Louis XVI, whose name is associated with everything great and good in his era, drew on his privy purse to award the abbé de l'Epée an annual sum for the upkeep of a certain number of deaf-mutes. Later on, the Estates-General decreed that all the establishment's expenses would be paid by the Treasury and set at thirty-three the number of pupils to be admitted at government expense. This number was raised to seventy, of whom a third are girls, housed in a separate building.
   The economy and expenses of the institution are entrusted to an agent who reports to the administrative council made up of five hon-orary members chosen from among the most highly esteemed person-ages. The general educational management is entrustd to a head teacher, the abbé Sicard. The assistant teacher, the abbé Salvan, is charged with the education of the girls. He is seconded by two teaching assistants, Mademoiselle Duler and Mademoiselle Salmon. There are four teach-ing assistants for the boys: the fourth teaching assistant, abbé Huilard, teaches the vocabulary of names for objects; the third teaching assist-

ant, Monsieur Pissin, teaches verbs; the second assistant, Monsieur Paulmier, teaches conjugation, prepositions, and elementary grammar; the first assistant, the deaf-mute Massieu, teaches grammar, history, geography, and religion. Also at the institution is a teacher of drawing, of shoemaking, of tailoring, and of carpentry. So after five years the pupil is restored to his family, bringing back with him the ability to earn a livelihood.

12. For us the vowel and consonant letters represent simple or modified sounds; but the deaf person, with no awareness of sounds, can see in letters only elementary lines of various shapes making up more complicated characters that represent ideas and that we call words. For him each word is a complex shape, a kind of hieroglyph with several parts, but forming a single character. In the same way the letter M to our eyes is made up of four lines, yet remains a single letter, a single character. With the same lines, we could make a V or L or N, but in themselves they represent nothing. This is what letters are for the deaf.

13. It is true that for all the poor pupils this time is spent learning a trade. But that does not prevent them from finding time for study. Later on, the less time they have to study, the more they must forget. Hence the greater importance of a means for recalling, as need be, what they have learned.

Finally, this institution is not reserved just for the poor, trade-learning deaf-mutes. The rigors of nature make no distinction between social classes, and deaf-mutes from every class must find there instruction appropriate to their position in society. It is obvious that the study of drawing cannot take up their every moment.

14. [Here Bébian quotes Pierre Desloges, above, material pp. 36—37, beginning, "In intercourse with his companions the deaf child soon acquires . . ." to ". . . strong and great emotions."]

15. This is merely a manner of speaking with no implications about the mechanism of sensation or of memory. The same is true of the word "image."

16. It might also be productive to study the intellectual development of the blind. But only an incisive, patient, and totally theory-free observer could get reliable results. The blind are much less open than the deaf. In general, the blind are mistrustful, vain, and clever in concealing their ignorance. They talk like us, but how do we know whether they attach a precise meaning to words? In a different way it is the same with normal children. They are taught everything except to understand what they are saying. But if Fénélon is to be believed, it is never too early to give them accurate ideas. "Before they can talk," he says, "they

can be readied for instruction." In the explanations given them, "the words must be accompanied with stresses and gestures" (*Education des filles*).

17. "Six weeks at most are sufficient to become reasonably familiar with this language. Now where is there a language that even the most gifted genius can learn in six weeks?" (Desloges, *Observations d'un sourd et muet*, p. 12.)

7. F. BERTHIER

1. Aristotle, *History of Animals*, chap. 9: *Metaphysics*.

2. *Quod vitium ipsum impedit fidem; nam surdus natu litteras quibus lectis fidem concipiat, discere non potest* (The abbé de l'Epée, letter 2 to the abbé *** in 1772).

3. Aristotle, *De anima*, book II, chap. *De discendi ratione*.

4. Charles-Michel de l'Epée, *Institution des sourds-muets*, (Paris: Nyon, 1776) pp. 3–4.

5. R. A. Sicard, *Cours d'instruction d'un sourd-muet de naissance* (Paris: Le Clère, 1800), p. 10.

6. Jérôme Cardan, *Paralipomenon*, book III, chap. 3, vol. 16 of his collected works, p. 462.

7. Jérôme Cardan, *De utilitatae ex adversis capiendâ*, book II, chap. 7, vol. II of his collected works, p. 73; *De subtilitates*, book XIV, p. 425 (Basel edition).

8. François René de Châteaubriand, *Le Génie du Christianisme* (Paris, 1802), part 1, p. 77.

9. J. M. de Gérando, *De L'Education des sourds-muets de naissance* (Paris: Mequignon, 1827), vol. 1, p. 496

INDEX